89   5 °   40

40 4 ' 46

49 1 5" 2 4"

23   3 0"

7 2° 4 5° 2 4"

ENGLISH *for the* Armed Forces

ENGLISH for the Armed Forces

WRITING, SPEAKING, READING

by

LIEUTENANT COLONEL A. G. D. WILES
Professor of English

LIEUTENANT ARLIN M. COOK
Assistant Professor of Speech

LIEUTENANT JACK TREVITHICK
Assistant Professor of English
The Citadel
The Military College of South Carolina

With a Foreword by
GENERAL CHARLES P. SUMMERALL
Former Chief of Staff, U. S. Army

New York : London

HARPER & BROTHERS PUBLISHERS

This book is complete and unabridged
in contents, and is manufactured in strict
conformity with Government regulations
for saving paper.

CONTENTS

FOREWORD

Every officer of the armed forces is likely to be called upon and most officers will be called upon to write important studies, orders, reports and letters and to speak in conferences and in public upon military or naval subjects. It is unfortunate in too many cases that officers are not skillful and often are not capable of doing justice to themselves or to the services. Knowledge of a subject does not imply the ability to express that knowledge in writing or in speaking. Indeed, the possessor of such ability is exceptional.

The essentials of military composition are clarity, orderly arrangement, and brevity. In speaking, there must be added facility in vocabulary and in enunciation and in poise.

Every officer can greatly improve his ability and many can acquire skill by learning the methods and the mechanics of the art of writing and speaking.

These have been set forth with commendable simplicity by Lieutenant Colonel Wiles, Lieutenant Cook, and Lieutenant Trevithick in their book *English for the Armed Forces* and I commend it heartily to those for whom it is intended.

Charleston, S. C.
May 24, 1943

C. P. SUMMERALL
General, Retired
President, The Citadel

TO THE TEACHER

No teacher worth his salt needs to be told how to use a textbook. But before he chooses a text, the teacher will certainly be interested in a statement of the objectives of that text as set forth by the authors. In brief compass, these are the objectives of *English for the Armed Forces:*

Purpose. This book is especially written for the War Training Program in English. It is not designed for use in the traditional freshman English courses which are taught in a leisurely fashion to peacetime students; it is written in a person-to-person manner for the man who will soon be marching to the sound of the guns.

Point of view. The authors have tried to present English as a practical tool, as a weapon which the fighting man will carry with him, along with his mess kit and Garand rifle, to the battlefront. This book is based upon the principles of composition which make for direct, clear, and forceful English, qualities which all English instructors try to teach their students; it is only the method of approach that has been changed.

Scope. This book includes the three divisions of explanatory communication—writing, speaking, and reading—which the authorities responsible for the War Training Program insist shall be taught to students in English. The scope, however, is flexible: the book may be used in a 36-hour course or in an 84-hour course.

Practicability. The authors believe that the best way for a person to learn to write, speak, and read is through practice. The variety and abundance of the exercises, based on semi-technical material, will afford ample opportunity for constant drill in all the skills taught.

ACKNOWLEDGMENTS

For generous assistance and advice the authors express
their warm thanks to Lieutenant Karl H. Koopman, of
The Citadel Library; Colonel Louis Shepherd LeTellier,
Chairman of the Department of Civil Engineering at The
Citadel; and General Charles P. Summerall, President of
The Citadel.

A. G. D. W.
A. M. C.
J. T.

ENGLISH for the Armed Forces

CHAPTER I

ENGLISH

The Importance of English to the Armed Forces

When you heard that English would be a subject in your training program, probably some of you recorded a silent protest. It is easy to imagine such comments rising in your mind as "Why do we have to take English?" "What good is English in the Army or the Navy?" "This is a time to learn to fight, not to learn to talk!" "Teach us mathematics so that we can work the problems involved in bridge building or navigation; physics so that we may become specialists in radio and meteorology; any of the sciences that will help us in our job; and then stop. English can do us no good now."

Sharply contrasted with this attitude is the attitude of an experienced and respected Army officer, now retired. He has said in effect: "English is the most important weapon of the Armed Forces. The machine gun is called a 'weapon of opportunity,' that is, a weapon used when opportunity arises. In the same sense, a field artillery piece, a plane, or a battleship is a weapon of opportunity. But English is a constantly used weapon upon which the successful use of all other weapons depends."

A bit of thought fully confirms his statement. English *is* a constantly used weapon upon which the successful use of all other weapons depends. It is through the medium of English that men are trained to man the guns, the ships, and the planes. In the last analysis, it is English that makes the gun speak, the ships move, and the planes rise. If that English is misused, men may sail or rise to their death.

No Magic Formula for the Successful Use of English

English is a complicated weapon that cannot be mastered without effort, any more than flying or bridge building can be mastered without effort. It requires a good working knowledge of the basic principles governing writing and speaking, that is, a knowledge of grammar, sentence construction, punctuation, and paragraph structure. It requires patient and thoughtful practice in writing and speaking, a requirement that many students refuse to recognize, much to their own detriment.

Practical English

The English predominantly used by the armed forces might be called practical English. It is English that presents hard facts and well-considered ideas in such logical order and such direct and clear language that they cannot be misunderstood. It is really explanatory English, or English that explains something; for the hard life of school, camp, or battlefield is one ceaseless round of explanation, and of absorbing and applying explanation. The instructor in the use of the 60 mm. mortar explains the process by which his piece works; the instructor at the submarine school explains how a crash dive is made; the operations officer of an air unit explains the mission for the night; the commanding officer of a post issues a memorandum explaining that the grounds must be better policed; and so on through the whole routine of the profession of arms.

Therefore, it is clear that you prospective officers must learn how to explain, both orally and in writing, for the purpose of both understanding and instructing. You are not here concerned with the niceties involved in telling a good story or in describing a beautiful scene that has aroused you emotionally. You are rather concerned with the logical presentation of facts and inferences based on facts in such a direct, concise, and clear language that your meaning cannot be misinterpreted. This is equally an art, and one that will prove of inestimable value to you in any walk of life.

Types of Explanatory Communication

It would be possible to enumerate a surprising number of types of explanatory communication, but you will need to master only the most important ones. You will certainly find frequent use for the following:

1. The explanation of an object, which is nothing more than describing an object (for example, a rubber pontoon) so clearly, in whole or in specified parts, that the reader or listener is able to see it with the eye of his mind.

2. The explanation of a process, which is a clear and accurate tracing of the steps by which some machine functions or some action is performed.

3. The explanation of an object and of a process in combination.

4. The explanation of an idea, which is a setting forth of one's thoughts upon a subject in such a fashion that they will be readily understood.

5. Report making, which usually combines the explanation of an object, of a process, and of an idea in a fairly formal structure.

CHAPTER II

THE EXPLANATORY PARAGRAPH

Before you will be ready to write a long composition, you must be able to write an effective explanatory paragraph. There are two reasons for this fact. One is that of two forms governed by the same general principles we have always found it wise to master the simpler first. The other is that the long composition is made up of paragraphs; we cannot create the whole until we can first create the parts.

In your study of the paragraph you should remember that you are dealing with a form the usefulness of which extends beyond the art of writing. Good speaking too requires the knowledge and application of the principles of the paragraph, though the use of these principles may be less easily detected in speech than in writing. Furthermore, it is only by understanding the principles of the paragraph that one can read with ease and intelligence. You should, then, look upon your study of the paragraph as of great value to your writing, speaking, and reading.

Definition of the Paragraph

The paragraph may be defined as a series of sentences that amplify a single idea in an orderly manner. You should note three important details in this definition: (1) a single idea, (2) the amplification or enlargement of it, (3) order.

How to Write a Good Explanatory Paragraph

Whether you wish to write a paragraph as a separate composition or as part of a long composition, you must follow certain established principles.

1. **You must treat but one idea.** The paragraph must

have singleness of idea, or unity, above everything else. In other words, you may not write about carrots and compasses in the same paragraph, because they represent two wholly separate ideas; nor, for the same reason, may you write about the discovery of coffee and how to make coffee in the same paragraph.

Since the paragraph is a relatively small unit of thought, normally not exceeding two hundred and fifty words in length, you should limit the scope of this single idea which it treats. Otherwise, you will be unable to give the idea substantial development. For example, you should not try to present in a paragraph such a broad idea as the role of Russia in World War II, or the generalship of Marshal Timoshenko, or the tactics of the Cossack cavalry. These are ideas not for paragraphs but for books. You might, however, write an effective paragraph on such a limited idea as the Cossack cavalryman's skill in terrifying noise-making, or the dress of the Russian ski trooper, or the structure of the "Molotoff Cocktail."

You should usually express this idea in the first sentence of the paragraph. Doing so is advantageous to you as the writer, because it sets your topic idea before your eyes and thus tends to prevent you from wandering from it. But it is more advantageous to the reader, because it enables him to know at once what the paragraph is about and thus to have a sure guide in his reading. In the following paragraph note the author's statement of his idea in the first sentence, and the unmistakable direction it gives to the content of the paragraph:

For a while the U-boats working against the convoys adopted a very clever ruse that paid them excellent dividends. One submarine was placed on one side of the convoy, the rest of the pack on the other. The lone submarine purposely created a diversion, causing the destroyers to leave their assigned stations and go charging after it. This left huge exposed and unprotected gaps in the convoys. Before the destroyers could detect the trickery, the rest of the submarine pack had closed in at full speed and taken a terrific toll of the convoy, and were away before they could be fired upon or even sighted by the destroyers. But escorting destroyers can no longer be lured away by such trickery.[1]

You may occasionally, however, find it desirable to state your topic idea at some other point in the paragraph, especially at the end. When it is withheld until the end, the statement of the topic idea may achieve the effect of climax, of final, forceful clarification of the gist of the whole paragraph.

2. **You must amplify the topic idea as fully as your purpose requires.** In other words, you must give the paragraph substance, say something really significant about the idea. There are numerous ways of amplification, the more common of which are mentioned below.

a. **Details.** You may give the details that are naturally suggested by the topic idea. This method of amplification is most natural when the idea involves the explanation (or technical description) of an object, such as the recoil mechanism of the Garand rifle, a fireman's axe, or a spark plug. Note how the author of the following paragraph brings detail upon detail in explaining the Japanese stick grenade:

This grenade is made up of a cylindrical cast-iron pot which is two inches long, two inches outside diameter, and one and one-half inches inside diameter. It is open at one end and closed at the other and is of uniform thickness. Inserted in this shell is a charge consisting of two ounces of lyddite in the form of a plug with a hole through the center to receive a detonator. It is covered by a thick paper cylinder to prevent the charge from coming in contact with either the detonator or the cast-iron shell. This charge is two inches long, and the detonator hole five-sixteenths of an inch in diameter. A wooden handle is placed in the top of the iron cylinder to a depth of three-quarters of an inch, and it is secured by three small screws which pass through the iron shell. This handle is five inches long and is drilled lengthwise through the cylinder with a three-eighths-inch hole.[2]

[1] From *Serpent of the Seas* by Commander Harley F. Cope, Funk & Wagnalls Company. Reprinted by permission of the author and the publisher.

[2] From "Japanese Tactics and Materiel," *Coast Artillery Journal*. Reprinted by permission.

This method is also a natural one to use if the topic idea involves the explanation of a process or an action. Note how the author of the following paragraph details the steps of the procedure which is the topic idea of the paragraph:

While it is not strictly an engineer function, an account of the means by which water actually reaches the soldier after it has left the water point is necessary if this picture of water supply in the Army is to be complete. Like all systems which function well in the field, the one used by the units to get their water is very simple. The units simply load up an appropriate number of trucks with receptacles, and send them to the water point. There, the receptacles are filled in a manner already described [by pumping or by gravity], the trucks return to their units, the soldiers fill their canteens, and the mess sergeants fill their cans. The final step of the water supply problem has been solved.[3]

b. Comparison or contrast. You may amplify the topic idea by the use of comparison or contrast, that is, a statement of the similarities or dissimilarities between two things. You will find this method particularly advantageous when you have to explain an object or a process with which your readers are likely to be unfamiliar. Let us say that your topic idea concerns a description of the physical device by which engineers are enabled to tunnel under rivers. Since most people are unfamiliar with this device but are thoroughly familiar with the telescope, you could best explain the device by comparing it to a huge steel telescope progressively pushed open from the large end. In writing a description of the new Garand rifle, unfamiliar at least to most civilians, you might contrast it with the more familiar Springfield.

c. Examples. You may present examples that reveal the truth of the topic idea. This method of amplification is often useful when the central idea concerns not concrete things such as objects and processes, but abstract

[3] From *What the Citizen Should Know About the Army Engineers* by Lieutenant Colonel Paul W. Thompson, W. W. Norton & Company, Inc. Reprinted by permission.

things. In other words, it is used mainly in the type of explanation known as the explanation of an idea. For instance, if your topic idea is "The Hollander has proved a good colonizer," you might develop it by citing as examples what he has done in Java, Dutch Guiana, and elsewhere. In the following paragraph an example is used to amplify the idea that home environment plays a significant part in the development of "the flying cadet type":

There is no gainsaying that family and home environment play a tremendous part in the development of the flying cadet type. Not long since, into one of our squadrons came a young flyer who almost from the beginning manifested evidence of lack of sufficient co-operativeness; he had a stubbornness and a failure to assimilate or accept the necessary tenets of military discipline. His flight leader and squadron commander, and eventually his group commander took him personally in charge and made every effort to correct his attitude, but without success. Eventually a flagrant breach of discipline on his part was a factor in the death of one of his fellow flyers. Eventually it was necessary to eliminate him from the service. A study of his previous record revealed that he was an only child. He had probably been pampered and spoiled from babyhood. The system for selection of flying cadets, careful and stringent as it is, had failed to find and eliminate him, with the result that his government lost the thousands of dollars spent in his training, an airplane costing more than $25,000, and the life of a very fine young flyer. Examples such as these indicate the reasons for the careful selection of young Army flying men.[4]

d. Causes or effects. You may state the causes or the effects (or both) of a condition or a phenomenon pointed out by the central idea. The following paragraph is developed mainly by a statement of causes:

If a cell [dry cell] should cease to function, one of three things may have happened: (1) The zinc has been eaten away. If this is the case you have received your money's worth from the cell, for you have burned up all the fuel for which you paid. (2) The cell may have lost a good deal of its

[4] From *Army Flyer* by Lieutenant General H. H. Arnold and Brigadier General Ira C. Eaker, Harper & Brothers. Reprinted by permission.

water through evaporation. If this happens, since there is no water to ionize the ammonium chloride, the cell cannot produce a current. If one or two holes are carefully punctured in the zinc container and the cell left to stand in a dish of water, the water will be absorbed through the holes and the cell can be restored. (3) Polarization may occur if much current is drawn from the cell for any extended time, for hydrogen then forms faster than it can be absorbed by the depolarizer. By allowing the cell to rest, it will "recuperate." Sufficient time must be allowed for the depolarizer to remove the excess hydrogen.[5]

The next paragraph, on the other hand, is developed by a statement of effects:

If gasoline is allowed to flood automobile cylinders it may by-pass the piston rings and descend into the crankcase. The gasoline in the crankcase dilutes the oil. At the same time, it has momentarily removed the lubricant from the cylinder walls and piston rings.[6]

   e. Definition. Finally, you may amplify the central idea by the use of definition, formal or informal. **A formal or scientific definition** states the class to which a thing belongs and the peculiarities that set it off from other members of that class. Note in the following paragraph, in which the author defines an alternating current, that he first states the class to which an alternating current belongs—that is, electric current—and then states the peculiarities of it:

An alternating current is one [that is, an electric current] which constantly changes direction at regular intervals. The current increases from zero to its maximum strength and decreases to zero with the current flowing in one direction; then, with the current flowing in the opposite direction, similarly increases to a maximum and again decreases to zero.[7]

An informal definition sets forth details or examples that clearly characterize the thing to be defined. In the follow-

---

[5] From *Fundamentals of Electricity* by Theodore C. Benjamin, Charles Scribner's Sons. Reprinted by permission.

[6] From *Fundamentals of Machines* by Alexander Joseph, Charles Scribner's Sons. Reprinted by permission.

[7] From *Fundamentals of Electricity* by Theodore Benjamin, Charles Scribner's Sons. Reprinted by permission.

ing paragraph the authors effectively use an example to define moral courage:

Moral courage is too frequently overlooked as one of the desirable characteristics of the fighting man. Some years ago, a group of flying officers were en route to a distant station for the performance of an unusual flight undertaking. At their first stop en route, all stayed for the night in a common room at an officers' club. As they were retiring for the night the junior of the crew knelt beside his bed, bowed his head, and prayed for a full minute before climbing upon his army cot. That took moral courage of no mean order. His associates were a hard-bitten group of older officers. He might well have expected derision or ridicule. This he faced to carry out a custom of childhood. One of those fellow flyers said later that this real-life repeat of *Tom Brown's School Days* sold him immediately on the fact that the youngster had courage and fortitude of high degree.[8]

It is obvious then that there are numerous ways of amplifying the central idea of a paragraph. The important thing is that you develop the habit of analyzing your central idea in order to arrive at the most effective way of enlarging upon it. Ask yourself this question, "Would this idea best be amplified by the use of details, comparison, contrast, examples, causes, effects, or definition?" If after analyzing your central idea you find that effective amplification calls for the use of several methods in combination, you should not hesitate to go ahead on that basis. Indeed, a good paragraph often represents a combination of several ways of amplification.

Exercise A

In each of the following paragraphs underline the sentence that expresses the central idea and determine the way (or ways) used for amplifying that idea.

I

Roads have always exercised a dominating influence on the conduct of war. The military strength of Rome rested

[8] From *Army Flyer* by Lieutenant General H. H. Arnold and Brigadier General Ira C. Eaker, Harper & Brothers. Reprinted by permission.

squarely on its system of roads, the model for which was that greatest of all military roads, the Appian Way. The heroic defense of Verdun—one of the proudest pages in French history —succeeded because French engineers performed the prodigious feat of keeping open the single slender road over which all supplies for the fortress had to pass. The French have a name for that slender road. They call it "the Sacred Way." [9]

2

A good officer, like a good foreman in civil life, has the knack of securing co-operation from his subordinates without toadying, coddling or self-abasement. Firmness without cruelty; impartiality, fellow feeling, consideration, sympathy, understanding—these are the qualities which make for esteem and high regard by soldiers for their officers. Fortunate is the officer who has the character to make the right impression on his men. [10]

3

Each composition, or article, is a stone in the temple of knowledge, some mechanism useful in the shaping of the stones, or some revelation concerning the blueprint of the unknown plan of the temple or the use of the functioning portions of the edifice. A writer, once he has ascertained that his stone is compounded of and is foursquare with truth, should not be fearful concerning its place in the temple because its place seems to be far from the foundation. It may be the foundation stone for a very useful flying buttress, or a new wing. Nor should the contribution be despised because it is just one stone in the slowly rising walls—for of such is the temple constructed, and without them there would be no structure of knowledge. [11]

4

The topographic company . . . consists of a headquarters and three platoons, the functions of which are indicated by their titles: survey platoon, photomapping platoon, and re-

[9] From *What the Citizen Should Know About the Army Engineers* by Lieutenant Colonel Paul W. Thompson, W. W. Norton & Company, Inc. Reprinted by permission.

[10] From *Army Flyer* by Lieutenant General H. H. Arnold and Brigadier General Ira C. Eaker, Harper & Brothers. Reprinted by permission.

[11] From "Expression as an Engineering Technique" by John J. O'Neill, *Journal of Engineering Education*. Reprinted by permission.

production platoon. The survey platoon is equipped with theodolites, levels, and other such instruments. The photo-mapping platoon is equipped with "stereocomparagraphs"—instruments which operate on the principle of the old parlor-game stereoscope, and which enable the operators to interpret and develop maps from aerial photographs. The reproduction platoon is a printing establishment, equipped with facilities for turning out thousands of copies of maps per hour. The chief item of equipment in this platoon is a printing press operating on the lithographic principle.[12]

5

An explosive is a substance or mixture of substances which is likely, on the application of heat, friction, or a blow to a small portion of the mass, to be converted in a very short interval of time into other more stable substances largely or entirely gaseous. A considerable amount of heat is also invariably evolved, and consequently there is a flame. The very sudden or violent transformation of the explosive into the more stable gases is called an explosion.[13]

6

The antitank ditch is an obstacle which has the obvious advantage of requiring no steel, gravel, cement, or other material. On the other hand, its construction requires tremendous amounts of labor, or, instead, the services of earth-moving machines. To be effective against modern tanks, ditches must be at least 6 feet deep and at least 18 feet wide. The friendly side, and preferably both sides, should be close to vertical, and, preferably, should be revetted (otherwise they may disintegrate with the weather, or be shot to pieces by the tanks' guns). The antitank ditch is well exemplified in the extensive system of field fortifications thrown up by the British along the Franco-Belgian frontier during the winter of 1939–40. (Unfortunately, that British line was outflanked, and so never had a test.) [14]

3. You must arrange the amplifying material in some order that gives it effectiveness. It is only by hav-

[12] From *What the Citizen Should Know About the Army Engineers* by Lieutenant Colonel Paul W. Thompson, W. W. Norton and Company, Inc. Reprinted by permission.

[13] From "Explosives and Their Military Applications" by R. H. Kent, *Journal of Applied Physics.* Reprinted by permission.

[14] From *What the Citizen Should Know About the Army Engineers* by Lieutenant Colonel Paul W. Thompson, W. W. Norton and Company, Inc. Reprinted by permission.

ing orderly progression in your thoughts that you can achieve that ultimate goal of all communication—clarity. There follow several commonly used methods of arranging the materials in a paragraph.

a. Order of Space. In a paragraph that is concerned with the explanation of an object (a machine or a landscape, for example), you should use the order of space. That is, you should proceed in your description from the left to the right of the object, or from top to bottom, or from near to far, or from outside to inside, or the reverse. Refer to the paragraph on the Japanese stick grenade (page 6) and note how clear a picture the author gives of it by describing first the outside details of the grenade proper, then the inside details, and finally the stick and how it is attached.

b. Order of Time. In a paragraph that is concerned with the explanation of a process or of anything that entails a time sequence, you should use the order of time. In the paragraph on water supply (page 7), note that the author presents the steps of getting water to the soldiers in the exact time order in which they occur.

In the explanation of an object or process, arrangement of materials should not prove difficult for you, since these types of explanation naturally suggest the methods of arrangement described above. In the explanation of abstract things, however, arrangement will not be so obvious. Here you must study your materials to discover an effective logical order in which to present them. Normally you will find that one of the following logical methods of arrangement will help you in your problem.

c. Order of Increasing Significance. This order involves your proceeding from the least important point among your amplifying materials, through the more important points, to the most important point. Its value lies in increasing the interest of the reader to the end and in placing the most important part of the subject in the most emphatic position, which is the end. It is frequently used by writers and speakers who want the effect of a strong clincher at the end of their discourse. President Roosevelt's "We can. We will. We must." offers a brief example of this method of arrangement.

d. Order of Decreasing Significance. In spite of all that has been said against this order as one that loses the interest of the reader, there are times when it is the best one to use. For example, if you were asked to state your reasons for advocating a particular course of action and you had one that was overwhelmingly persuasive, while the others were minor beside it, would you not want to present the important one first, to call attention to it at once in order to make sure that it was considered?

e. Order of Strictly Logical Relationship of Thought. Upon considering your amplifying materials you will sometimes find a very close thought relationship existing among them. One thought seems naturally and inevitably to lead to another in an unbroken chain of logic. When you can make this discovery, you have the best order of all.

Exercise B

In each of the following paragraphs underline the sentence that states the central idea and determine the method of amplifying that idea and of arranging the amplifying materials.

I

The meeting [for the Atlantic Conference between President Roosevelt and Prime Minister Churchill] was, therefore, symbolic. That is its prime importance. It symbolizes, in a form and manner which every one can understand in every land and in every clime, the deep underlying unities which stir and, at decisive moments, rule the English-speaking peoples throughout the world. Would it be presumptuous for me to say that it symbolizes something even more majestic, namely the marshalling of the good forces of the world against the evil forces which are now so formidable and triumphant and which have cast their cruel spell over the whole of Europe and a large part of Asia?[15]

[15] From Prime Minister Churchill's speech to the world concerning the Atlantic Conference.

2

The *kaong* is a palm commonly found in forests and open regions and along valleys and creeks, up to altitudes of 1500 to 2000 feet above sea level. The plant reaches a height of thirty to fifty feet and has a trunk diameter of ten to fifteen inches. It has long feather-like leaves, each fifteen to twenty-five feet long, and the base of each leaf is covered with black fibers. Each long leaf is made up of ninety to one hundred pairs of linear leaves, three to five feet long. These smaller leaves are lobed at the tip and notched or ear-shaped at the base. The fruit of the kaong consists of clusters of green nuts which turn yellow when they mature. This fruit causes irritation to those who do not know how to handle it. The covering of the fruit contains numerous microscopic needle-like hairs and when handled with the bare hands, especially when the fruit is decaying, the hairs cause irritation of the skin.[16]

3

The Spencer Microfilm Reader, developed as a result of studies by the Committee on Scientific Aids to Learning, is the first inexpensive instrument designed to reproduce the almost microscopic characters of microfilm with brilliant fidelity. The instrument consists of a projection head, a glass film book, and a shadow box and screen. The projection head incorporates an inexpensive spotlight type of long-life bulb, the proper condensing system, and a specially designed projection lens. This head is held by spring clips to the shadow box, which also serves as a support, and may be rotated to project the film in either a vertical or horizontal meridian as desired. Operation of the instrument is simple. The microfilm is placed in a convenient glass film book which consists of two pieces of glass, hinged and bound at the edges with transparent Cellophane tape. This tape serves to space the film properly to protect it from scratching and to orient the film in relation to the focal plane of the objective. The image is projected into the screen and is so protected by the shadow box that a darkened room is unnecessary. The image is flat and undistorted and should not cause optical fatigue or discomfort.[17]

4

The photoengraver makes his photograph print on a zinc or copper plate sensitized with a mixture of glue and potassium

[16] From "Jungle Warfare," Part Two (condensed from Field Manual 31–20), *Coast Artillery Journal.* Reprinted by permission.

[17] From "Innovations in Instruments," *Journal of Applied Physics.* Reprinted by permission.

chromate. When exposed and the unexposed sensitizer washed off, the plate will have a positive image in dots composed of the hardened sensitizer. Where the original was black there will be dots of hard sensitizer close together on the plate; where it was gray these dots will be farther apart; where it was white there will be empty squares. All this dotted surface is now further hardened by heat and dusted with an acid-resistant resinous material called, in the trade, "dragon's blood," which in turn is heated to make it stick to the dots. All this is done in such a way that only the dots will be protected by dragon's blood, the spaces between them remaining vulnerable to the acid. The plate is put in an acid bath and all the metal is bitten except the dots. What comes out of the bath is a plate ready for printing, made up of dots in relief. When this plate is printed from, the picture appears to consist entirely of tones, and only under the magnifying glass, when the black and white dots are visible, is the deception evident. To the naked eye, a photograph has been perfectly reproduced in printer's ink.[18]

4. You must show the relationship of your successive thoughts by the use of connective expressions (frequently called transitional expressions). Otherwise, even though you have arranged your materials in an orderly manner, a good bit of your writing will lack clarity. Connective expressions in writing are like the cement in bricklaying. They join the bricks of thought solidly and unmistakably together. Here are two successive thoughts unjoined by the connective cement:

We want to defeat Hirohito. We must defeat Hitler first.

Note how insecurely these thoughts stand together, even though they are successive thoughts. Now let us apply the connective cement.

We want to defeat Hirohito. *However,* we must defeat Hitler first.

Note the solid joining of the two thoughts. There can be no lack of clarity now.

There are three classes of connective expressions that

[18] From *Engines of Democracy* by Roger Burlingame, Charles Scribner's Sons. Reprinted by permission.

Paragraph Topics for Writing and Speaking

Explanation of an object:

1. A pontoon
2. The compass (either the direction compass, or the mathematical instrument)
3. The gas mask
4. The oxygen mask
5. A bangalore torpedo
6. A pedometer
7. A spark plug
8. A primer (on an automobile)
9. The Army helmet
10. A fire extinguisher
11. A depth bomb
12. The Garand rifle
13. The Browning machine gun
14. An anemometer
15. The barrage balloon
16. The thermometer
17. An anchor
18. The Army .45 caliber
19. The Navy Colt
20. The hand grenade
21. A fireman's axe
22. A crosscut saw
23. A brace and bit
24. A headphone
25. A modern submarine torpedo

Explanation of a process, procedure, action:

1. How to do Dress Right
2. How to do Parade Rest
3. How to put up a pup tent
4. How the Army makes a bed
5. How the bicycle (or automobile) pump works
6. How to patch a punctured inner tube
7. How the American salute is rendered
8. How to read an aerial photograph
9. How to pack a parachute
10. How to plot the course of a vessel
11. How to plot the course of an airplane
12. How to change a tire
13. How to clean a rifle (or any kind of gun)

may be used within the paragraph. The first two classes will appear rather naturally in your writing; the third, not so.

a. Reference words, consisting of personal pronouns (especially those of the third person: *he, she, it, they*) and demonstrative adjectives (*this, that, these, those, such*). When the antecedent of the pronoun or demonstrative adjective is in the preceding sentence, the pronoun or demonstrative adjective becomes a natural link between the thoughts of the two sentences.

> *Example:* The New York Yankees will not find things easy without Joe Di Maggio. *He* was a great source of strength to the team.
> *Example:* The cause of peace is the only one in which man should fight naturally. *This* cause should stiffen the muscles of all of us.

b. Repeated words, phrases, or clauses.

> *Example:* In the name of liberty we cry to you for help. *In the name of liberty* we expect *help.*

c. Directive expressions: *first, second, third, in the first place, in the second place, in the third place, when one enters upon the fourth phase, next, then, finally, further, moreover, on the one hand, on the other hand, however, nevertheless, consequently, therefore, hence, as a result, indeed, in fact* (and many more). To such expressions you must give your careful consideration; you cannot expect them to appear naturally—and correctly—in your writing. Yet they are invaluable, not only to show the relationship between successive thoughts, but also to point out to the reader the larger divisions of the thought. In the latter capacity they say in effect: The writer has now completed one phase of his explanation and is going on to another.

Do not overload your paragraphs with these directive expressions. Use them only when they are necessary for clarity.

In the following paragraph all connective expressions are italicized and their classes indicated in the margin:

> The subject of roads, their construction and maintenance, tends to be a little dull. "All that is required to *build and maintain* a *road*," runs an axiom springing from experience in the AEF of 1918, "is to get the rock on and the water off." *However,* the act of *getting the rock on and the water off* may be very simple, or very difficult, according to circumstances. If the *road* net in the theater of operations is dense and good, if the weather holds fair, and if the campaign is short, *road maintenance* will cause little concern. An example of *such* a happy situation is found in the *campaign* of 1940 in France, or in our own Carolina maneuvers of 1941. *On the other hand,* if the *campaign* is long, and if it includes much bad *weather,* the best of *roads* will deteriorate. The prime example of *this* we have already cited [in preceding paragraph]: the France of 1918. *If the road net* existing *in the theater of operations is* sparse and poor, the resulting *road problem* may transcend every other one in difficulty and importance. An example is the Abyssinian *campaign* of 1935, in which entire Italian army corps were diverted to assist the engineers *in building and maintaining roads.*[19]

Margin notes (top to bottom): Rep. / D.E. / Rep. / Rep. / Rep. — Ref. Wd. / Rep. / D.E., Rep. / Rep. / Ref. Wd. / Rep. Rep. / Rep. / Rep.

Exercise C

In the following paragraph select the sentence that states the central idea, determine the method of amplification and the method of arrangement, and underline and be prepared to classify all connective expressions.

The Army Engineers are the mapmakers for the Army. As we have seen in Chapter III, there are in the Corps of Engineers certain "topographical" units. These units form something of a corps within a corps. Their high responsibilities, their complex equipment, and the special skills which their work requires, combine to give them the feeling of being an elite group. The Army, however, needs a great deal more than gasoline company maps. Indeed, the map needs of

[19] From *What the Citizen Should Know About the Army Engineers* by Lieutenant Colonel Paul W. Thompson, W. W. Norton and Company, Inc. Reprinted by permission.

the Army are almost limitless. The commanding general demands a map which gives him "the big picture"—that is, a map which shows him the situation throughout the theater of operations, practically at a glance. The platoon commander would find such a map worse than useless. The latter demands a "large-scale" map which shows every road and trail, and on which he can spot the very clump of woods in which he is to bivouac his unit tonight. The artillerist is most exacting. He demands a large-scale map on which he can identify his target, and from which he can scale the data necessary for the calculations which will enable him to hit the target. This calls for a high degree of accuracy in the map.[20]

Writing the Paragraph

You can see from the preceding discussion that writing a unified, substantial, and well-organized paragraph is not an achievement with which a person is born. It requires thoughtful practice. If you desire to get the most from that practice, you should take the following steps in preparing a paragraph:

1. You should first formulate and write down the central idea in sentence form; for until you have written down the central idea, you will most likely be floundering.

2. As your second step, you should jot down in the form of brief notes the materials that suggest themselves for the amplification of the central idea.

3. Then you should scrutinize these notes, crossing anything trivial and unimportant, adding anything important that has been omitted.

4. You should then study your notes again to determine an effective arrangement of your materials. Having decided upon your method of arrangement, you should number or renumber your materials in order to show method.

5. Guided by your simple outline then built, you write the paragraph, always remembering the importance of connective expressions in establishing clear relationship between successive thoughts.

[20] *Ibid.* Reprinted by permission.

Explanation of an object and a process in combination:

1. The recoil mechanism of the Garand rifle
2. The oxygen mask
3. The gas mask
4. The pedometer
5. The gravity filter
6. A primer
7. The electric razor
8. The emergency brake
9. The vacuum cleaner
10. The slide rule
11. A cash register
12. A stop watch
13. The direction compass
14. The accelerator (on an automobile)

Explanation of an idea:

1. Current difficulty of getting farm machinery
2. Effects of the war on some aspect of American life
3. Why I want to be an Army or a Navy pilot
4. Why I want to be an Army Engineer
5. Reasons for rationing
6. Relative speeds of Allied aircraft
7. When to (or not to) salute
8. The thrill of Retreat Formation
9. Effectiveness of the air-borne torpedo
10. Effects of dive bombing on physical well-being of airmen
11. Virtues of the P-T boat
12. The man who did not button his lips
13. Government censorship in time of war
14. The meaning of patriotism

CHAPTER III

THE COMPLETE EXPLANATORY COMPOSITION [1]

Definition of Complete Explanatory Composition

The term *complete explanatory composition* is used here to represent various terms, such as *article, theme, thesis, informative essay,* and *report*. A complete composition usually consists of a series of paragraphs, although a single paragraph may occasionally be a complete composition. Just as a paragraph is usually composed of a series of sentences, so a composition usually contains more than one paragraph. A composition may consist of only two or three paragraphs, or it may be of book length.

A complete composition presents, even as a paragraph, a single topic, but normally the topic of a composition will be larger or more extensive than the topic of a paragraph. The single topic of a composition must be completely developed, but the phrase *completely developed* may have more than one meaning. It would be more accurate to say that a composition must be completely developed in relation to the function that it is expected to perform. Complete development will mean one thing for the writer who is preparing a composition on the geology of the Mississippi basin to be used as a single chapter in a book on the geology of the United States; it will demand somewhat more of the writer who is preparing an entire book on the geology of the Mississippi basin. Yet the composition of each writer will be complete in its own way. A simple

---

[1] Although the terms *writer* and *writing* will be used in the following, you are reminded that for these terms you can substitute the terms *speaker* and *speaking,* for many of the general principles governing spoken and written compositions are identical.

analogy from another field may help. Imagine two measuring instruments, one the coarsely graduated ruler of the schoolboy, the other the minutely graduated steel rule of the machinist. They are quite different, yet each is complete enough for the job for which it is intended.

The topic of a composition must be presented in an orderly manner. Orderly presentation is attained by the general process of breaking the topic into its component parts, of sorting these parts, and of arranging them according to some plan.

Armed with this definition, you are now prepared to learn from the beginning how to write an explanatory composition.

Preparing to Write Explanatory Compositions

Choosing a Topic. Later, during your professional or business career, your topics will usually be decided for you by circumstances or command; but as long as teachers of English composition persist, students will probably be asked to select topics for themes and compositions. Therefore you should know how to pick topics for compositions. You should be guided by the following suggestions in the selection of your subject.

Be sure that you have picked one topic and only one topic. It is fairly obvious that this principle would be violated by a composition on Diesel engines and gasoline engines. There would, however, be no violation of this principle in a composition which presented comparative costs for Diesel engine upkeep and gasoline engine upkeep; the unifying principle would be in the comparison.

You should decide whether you will be able to gather sufficient material for an adequate development of the topic that you are considering. Is your library, or laboratory, or whatever the source of your material, adequately supplied with the materials you will need?

Examine the topic that you are considering to be sure that it is not too large in its scope. Your topic must be limited enough in scope so that you will be able to give the reader or listener a full understanding of it within the limits of the space or time that will be available for your presentation. This consideration is especially important for the speaker, for the time allotted to him is usually limited.

Mastering Your Topic. You must acquire a thorough mastery of your topic before you are ready to start writing. Know your subject thoroughly, completely, through thinking, or reading, or observation; remember, for knowledge there is no substitute. In fact, if you have any hope of being taken seriously as either writer or speaker, you will have to make it an invariable rule to know more of your topic than you will need to tell. Even go so far as to learn as much as you can about related subjects, those which have a bearing upon your topic although they are not a part of it. It is only through solid understanding of his subject that a writer can see it in its proper perspective.

Organizing Your Topic. You will approach the actual writing by a series of steps, each step representing a distinct advance along the road from a vague idea to the finished composition. Let us suppose that you have decided to write on tennis, and that after some thought you have limited this topic to serving in tennis, one aspect of your subject that can adequately be dealt with in a short composition. From playing this game and watching others play it, you believe that your own experience will supply you with enough material. Moreover, this is not the kind of topic that readily lends itself to research in a library.

Deciding Upon a Central Idea. Your first step is to decide what part of your topic you are going to develop as your central idea. After some careful thinking, you should be able to make a clear statement of this central idea, not in a phrase such as a title, but in a single, complete declarative sentence. This sentence should indicate both the extent and the limitations of the composition. For the proposed composition on tennis your central idea sentence might read something like this:

The server in tennis holds a distinct advantage over his opponent.

Jotting Down Rough Ideas. Your next step is to jot down, on a piece of scrap paper, rough ideas about your central idea. These jottings should be committed to paper in the helter-skelter fashion in which they pour into your mind. Do not try to order them in a logical sequence; do not strive for finished phrasing. Your object here is simply to empty your mind of all it contains on your central idea. Here are some of the jottings that might occur to you if you were writing on the advantage which the server holds in tennis:

The server has two serves.
If he nets one, he still has a second chance.
Position of the server on the court after he has served.
Next play.
Serving to the opponent's backhand.
Cutting the corners of the service square.
Perhaps an ace.
Force your opponent to return the kind of ball you want— making him play your kind of game.
Take advantage of his position.
The offense has it all over the defense.
Compare with military strategy.
Deception: a soft ball first and then a hard one.
The various kinds of serves.
Describe the American serve, comparing it to the European.
Mention the difficulties Bill Harris had with my serves in our game last Friday.
Good comparison: compare serving to lashing a whip.

Classifying and Arranging Your Notes. Your third step is to classify and arrange your rough notes. Group together those that are logically related, and arrange these groups in the probable order in which you think you will finally present them.

Of course you will not want to use every rough idea; do not hesitate to discard those which are irrelevant. Hard thinking will convince you, for example, that the note which reads "Describe the American serve, comparing it to the European" contains an idea which does not come under your topic. A comparison of the various types of serves, while more or less related to the idea of the advantage which the server holds over his opponent, is not a logical part of that idea. The act of grouping your notes likewise may suggest additional ideas to you; write down these ideas in their proper groups. And it is not too early to think of each of these groupings as a major heading in the sentence outline or as a paragraph in the finished composition. The rough jottings for the composition on tennis might be grouped somewhat as follows:

1 {
The server has two serves.
If he nets one he still has a second chance.
The offense has it all over the defense.
Compare with military strategy.
Deception: a soft ball first and then a hard one.
Serving to the opponent's backhand.
Cutting the corners of the service square.
Perhaps an ace.
Take advantage of his position.
}

2 {
Force your opponent to return the kind of ball you want—making him play your kind of game.
But the server must possess the proper equipment, and he must know something about strategy.
Lobbing: chance for an easy kill.
A low ball over the net; chance for another easy kill.
With a difficult serve your opponent is content merely with returning the ball, generally to your forehand. (Notice the additions here.)
}

3 {
Position of the server on the court after he has served.
Plenty of time to rush to the net.
Or to stay in the back court.
The server can play the game where he wants to.
}

Outlining. Your next step is to make a complete sentence outline. This should be prepared with as much care as you would give to the actual writing of the composition. An outline is like the blueprint which an architect prepares for the builder; in itself it has no value, but as part of a process it is indispensable. Look upon your outline as an orderly plan for your composition; it will serve you as a guide in writing, and your use of it will aid your readers in understanding. There are several types of outline, but most useful is the sentence outline, in which all topics and subtopics are in complete declarative sentences. Here is such an outline based on the groupings of ideas developed in the preceding paragraph:

Central Idea: The server in tennis holds a distinct advantage over his opponent.
I. The server holds the initial advantage that always belongs to the offensive.
  A. He is legally entitled to two serves.
  B. He can serve a soft or hard ball at will (provided he has mastered these techniques).
  C. He can take advantage of his opponent's position on the court.
    1. The opponent may be playing too shallow or too deep.
    2. The opponent may be playing too far to the left or too far to the right.
II. The server can force his opponent to return the kind of ball the server wants.
  A. The server can force his opponent to return a high lob, which is easily killed.
  B. The server can force his opponent to return a low ball over the net.
  C. With a difficult serve the opponent is generally content with playing to the server's forehand, the easiest kind of shot to handle.
III. The server can also place himself in an advantageous position on the court.
  A. He will know where to go to play his opponent's ball.
  B. He will have plenty of time to go to the net if necessary.
  C. Or he can stay in the back court if necessary.

The method of numbering and indentation for a sentence outline will be suggested by the foregoing outline. The main headings should be numbered with Roman numerals and should indicate in single, complete declarative sentences the main parts of the central idea, or the main steps of which that idea is built up. Study the following diagram:

```
I. ..........................................................
   A. ....................................................
      ..........................
   B. ....................................................
      1. .................................................
         .....................
      2. .................................................
      3. .................................................
         a. ................................
         b. ................................
II. ................................................. etc.
```

The degree of division and subdivision advisable for a particular outline will be determined by the length and complexity of the subject to be developed. For a short or simple composition, merely a list of sentences representing the main headings may be sufficient division of the central idea. But for longer or more complicated compositions, division and subdivision to the third or fourth degree will be necessary.

Writing the Explanatory Composition

Everything up to this point has been concerned with the preliminaries to actual writing, such as acquiring knowledge of the subject, planning, outlining, etc. Now comes the actual writing, which should be less difficult if you have given careful attention to the preliminaries. Work from the sentence outline into good paragraphs. Generally speaking, each major heading of your outline will provide the material for a paragraph. Often the major heading will be developed and expanded by the use of its subheadings.

During the process of actual writing some thought must be given to an adequate use of definitions. You will need to define strange terms or terms that might be understood in a way that you do not intend. Such definitions as you need in order to make your composition clear should appear at the point at which they first become necessary to an understanding of the meaning.

Especially in explanatory compositions dealing with objects and processes, visual aids should be used, where practicable, to make the machine or any part of it, the process or any step of it, clearer to the reader. For instance, a sketch or diagram is often helpful in explanation, but it should be used only to aid the written word, not to take the place of it. A sketch or diagram should always possess the following traits: It should show only the essential parts of the object; parts which are unessential to your explanation should be carefully omitted. It must be absolutely accurate, for an incorrect or disproportionate sketch does more to retard than to advance your explanation. It should have a careful labeling of the parts with letters or figures for the reader's convenience in referring to the parts, and under the sketch should be a key to the letters or figures and the parts which they represent. Lastly, such illustrations must be neat and orderly.

It is often helpful to your reader if you draw a comparison between the unfamiliar machine or process that you are trying to explain and an object or process with which he is likely to be familiar. Thus, if you were trying to explain a commonly used type of automotive shock absorber, you might suggest that it resembles the human arm from the wrist to the shoulder, with stiffness in the elbow joint which prevents rapid bending and unbending. You could further suggest that the arm is fastened at the shoulder to the frame of the automobile, and at the wrist to the axle. Of course comparisons of this sort should not be used indiscriminately. Each one should be examined for its clarity and accuracy. Does the comparison really help the reader to see the object or process that is being explained? Is the similarity between the familiar object and the unfamiliar object fundamental or superficial?

Whenever time permits you to do so, make a preliminary draft of your composition. Likewise, if time permits, put your preliminary draft aside for a while. Sleep on it. Then you are ready to come back to the revision and polishing of this draft. In this final retouching process you should take the following steps: check and if necessary revise the arrangement; smooth out the phrasing, striving for the exact word; add connective words and phrases where they will clarify the direction of the progressing thought and aid the reader in following the development of the thought.

Finally (from the revised preliminary draft) make a clear, clean copy, the final draft. Do not attempt any extensive changes while you are making the final draft. It should conform to the directions which have been given to you for preparing the manuscript of a composition.

Types of Explanatory Writing

Explanatory writing will here be divided into five types. It is conceded at once that this particular division may seem rather arbitrary, but there are those who object to any division of writing into types. Some maintain, and with considerable justice, that writing is writing and that's all there is to it. The division that has been made here is entirely in the interest of simplification in the presentation of the techniques involved in various sorts of writing. The five types are:

1. Explanation of an object
2. Explanation of a process
3. Explanation of an object and of a process in combination
4. Explanation of an idea, a relationship, or an organization
5. Report writing

It must be explained at this point that in actual writing the first two types, the explanation of an object and the explanation of a process, rarely occur in their pure forms. For the explanation of an object usually must recognize the function of that object, its part in a process; and the explanation of a process usually must include an explanation of the objects involved in that process.

However, because each of these types of explanation has its own problems, the two types are here isolated so that you can segregate and master one sort of skill and then go on to another. Actually a so-called explanation of an object is merely one in which there is a temporary emphasis upon an object. The topic of such an explanation is static; the problems of such an explanation are those of seeing the object, arranging the details, and discovering the over-all pattern. In the explanation of a process, the subject is dynamic; there is a temporary emphasis upon the process, the function.

Explanation of an Object

Before you are ready to do this type of writing, you must make a careful and thoughtful observation of the object. Through observation you should seek to discover the parts that make up the whole object, the relation of these parts to the whole, and the relation of these parts to one another.

As a simple illustration, take a good look at the classroom writing chair that you have probably used many times. First of all, there is a seat which is just about as wide as it needs to be; its length is nearly the same dimension. Hence, the seat is nearly square, unless it narrows toward the back. It is supported by four legs which are placed near the four corners of it; they are long enough so that the legs of anyone sitting in the chair will reach the floor—unless his legs are very short. You will notice that there are rungs between the legs and that these rungs are differently arranged on the sides than they are in front. Skipping over the back, notice the placing of the writing arm. It is supported at two points: at the back it is fastened to the back rest of the chair, and toward the front it rests upon an extension of the front right leg. And so on —for there are still a great many details to examine; as yet you know almost nothing about that chair. And to think that you had never before noticed much more than the generations of initials carved upon the upper surface of the arm. Now, as an exercise, you might try the same sort of analytical observation with a bicycle wheel as the object.

Even at this stage, that of observation, you should know the readers for whom you are writing your explanation. Are you writing for amateurs? Then you should give your topic a general or popular treatment. If, on the other hand, you are writing for specialists, you may usually assume that they will wish a more technical treatment of your topic. The same considerations apply equally to other types of explanatory composition. Such a recognition of the interests of your readers is needed for the next step in the analysis of your problem.

Your next step is the selection of significant details and the discarding of irrelevant details. Thus, about a piece of machinery, color and material will interest a camouflage officer; size, shape, and weight will interest an air transport officer; and the source of power will interest an officer of the Quartermaster Corps. So you can see that if you are going to perform this step successfully, you will have to get used to putting yourself in the other man's boots and seeing the object through his eyes.

In the explanation of an object the arrangement of details will be according to their order in space. The details may be arranged in your composition in the order in which they are found from left to right. Other bases for arrangement are the following: top to bottom, inside to outside, near to far, large to small, or the opposite of any one of these. In explanations of rather simple objects a single plan of arrangement may suffice throughout your composition. Usually the plan should be announced in the paper. In explanations of more complicated objects it may be necessary to use more than one plan of arrangement; if you do use more than one, you must be careful to inform your reader when you shift from one to another.

Now go ahead to the study of the illustrative explanation of an object which follows the list of topics. After you have analyzed the illustrative passage, you should be ready to write explanations of objects, drawing upon your experience or your present courses for your subject matter. The following list of topics is intended to be merely suggestive of the great variety of topics which you·could use. Such explanations could be made in either speaking or writing, or both.

Suggestive Topics for Writing and Speaking: Objects

1. A sea anchor
2. The sling of a rifle
3. The bipod of a trench mortar
4. The surveyor's plumb bob
5. Any one or a group of drawing instruments
6. A simple electrical switch
7. The harness for skis
8. Camouflage of a Bofors A.A. gun
9. Automotive oil filters, or air cleaners
10. The Very pistol
11. A sextant
12. Powdered metal self-lubricating bearings
13. Identification of some type plane
14. Army K rations

SNUG IN THE SNOW AT FORTY BELOW [2]

The Russo-Finnish affair may change some of our ideas as to winter warfare, for in modern times a large-scale war had never before been fought under such conditions. But if other things are equal, it seems certain that the troops with the best winter clothing and the best shelter should win because the bitter Arctic cold will quickly kill off those not adequately prepared to meet it.

It is conceivable that we may some day be faced with a winter campaign in Alaska. If Alaska is invaded, defense will be much harder than in Finland. Alaska is underpopulated and the defending forces will not have thousands of warm farmhouses from which to base their operations.

When the thermometer drops far below zero, man must have shelter or he will freeze to death. At present we have no shelter adequate for winter campaigning. The double shelter

[2] Copyright by The Infantry Journal, Inc. Reprinted by permission.

tent does not provide enough protection, for it cannot be heated properly. Candles and canned heat are the only means of heating double shelter tents—and this in a land that abounds in firewood. The pyramidal tent with the Sibley stove would be fine except that it is too heavy and the air space to be heated is too large. Equipment must be light so that it can be carried on the dogsled or even packed by the soldiers when necessary.

A heated shelter, light enough to be packed by the men using it, and large enough to allow them to remove their heavy outer clothing before getting in their sleeping bags is what we need.

An experimental tent to meet these requirements recently was constructed at Chilkoot Barracks, Alaska, from salvaged shelter halves. For want of a better name this tent will be termed the Chilkoot tent. Imagine four shelter tents pitched with the open ends meeting on the four sides of a square with the corners of adjacent tents overlapping. Now imagine another tent enclosing the open space over this square, with flaps to hang down and close the open spaces between the shelter tents.

The Chilkoot tent combination meets all requirements for an Arctic tent. It is light enough for the eight men it shelters to pack it. It provides a means of burning wood to furnish heat. It is large enough so that four men can stand erect to dress at one time.

The Chilkoot tent is seventy-two inches square with a forty-eight inch wall and a pyramidal roof. The roof ends in a seventeen-inch square top. This flat top is covered by a sheet of galvanized iron securely riveted to the top of the tent. A three-inch hole in the center of the top allows the stovepipe to protrude from the tent. Each wall has a V-shaped opening provided with buttons, buttonholes, and grommets so that a shelter tent can be securely fastened to it. The tent pole is made of three sections of iron pipe, each section thirty-one and a half inches long. The bottom section is screwed into a fitting with two arms riveted to it. These arms are turned at right angles to prevent the pole from sinking into the ground after the heat from the stove has thawed it. The top section is threaded so that it can be screwed into the fitting to which the wires holding up the tent are attached. This pole goes inside the stove and stovepipe when the tent is pitched.

Materials Needed

1 Chilkoot tent
1 stove

3 sections stovepipe
1 jointed pole
8 shelter halves
4 shelter tent poles
20 shelter tent ropes
8 metal pins with hook
4 spruce poles 22 feet long (cut at site)
4 spruce poles 50 inches long (cut at site)

Note: If only short poles can be found they can be lashed together to make the 22-foot lengths.

Explanation of a Process

In preparing to write an explanation of a process, you will follow the same general steps you went through in preparing to write an explanation of an object. First come careful observation and study of the process so that you can gain a thorough understanding of the steps in it and their relation, both to one another and to the complete process. Next come the selection of the important details or steps and the elimination of irrelevant or unimportant details. You will of course bear in mind, as you do this selecting and eliminating, that the interests of your reader will form the basis for your selection.

The arrangement of the parts or steps in an explanation of a process is always chronological, that is, according to the occurrence of the steps in time, such as early and late, or past to present to future. Thus, in the process of dressing, you must pull on your shoes before you lace them, and you must lace them before you tie the laces in a knot. But in undressing, the steps are reversed, and hence the order in which they are arranged will be reversed—if anyone cared to write about putting on and taking off shoes. Your mother's recipe file furnishes simple illustrations of chronological arrangement. Recipes usually follow the pattern of first listing the materials and equipment that will be needed and then telling what is to be done with them, in order of time, first to last.

Cautions. For clearness in the presentation of a process it is especially important that you try to complete one step at a time and thus avoid any overlapping of steps. As much as possible you should avoid reference to a step which has been completed and left behind. Although backward reference should usually be avoided, a much more serious fault in process explanation is forward reference. It is safe to say that there should never be a reference to a step not yet explained and hence unknown to the reader. You can also help the reader to find his way through a process by giving him signals, such as "in the second stage," "From the shaping machine it goes to the finishing room," etc. Such phrases are known as connective expressions; they are a great help to the reader trying to understand a process. (See pages 16–17.)

When to Use Introductions and Conclusions. In the explanation of a simple process it is best to dispense with formal introductions and conclusions. You should at once get down to the business of explaining the process, and stop when you have completed the explanation. In the explanation of a complex process, however, there may be a need for an introductory paragraph in which you trace briefly the main course of the process so that the reader may have a basis for a better understanding of the detailed explanation to follow. In other words, you will probably do well to let your reader have at least a glimpse of the forest before you thrust him into the midst of the trees. A concluding paragraph will ordinarily not be necessary.

Another contingency should be mentioned. The process you are explaining may be only a part of a larger process. If you have to explain a partial process, you can use an introduction to summarize what has gone before the partial process, and a conclusion to summarize what will come after this process. For example, if you had occasion to write on the heat treating of castings, you could in an introduction glance back to the casting process, and in a concluding section explain why the heat treating has to precede the final machining of the casting.

Now go ahead to the study of the illustrative explanations of processes which follow the list of topics. After you have analyzed the illustrative passages, you should be ready to write explanations of processes, drawing upon your experience or your present courses for your subject matter. The following list of topics is intended to be merely suggestive of the great variety of topics which you could use. Such explanations could be made in either speaking or writing, or both.

Suggestive Topics for Writing and Speaking: Processes

1. Rigging a sea anchor
2. Adjusting the sling of a rifle for different uses
3. The correct carry for the 81 mm. mortar
4. How to set up the surveyor's transit
5. Jury-rigged mast for a surf boat
6. Adjusting troop advances to rocky terrain
7. Automotive brake equalization
8. Construction of a field oven
9. "Shooting" the sun
10. Rigging an overhead power shaft
11. Adjusting camouflage to flat, marshy terrain
12. An emergency hand laundering

TAKE UP THE SLACK [3]

Before we go into the positions, it is important to know how to take up the slack in the trigger. This is part of the position exercise because the slack must be taken up by the finger as soon as the correct position is assumed and before careful aiming is begun.

The "slack" in the trigger of a rifle is like the "play" in the clutch of a car. That "play" is built into the clutch by the manufacturer as an extra safety allowance—a preparatory motion that enables both the car and you to get set for a shift in gears. There's "play" in the brake too—if there weren't, you'd stop so suddenly that you'd break your teeth on the dashboard the moment you pushed down on the brake pedal.

Your rifle also has this "safety allowance"—a small amount of slack that brings the trigger lug just to a point where it begins to release the hammer. Squeeze the trigger beyond the slack and the trigger releases the hammer. This causes the rifle to fire.

[3] From a brief résumé of *How to Shoot the U.S. Army Rifle, Infantry Journal*, Vol. LII, No. 4 (April, 1943), p. 34. Copyright by The Infantry Journal, Inc. Reprinted by permission.

The entire amount of slack in the trigger is taken up by one positive movement of the finger.

Take up the slack as soon as the correct position is assumed, and before careful aiming is begun.

SHOWMANSHIP [4]

The effective use of drama for the purpose of instruction has been a by-word among members of the teaching profession for years. Any course can be made interesting, instructive, and impressive through the use of this device.

At The Stockton Quartermaster Motor Transport School this idea of dramatization has been incorporated to a high degree in the Preventive Maintenance Course C for Field and General Officers. During the presentation of PMS 2, 3, 4, and 5, a truck representing a unit in a convoy is driven into the shop building by two typical enlisted men acting as the driver and the assistant driver. As the truck comes to a halt an act is presented showing the wrong way and then the right way to perform the "at halt" inspection. The enlisted personnel remain in the cab of the truck after it has been brought to a full stop and discuss everything but the checking of the prescribed operation. Their discussion is picked up by a microphone and transmitted through loudspeakers for the instruction and entertainment of the student officers. Finally, the assistant driver suggests that it might be a good idea to perform the "at halt" inspection, but the driver states that this is a useless procedure since everything has been working in a satisfactory manner. The driver performs this "inspection" while seated in the cab by merely checking everything "O.K." on the inspection report. Meanwhile, the truck has been prepared so that it is low on water and oil, the tires are under-inflated, the water pump leaks, the tarpaulin is not properly tied, etc. The repair sergeant then steps into the picture and inspects the truck. All of the items that are not up to standard are called to the attention of the operators and disciplinary action is taken. The sergeant then has the driver and assistant driver go through the correct procedure. This act has made quite an impression on the officer students.

After the class has become thoroughly familiar with the correct procedure as established by the various PMS schedules, a three-day convoy is arranged where the students do all of the driving and perform all of the operations and inspections, thus putting into actual use the information they have just

[4] Captain Clement J. Powell, "Showmanship," *The Quartermaster Review*, Vol. XXII, No. 2 (September-October, 1942), p. 60. Reprinted by permission.

acquired. Even though the route of the convoy has been over difficult mountain roads, no accidents or breakdowns have occurred. The students have been greatly impressed with the number of small items that were caught at these various PMS inspections. The immediate correction of these small defects, such as low oil and water, water pump leaks, loose fan belts, loose transfer cases, etc., eliminated the development of major defects. Many letters received from officer students reporting the results obtained since return to their home stations have demonstrated the importance of these inspections.

Drama has also been used in the presentation of the various lecture material through the use of a "horror chamber" of damaged parts. These parts were obtained from the Base Shop where they had been removed from vehicles which had suffered from abuse and lack of attention. The parts are presented, piece by piece, and the various reasons for their failure are explained to the students. This has proven much more effective than the usual conference lecture procedure.

After the demonstration has been completed, an IC vehicle is rolled down an incline into difficult terrain and its recovery is then made a class problem. Members of the class must decide among themselves upon the quickest and most effective way of returning it to its original position with the least possible damage.

During the presentation of the engine lecture a working cutaway model, obtained from an automotive manufacturer, is used. All lights are turned off, except for several spotlights, which are focused on the engine. This spotlighting device makes it easy for the students to concentrate their attention on the items discussed.

These are only a few examples of the ways in which drama has been incorporated in this course. These officer students gain a vivid and lasting impression of the material presented. This, of course, leads to more action and better results.

KEEPING A FUND IS DUCK SOUP [5]

Perhaps no other single item of administration is conducive of more serious trouble than the management of a company fund. The unfortunate part of this situation is that most of the trouble can be easily avoided if the custodian will only exercise a little common sense and devote a little time to his fund, particularly from the very outset. Carelessness rather than dishonesty is responsible for 99 percent of the trouble.

[5] Major Jack W. Rudolph, "Keeping a Fund Is Duck Soup," *Military Review,* Vol. XXIII, No. 1 (April, 1943), pp. 54-55. Reprinted by permission.

The first rule of a commander assuming responsibility for a fund (particularly for the first time) is never to be afraid of it. He has far more serious responsibilities. If he familiarizes himself with the mechanics of supervising the fund and keeps it up to date, he will have no trouble from that source.

The information necessary to run a fund efficiently can be found in three documents. TM 12–250 (Administration) discusses company funds in a general way, and AR 210–50 covers them in detail. Also, the company fund council book itself contains much valuable information. If, upon assuming a fund, you will read these manuals and regulations carefully and then follow their simple rules, you will be all right. If possible, have copies of TM 12–250 and AR 210–50 available for reference at all times.

Having familiarized yourself with the regulations governing funds, you should adopt one important rule and live up to it. *Never receive a penny for the fund and never pay out a penny without making the proper entry in the council book at once.* If you put off this step you are only asking for trouble, because you will probably forget it and gum up your bookkeeping. Nothing is so nerve wracking as the job of finding out why your bank statement doesn't balance with your council book totals.

Upon making a payment or receiving money for the fund, a voucher is mandatory to cover every transaction. This voucher need only be the duly receipted bill for which payment was made or it may be a certificate of a party to the transaction. In any event every fund transaction must be supported by a voucher. While it is possible, and frequently it is a practice, to wait until the end of the month to prepare vouchers in time for an audit, much time and effort will be saved by preparing vouchers as quickly as possible after a transaction has taken place. If vouchers keep pace with council book entries, the fund may be quickly and accurately closed at any time with a minimum of effort.

Paragraph 48 of TM 12–250 utters a vital warning to all custodians that should be gospel for everyone connected with company funds. "Every transaction," it states, "should be handled with the most scrupulous attention to detail. Failure to observe these and similar precautions has ruined the career of many an officer." While at first glance these details may appear picayune, it must be remembered that fund keeping procedure has grown up through long experience and is designed to protect the responsible officer as well as the fund itself. The rules are simple and if followed will afford such protection. If neglected, the results can be tragic.

Remember, that fund responsibility is a duty that cannot be delegated. While it may be possible to place the task of maintaining the council book and fund records in the hands of a subordinate officer, the custodian himself is accountable for every cent and in self-protection should know the status of his fund at all times. Under no circumstances should the fund ever be turned over to an enlisted man, whatever his honesty.

Another point—don't keep a large amount of cash on hand and *never* mix such cash with personal funds. If at all possible, don't keep any cash in your possession. Bank it at once and carry on your business by check—the check book and cancelled checks make excellent supporting evidence and greatly simplify your bookkeeping.

In your bookkeeping be neat and meticulous. A neat council book and well-prepared vouchers are almost invariably an indication of a carefully handled fund and pay dividends at inspection. On the other hand, a sloppy book, incomplete or poorly prepared vouchers, and carelessness in handling cash will result in mistakes and "skins" at periodic audits.

The method of keeping a fund is simple and requires little time if properly followed. Ten minutes a day spent on it will save many hours of perspiring at the month's end and may save considerable money and trouble—serious trouble—as well. Too many officers make a nightmare of keeping a fund when a minimum of effort will keep everything running smoothly.

In conclusion, follow these simple rules and you can't go wrong.

1. Know your regulations and follow them.
2. Never make a transaction without recording it immediately.
3. Be neat in keeping your records.
4. Pay attention to details.
5. Never mix fund money with personal cash.
6. Keep little or no cash on hand—if possible do all business by check.
7. Never try to delegate responsibility—it can't be done.
8. Keep your fund up to date.

The above items are no more than an expression of the care a man takes with his personal funds or property. If followed, they will keep you out of difficulties, make fund maintenance a light burden, and will pay dividends to your outfit in benefits which only an efficiently administered fund can give and which are, after all, the only purpose for having such a fund.

Explanation of an Object and of a Process in Combination

The principal problem in explanations involving both objects and processes in combination is that of maintaining some progressive order. To put the problem in another way, there is a danger that the writer will vacillate between object and process in such a manner that the reader will be confused. Thus, in explanations of processes which involve the use of machines, it is often necessary to describe the machine itself and its essential working parts. In other words, the problem resolves itself into one of arranging the material.

The problem can often be solved by using an introductory paragraph describing briefly the general size, shape, proportions, or weight of the machine as a whole. It is likely, however, since a process is involved, that a brief statement of the general principle of operation of the machine will contribute more to the reader's understanding of the detailed explanation which will follow.

Descriptions of essential parts of the machine should be brought into the explanation of the process one by one as they are needed to make clear a step in the process. Stated differently, the various parts will be described with the step in the process with which they have the most to do.

Now go ahead to the study of the illustrative explanation which follows the list of topics. After you have analyzed the illustrative passage, you should be ready to write explanations of this sort, drawing upon your experience or your present courses for your subject matter. The following list of topics is intended to be merely suggestive of the great variety of topics which you could use. Such explanations could be made in either speaking or writing, or both.

Suggestive Topics for Writing and Speaking: Object and Process in Combination

1. The use of a portable belt-sander in boatbuilding
2. Replenishing aviation ammunition belts
3. Overcoming mud, or mosquitoes, along the Alcan Highway

4. Water, or gasoline, transportation
5. The use of kites in conjunction with balloons
6. Plywood or masonite hulls for small craft
7. Getting a plane off a flight deck
8. Towing, or firing at, a towed aerial target
9. U.S. Mail A.P.O.
10. Making odds and ends serve
11. Getting trucks across streams
12. The diamond goes to work

THE BEYETTE MOBILE PLATFORM [6]

Colonel H. W. Beyette, Commanding Officer of the Schenectady Quartermaster Depot, has developed a simplified method for unloading vehicles, making all straight track available for unloading operations. After a great amount of careful study, experimentation, and testing on all types of vehicles, from jeeps to ten-ton trucks, the Beyette Mobile Platform has proven to be a speedy, efficient device for handling quantity jobs of this nature. Experience has shown that, whether or not fixed loading and unloading facilities are available at depots, this method results in quicker handling than was formerly possible—averaging, under normal conditions, five to ten minutes per vehicle.

Construction of the Beyette Mobile Platform is simple, and the platform super-imposed on the trailer . . . can be built with approximately one hundred and fifty dollars' worth of lumber and material by two or three carpenters in one day.

At present almost all depot facilities are taxed to the utmost in performing necessary operations in a limited period of time. It is therefore necessary to utilize the very best and most modern methods of handling materials.

A considerable amount of mechanical handling equipment has been developed for the handling of various types of supplies in the warehouses proper. The loading and unloading of cars, however, is still an important operation on which a great many others depend, but for which only a limited amount of materials-handling equipment is available.

If we consider the importance of efficient handling in a depot operation, we will frequently find that it is possible to develop equipment or devices within the depot which will materially speed up the handling operation and increase the efficiency of loading and unloading crews. At the Schenectady Depot one of the most important operations in outside storage

[6] Lieutenant Robert C. Doyle, "The Beyette Mobile Platform," *The Quartermaster Review*, Vol. XXII, No. 3 (November-December, 1942), pp. 39–40, 127–129. Reprinted by permission.

is the loading and unloading of motor vehicles. The depot facilities provide a fixed unloading dock for this purpose. While this is a fine structure, its use is limited by the capacity of tracks available for unloading. A switching operation is necessary to pull aside the empty cars and place full cars at the dock for the next unloading.

Colonel Beyette, of the Schenectady Quartermaster Depot, recognized the limitations of his particular facilities for unloading vehicles. The dock at the Schenectady Depot has a capacity of about seven cars. It will therefore be seen that, when these seven cars had been unloaded, it was necessary to wait for the switching crew to remove the empties and place seven more full cars ready for unloading. Meanwhile the crews must wait while the switching operation was being performed.

Colonel Beyette studied this situation very carefully and gave much thought to the problem of speeding up the process of unloading with the limited fixed ramps and platforms available. To provide an additional ramp was an expensive proposition, and this would again be limited in its capacity by the amount of trackage available at the unloading dock. A survey made by Colonel Beyette disclosed the fact that there were two open tracks available which would be ideal for loading and unloading if some type of platform were provided. Each of these tracks was in an open area and had a capacity of thirty-five cars each, or a total capacity of seventy cars.

To construct a platform the full length of this track, however, did not seem practicable. Careful study developed the idea of a portable unloading dock or ramp. After the design was worked out, the ramp was not difficult to construct and was assembled in a very simple manner without a great deal of expense.

First, the basic piece of equipment used was a sixteen-ton trailer, Series 112, Type H–20–L–S–6, as used by the Corps of Engineers and furnished by the Rogers Brothers Corporation at Albion, Michigan. The trailer itself has an over-all dimension of 12 feet in width by 26 feet in length. This standard trailer was of the low-bed type, however, and was not of sufficient height to permit direct unloading from the cars to the bed of the trailer. Since it was necessary to provide a superstructure for the trailer in order to raise the trailer bed to the height of the car door level, it was felt that the size of the platform should also be increased. A simple wood platform was built on the trailer, increasing the platform-surface to 14 feet 2 inches wide by 26 feet long. At the end of this platform an inclined ramp, 12 feet wide and 13 feet 6 inches long, was constructed and attached to the rear of the trailer by means of four simple hooks. The ramp is thus detachable and can be placed on the platform in the event of a long haul from one operation to another. When the ramp is in operation close to the cars, however, casters located at one end permit it to trail without difficulty on ordinary road surfaces. The casters used can be anywhere from 6 inches to 12 inches in diameter, but it is felt that the larger casters are more practicable.

The platform or superstructure of the trailer is constructed of 2-by-10's running crosswise of the original trailer platform. On top of these 2-by-10's, which are also well braced, a platform of 2-by-8's running lengthwise of the trailer was provided, and on top of this was placed a decking of 1-by-8 ship lath. The upper decking provides a smooth platform on which a four-wheel heavy automobile jack can be used. The use of these jacks is essential in the unloading of heavy vehicles, and, unless the deck is smooth, there is difficulty in operating the small wheels of the jacks when the heavy load is imposed.

Since this unloading ramp must be operated early in the morning, late in the afternoon, and even at night, electric lights were provided. The platform was equipped with two 200-watt lamps, for which power is furnished by two ordinary automobile batteries. In night operations the interior of the car which is being unloaded is illuminated by means of the headlamps on the vehicles inside. It was felt that it was better to supply power by the battery method than to try to work with an extension cord from fixed outlets. Such fixed outlets are not always available, and, since the trailer moves every few minutes, constant connecting and disconnecting of the extension cord would have been the result. By making lights and batteries an integral part of the trailer, all such delay is avoided.

In constructing the platform on the trailer, sound wood should be used. The space between the platform and the deck of the trailer will be found most convenient for the storage of crowbars, sledge hammers, and various other tools which are constantly required in the unloading process. A simple railing, 3 feet 6 inches high, extending the length of the platform on the off side of the trailer, is a safety measure to prevent the operators from injuring themselves by walking or falling off the platform. The cost for such a super-imposed platform was approximately $150.00 for materials, plus the cost of labor. It was built by two carpenters in about one day.

A mobile platform offers many advantages over the fixed type of ramp. It eliminates the need for a switching engine and crew, especially if the tracks available provide sufficient space for thirty or more cars. This results in a saving from this standpoint alone. Another distinct advantage is that, with the portable ramp, vehicles may be parked temporarily along the line of freight cars after they are unloaded; whereas with a fixed ramp they must be driven away immediately in order to avoid congestion.

Experience also shows that where vehicles are being unloaded on a fixed ramp, the laborers must constantly move heavy steel plates from car to car and a great deal of time is lost in carrying tools and other necessary materials along the platform. Likewise, in working on a fixed platform a tremendous amount of labor is wasted in the switching out of empty cars and moving in of loaded ones. This loss is entirely eliminated with the mobile platform. The unloading crew, with all the necessary equipment, is confined to a small area and the cars are always readily available.

With the fixed type of ramp, having a seven-car capacity, it was possible to unload between fourteen and twenty-one cars in an eight-hour day. Now, with the portable platform, the average time for freight car unloading, under normal operating conditions, averages from five to ten minutes, depending upon the type of vehicle being unloaded. The Schenectady Depot has unloaded as many as 152 freight cars by this method in one day. It now has two of these mobile loading platforms in operation, which, together, have a potential unloading capacity of from 250 to 300 freight cars per day. It would be impossible to handle any such number with the fixed-platform method because of the time inevitably lost in switching cars.

By experimenting Colonel Beyette found that the most efficient procedure for unloading vehicles by means of a portable ramp is as follows: A line of box cars is spotted on any available straight trackage where it is possible to operate the trailer alongside the trackage at a given car level. A preparation group is set to work inside the cars, loosening the chains and removing steel strapping and blocks which hold the vehicles in place.

This group normally is composed of four men—two to a car. Since the vehicles are shipped without water, and with batteries disconnected, two additional men immediately follow the aforementioned group to check radiators and connect the batteries.

The vehicles are then ready for unloading, and the portable ramp is pulled up alongside the car. Four men are required for this operation—one to drive the tractor pulling the trailer from car to car, and to assist in unloading the vehicles; two drivers who actually drive the vehicles out of the car and spot them in the parking area; one additional man to manipulate the jack which is used when extremely heavy vehicles are being unloaded. The total crew required for full operation of the portable platform is, therefore, ten men.

It is not necessary to use a jack with jeeps, ambulances, weapon carriers, and other light and medium vehicles. It has been found advantageous, however, to use the jack with heavier vehicles, due to the very limited clearances around the car doors. The heavier vehicles may be driven out, but this is a waste of time because of the great amount of maneuvering inside the car which it involves.

Under present operating conditions no attempt is made, during the actual unloading process, to drive the vehicles to their eventual parking area. This would slow down the operation to a tremendous degree. Due to the fact that the platform is moving from car to car, space is, as a rule, temporarily available near the platform. Upon completion of the unloading work, the men of the unloading crew drive the vehicles to their more or less permanent parking area.

Colonel Beyette discovered that the unloading of the small jeep vehicles requires the greatest amount of time because these are shipped five to a car, with two vehicles suspended on steel ramps in the upper part of the car. It is therefore first necessary to unload the three jeeps from the floor of the car; then lower one of the two remaining vehicles, unload it, and again hoist the auto loaders or steel ramp deck inside the car before the final vehicle may be unloaded.

These auto loader ramps were formerly raised and lowered by hand, which process required husky men. This operation was greatly expedited by the use of an electric hoisting device, manufactured by the Evans Product Company at Detroit, Michigan, which may be used both for raising and lowering the auto loader ramps or decks.

Here again the mobile loading platform saves a great deal of time as compared with the fixed platform. The mobile platform pulls alongside the car, unloads the three jeeps stowed on the floor, and then proceeds to the next car; during which interval the preparation group is lowering the two remaining jeeps from the overhead ramps to the floor of the car. The unloading platform is then run alongside the car a second time, and the two remaining jeeps are driven out. If this operation is performed at a fixed unloading platform, a large portion of the crew remains idle during the operation of lowering the two jeeps from the upper deck to the floor of the car.

The use of a portable unloading dock has this further advantage. Where fixed platforms are not available, this portable device makes it possible to start unloading vehicles promptly and without any great expense. The platform is also quickly constructed. It can be placed within 4 to 6 inches of the car door, with the result that the use of the heavy steel plates, which are the cause of most minor accidents, is eliminated. No injuries of any consequence have occurred. Also, because the platform is close to the car, vehicles are seldom, if ever, damaged during the process of unloading.

The use of a portable unloading platform eliminates the construction of fixed unloading docks for motor vehicle unloading and speeds up the unloading operation. It permits the use of a complete line of trackage without any shifting of cars, and, altogether, makes it possible to unload cars more quickly, more safely, and more efficiently.

Colonel Beyette has been commended by many high-ranking military officials for this splendid innovation in the loading and unloading of supplies.

Explanation of an Idea

The explanation of an idea will likely be more difficult than explanations of an object or a process, because the former must deal with abstract and intangible matters, whereas the latter are concerned with concrete and tangible things. However, you are again reminded that neither the explanation of an idea nor the other types of explanatory composition should be regarded as mutually exclusive types of writing. For many explanations of ideas will depend, for their satisfactory development, upon the inclusion of an explanation of an object or a process at one point or another.

The explanation of an idea should not be confused with argumentation; the former seeks creation of understanding, while the latter seeks conviction or persuasion. However, any successful trial lawyer, whose work is thought to be argumentation, will tell you that successful argumentation usually rests upon a solid foundation of explanation. Neither a reader nor a listener can be expected to accept a belief which he does not understand.

A clearer conception of what is included in the term *explanation of an idea* can perhaps be found in some typical examples of topics that involve explanation of an idea.

For instance, there are explanations of relationships, as in "The Paratrooper's Dependence on Airmen." Or there are explanations of organizations, as in "The Jefferson County Sanitary Commission." And there are explanations of services, as in "Food and Supply Services for an Advance Survey Crew." There are explanations of value or efficiency or importance, as in "Efficiency of Diesel Power in Motor Transport." Also, there are explanations of proposals or recommendations, and explanations of similar processes or techniques—good or bad, efficient or inefficient.

Before you are ready to start writing an explanation of an idea, you must make yourself thoroughly familiar with the idea. This familiarity will include the ability to define any terms which might cause misunderstanding. Again, as in the preliminaries to the other types of composition, you must know your topic so well that you will be able to anticipate a reader's difficulties in understanding the explanation. You must be willing to do hard, close thinking about your topic to discover its parts and their relations to one another so that you can work out the most satisfactory arrangement of the material that is to go into the composition.

In the types of explanation previously discussed, the arrangement has been mechanical, that is, according to space or time. In the explanation of an idea, the arrangement will be logical. For a short explanation a single one of the systems of arrangement given below will suffice as an over-all plan. For a longer or more complex explanation it may be necessary to use two or more of these systems, either in combination or consecutively. The following are the conventional plans of logical arrangement: from cause to effect, from the familiar to the unfamiliar, from simple to complex, from what is most important to what is least important, from statement to proof, and from the general to the particular. Nearly all of these can be reversed.

Now go ahead to the study of the illustrative explanations of ideas which follow the list of topics. After you have analyzed the illustrative passages, you should be ready to write explanations of ideas, drawing upon your experience or your present courses for your subject matter. The following list of topics is intended to be merely suggestive of the great variety of topics which you could use, for either speaking or writing, or both.

Suggestive Topics for Writing and Speaking: Explanations of Ideas

1. The meaning of "Retreat" to the draftee
2. Lamps: kerosene to mazda to fluorescent
3. Adaptability of plastics
4. The importance of military insignia and ornaments
5. Polishing brass in the Navy, in the Army
6. The ideal Army chaplain
7. The difference between strategy and tactics
8. The average American and world affairs
9. Army Service Forces
10. New concepts of far and near
11. The return of a private
12. Reducing the tempo of life
13. Soldiering on the job
14. Qualities of leadership
15. The military, or naval, career man

WHAT'S AN AMATEUR?[7]

The amateur works because he cannot help it, impelled by a love of the work he does.

Today the amateur home mechanic is helping to win the war in at least three specific ways: as a "bits and pieces" machinist bending over a cellar lathe at home after regular working hours while the owls hoot outside; as a repairman reconditioning firearms for home-guard uses; and as a precision optician making parts of the optics of armament to fight Hitler.

All three of these amateur movements have been organized and are now in actual production. The results they have given are changing the meaning of the word amateur. What is an amateur?

The trouble with this two-headed word is that it means two different things that sometimes actually march in diametrically opposite directions. It means, first, a dilettante who makes a

[7] Albert G. Ingalls, "What's an Amateur?" *Scientific American,* Vol. 167, No. 2 (August, 1942), p. 61. Reprinted by permission.

superficial pretense. But it also means a man who practices an art for the love of it. Now, when it turns out, as it is turning out more and more often, that the man who practices an art for the love of it equals, or even excels, the professional who works mainly to earn a livelihood and sees little romance in what he does, the word *amateur* comes to connote something not derogatory but entirely good.

The program for home machinists has been described in other publications. Hundreds of lathes and other machine tools in cellar and attic shops have been put to work on bits and pieces of armament, their owners becoming sub-contractors.

The National Rifle Association has organized those of its members who are gunsmiths in a program for reconditioning old rifles of standard caliber. It also is endeavoring to round up for similar uses as many as possible of the old Springfield rifles which had been sold to private individuals and to put them to better uses than lying in attics.

Scientific American, since last autumn, has quietly organized in a program some of its thousands of amateur telescope makers. A limited number of these advanced workers have already demonstrated that the amateur who works mainly for the love of the work, or for the hate of Hitler's regime, can successfully do precision optical work of a grade of difficulty that is looked upon even by most professionals as ultra, and which some of them find it prudent not to tackle. Several of these amateurs now hold primary contracts, and some of them, if they continue to make good on the promise contained in their preliminary successes, will no doubt be able to expand their home shops into much larger plants.

There is today far less tendency to look down the nose at the amateur than there was a generation ago, for the amateur has proved up in too many ways. The classic example of this proof was the help given in World War I by the American Radio Relay League, about which everyone has often heard. The War Department discovered that it had among those amateur "hams" a huge reservoir of virtual virtuosi in radio engineering. Since then it has been far easier for amateurs of any kind to get a straight-faced hearing, and today the professional who low-rates the amateur is likely to be warned by some other professional that he had "better look out, or that fellow you scorn will soon be catching up and blowing on the back of your neck."

There is no longer even any need for the amateur to over-compensate by being cocky and assertive. In most places he meets with an honestly co-operative reception and an intrigued interest in what he is trying to do. Sometimes the professional envies him, for the amateur hasn't had his fun spoiled by having to make a living from it.

PAGING THE MILITARY NATURALIST [8]

The opening sentence in the War Department's *Basic Manual for Jungle Warfare,* FM 31–20, tells us: "In jungle warfare the soldier fights two enemies: man and Nature. Of the two, Nature is often the more formidable." It then devotes approximately 44 of its 79 pages to the problems of living in and off Nature, irrespective of human adversaries. We hope and believe that the introductory sentence in the *Manual* is truer than most of the sentences it contains on such important things as the identification of poisonous snakes. Reading the snake suggestions, one might suspect that they were written by fifth columnists intent on destroying our fighting men by giving them false information about Nature, the enemy that may be "more formidable" than man.

Life magazine in the first number of 1943 devoted a page to the dangers a soldier might expect if he did not examine carefully some of the things that live on the ground in the tropical and subtropical areas. It is highly doubtful if many experienced naturalists will agree with many of the recommendations made in this magazine article, or in the identification of and information about some of the snakes represented as being dangerous. It is equally doubtful if any naturalist who did not already know tropical natural history could use wisely the material to be found in the jungle warfare manual. If this is true of the naturalist, how much greater would be the probability that the untrained field Nature student would come to some dangerous conclusions by following this official guide.

The purpose of this article is not to disparage but to point out existing needs, and to make suggestions as to how these may be met.

Most units of our armed forces have officers whose responsibilities are highly specialized. Individuals may be charged with problems of transportation, of camouflage, of communication, or intelligence. Others may be expert in dropping bombs from great heights, while still others direct torpedoes from undersea positions. There are radio experts, airplane pilots, and sky-pilots. But where do we find the military naturalist whose primary responsibility is matching wits with Nature, which may well be "more formidable" than the human foes to be met?

[8] E. Laurence Palmer, "Paging the Military Naturalist," *Nature Magazine,* Vol. 36, No. 3 (March, 1943), pp. 157–159. Reprinted by permission.

Some Suggestions

This page proposes that officers be provided whose responsibilities may be somewhat as follows:

1. To provide military tacticians and other officers with valuable and reliable interpretation of the natural history of an area where action may be expected to take place; to be essentially liaison officers between Nature and those engaged in combat with men.

2. To provide adequate instruction of men who will go into action in strange country so that these men may remain as effectives as long as possible should they become detached from their units and be forced to "live off the land," and so that they may, in any situation, make a maximum use of whatever natural resources may surround them.

3. To prepare and distribute adequate guides and essential equipment for living off the land, carrying on communication, and if necessary maintaining cordial and effective relationships with natives in the area involved.

4. To gather and organize the significant literature, and the talent from enlisted personnel and elsewhere, to the end that both may be used wisely, and so that intelligent use may be made of valuable forms of Nature in a given area and dangerous forms avoided. This relates to the problems of transportation over extended lines, and where local supplies of food should be used so far as possible.

5. To provide a channel for guidance of the military forces in meeting natural history problems in areas that have been conquered, or in non-combatant areas where the responsibility for making decisions rests primarily with those whose chief training has been military.

6. To provide a reliable channel of information that may prevent the military posted in relatively peaceful areas from abusing established conservation practices by such things as wanton destruction of animals that may offer themselves as convenient targets. This should lead to a better understanding between the military and civilians on matters dealing with Nature.

Qualifications

The proposed officers probably should be recruited from the enlisted personnel, and should include those who already have a good background in natural history. Any needed additional training could well be provided in some of the colleges where there are trained field naturalists. Special training could be provided in or near the areas where the officers may expect to find action. The officers might also serve as advisors in the wise development of the natural resources of an area after the military emergency has passed.

The content of any course of training should be determined jointly by the military interests and by those who understand the problems of Nature. Without any intention of being presumptuous, the writer suggests that those planning the course should consider the following fields as being important.

Food Problems: The recognition of plant and animal food organisms, how they may be procured, prepared and stored for maximum use, and their suitableness for use for different purposes. This includes the techniques of the capture of animals, the recognition of species suitable or unsuitable for food, and suggestions for maintaining balanced diets from local resources.

Health Problems: This should supplement or be integrated with work already being done by the Medical Corps. It calls for recognition of pest species of plants and animals, of means of their control, and of the various climatic conditions that must be met. Some of these are mentioned, but most inadequately treated, in the *Basic Manual for Jungle Warfare*.

Human Relationships: There should be some understanding of the language, dialects, mores, and human nature of the natives of the area for which training is being provided, with some understanding, for example, of the sign languages used in the area.

Weather: The military naturalist should have basic training in meteorology and in weather prediction, with special emphasis on the part of the world where he may be expected to see action.

Physical Geography: The military naturalist should have significant training in meteorology, in map-making and reading, and in the problems of water supply and sanitation.

Engineering: The military naturalist should be able to help Engineer Corps men by knowing the values of woods to be found in a given area, and should be able to help provide suitable materials from local sources to supply the needs of engineers. This should include the use of local materials in camouflage and in other activities.

Outdoor Living: The military naturalist should, of course, know how to keep reasonably warm, free from hunger and thirst, healthy, safe, and oriented in a strange area should he be dropped there suddenly and find himself quickly on his own.

At least he should be able to make a maximum use of the resources he has or can find, and should be able to help others to do the same.

The content of the course should show recognition of the varied geographical areas in which combat will take place and not be limited to problems of dramatic jungles, deserts, and seas.

These are but a few of the fields that should be considered in training this new kind of military man. The program would call for a more dynamic contribution to the war effort on the part of our trained naturalists than is possible by the activities solely as appropriate for morale building in the camps and as competitors for the soldier's interest with the movies, dance-halls, saloons, and so on. It is true that any program such as this could not be developed without effort on the part of those responsible for it, but it is deserving of thought, effort and support. Since it is essentially identified with a new kind of Nature education, it is appropriate that it be proposed through the School Page of a magazine that has long pioneered in Nature Education. This does not imply that the program should be just "another school program." One way in which such a useful program might be stimulated would be through discussion by readers of *Nature Magazine*. The discovery of individuals or organizations who might be able to bring the idea to the military authorities might be one of the results.

Report Writing

Report writing depends for success upon the same basic principles as all explanatory composition. Usually failures in report writing are due not to failure of a writer to master the special techniques of reports, but to his failure to practice the general principles of explanatory composition.

The successful report is one that conveys specific information from the writer to a specific individual or group with clarity and accuracy and the greatest possible efficiency. Also, a report should be objective; it should avoid any reference to personal opinion or prejudice except in the conclusion, where opinions and recommendations should be stated. They should, however, be based entirely on a careful scrutiny and analysis of the facts contained in the body of the report.

A successful report can be written only after you have

gathered sufficient information on the problem, the material having come from experience, investigation, or study.

Parts of a Report. In their simplest form, reports consist of three parts:

1. A statement of the problem
2. An account of the procedure, which includes a description of the material or apparatus used (explanation of an object), a statement of what was done (explanation of a process), and a statement of the results of the process.
3. The conclusion, which may include recommendations.

The Statement of the Problem. This statement should be a concise, carefully considered phrasing of the single problem of the report, and should consist of a statement of (a) the general problem, and (b) the specific limitations of the investigation, as in the following. The specific limitations (b) are indicated by italics.

1. The object of this investigation was to discover a substitute for aluminum in pontoons *to be used in salt water.*
2. The object of this report is to demonstrate how production time could be cut in the Jones factory by the use of explosive rivets *in the sheathing process.*
3. The object of this survey was to discover the best route for a temporary road between Tobruk and Tunis, *the factors considered being economy of construction, distance, and economy of upkeep.*

The Procedure, or Body of the Report. Other than that already given, there is no simple definition or description of the procedure part of a report. It was said to consist of a description of apparatus or materials, an account of the work done or the process followed, and a statement of the results obtained. Beyond this simple, almost invariable pattern, the variety in procedures is unlimited. This variety is unavoidable because every report has its own particular problem. Each specific problem necessitates certain specific methods of procedure for its solution. These specific methods of procedure will, in turn, determine the nature of the details and the extent and arrangement of the material. In other words, even in such a pedestrian form of writing as the report, the writer retains both the responsibility and the privilege of exercising his intelligence and ingenuity. He will profit, however, by making a study of successful reports, especially those covering problems similar to his, and by trying to adapt to his own problem the tricks he has discovered.

Since the purpose of the report is to convey factual information to the reader with clarity and directness, it is advisable to use whatever mechanical devices and visual aids will be helpful. Some of these helps are:

1. Topic labels for sections or even for paragraphs; topic labels may be set off from sections and underlined. (In this book the topic labels have been set in bold face type.)
2. Special techniques of indentation to indicate degrees of importance or divisions, as in outlining
3. Numbering or lettering of the various sections
4. Diagrams, illustrations, sketches, photographs, charts, tables, figures, statistics. Any or all of these devices may be used, subject only to the test: Do they facilitate or detract from the communication process?

The Conclusion. The conclusion of a report, like the statement of the problem, should be carefully weighed and concisely expressed. It should be impersonal and objective. It may state only a general truth based on the procedure, as it usually will in a simple laboratory report. The conclusions of professional, technical, or engineering reports should, if possible, be considered even more carefully, for they will usually proceed to recommendations of future action, policy, or technique.

Letters of Transmittal. Some reports require a letter of transmittal, which is to a report what the introduction or preface is to a book. It is from the writer of the report to the reader of the report, and states the reason or author-ization for the report, any special problems or difficulties that have arisen during the procedure, the report's limita-tions, and, if it is needed, an acknowledgment of indebted-ness for assistance that has been given the writer. It may sometimes contain a brief statement of the conclusions ar-rived at in the report.

Table of Contents. Longer reports should be preceded by a table of contents which lists both the general headings (statement of the problem, the procedure, and the conclu-sion) and the topic labels or divisional headings of the procedure. It also gives the page numbers of these head-ings.

Bibliography. Reports involving readings in books, magazines, journals, or other reports should contain a selective bibliography. The purpose of this bibliography is not to impress the reader with the writer's diligence or scholarship but to supply him with a starting point for further efficient study of the problem of the report.

No example of report writing is included here because, as has been suggested, variety in reports is infinite except for the three main parts and various mechanical and visual aids which have been described. Anyone who is seriously interested in the writing of reports because he has to write one should look up some which have already been done in his field of investigation. Just any report will not help him. Thus, a city engineer who has to prepare a report on his inspection of boilers will not get much assistance from studying the report by the president of a public utility to his stockholders.

Conclusion

You should remember that there are no substitutes for a sound knowledge of your subject, conscientious thought, good planning, and careful composition. These are the qualities that make good writing.

CHAPTER IV

A VOCABULARY OF GRAMMATICAL TERMS

You will use this chapter largely for reference; here you will find brief explanations of those grammatical terms with which you may be unfamiliar. You may discover, however, perhaps from the comments that your instructor puts on your written work or perhaps from your inability to handle the material in the chapters on sentence construction and punctuation, that you do not possess a sufficient knowledge of the fundamentals of grammar. In that event, you should work the exercises at the end of this chapter (and similar exercises which your instructor can suggest), in this way briefly reviewing the principles of grammar.

Absolute construction. An absolute construction (usually consisting of a noun or pronoun, a participle, and their modifiers) is independent, grammatically, of the rest of the sentence.

> *The storm having at last abated,* we proceeded on our journey.

Active voice. See **Verb.**

Adjective. An adjective is a word that describes or limits a noun or pronoun.

> The *red-headed* girl sang a *Russian* folk song.

Adjectives have three **degrees of comparison.**

1. **Positive**	bright	good	hopeful
2. **Comparative**	brighter	better	more hopeful
3. **Superlative**	brightest	best	most hopeful

Distinguish between adjectives and adverbs when they are used after such verbs as *look, seem, sound, feel, smell, taste,* etc. Such a verb must be followed by an adjective when the subject is being described, and by an adverb when the verb is being modified. Distinguish sharply between the meanings of these two sentences:

The little girl looked *shy*. (This sentence means that the girl was shy; therefore, *shy* is an adjective modifying *girl*.)

The little girl looked *shyly* at the newcomer. (Here *shyly* describes the manner of looking; therefore, *shyly* is an adverb modifying the verb *lŏoked*.)

Adjective clause. See **Clause.**

Adverb. An adverb is a word that modifies a verb, adjective, or another adverb. (For use after such verbs as *look, seem, sound, feel, smell, taste,* see under **Adjective.**)

1. Adverb modifying a verb: ran *quickly*, fought *well*.
2. Adverb modifying an adjective: *unusually* bright, *very* military.
3. Adverb modifying an adverb: *justly* proudly, *quite* satisfactorily.

Adverbs denote **manner** (how?), **degree** (to what extent?), **time** (when?), **place** (where?), **number** (how many?), and **affirmation** or **negation** (yes, no).

Like adjectives, adverbs have three **degrees of comparison.**

1. **Positive**	well	rapidly	happily
2. **Comparative**	better	more rapidly	less happily
3. **Superlative**	best	most rapidly	least happily

Adverbial clause. See **Clause.**

Antecedent. See **Pronoun.**

Appositive. An appositive is a noun which is used with another noun to explain or limit it, and which is identical with it in meaning. The second noun is said to be **in apposition** with the first.

Dick Wright, my *friend,* recently was sent to Bedford, a *town* in the central part of England.

Auxiliary verb. See **Verb.**

Case. Case is the form of a noun or pronoun determined by its use in the sentence. There are three cases in English: **nominative, possessive,** and **objective.**

A noun or pronoun may be used in the **nominative case** in the following ways:

1. As **subject of a verb.**
    The *girl* smiled only when *she* was deeply amused.
2. As **subjective complement.** A subjective complement is used to complete the meaning of such linking verbs as *be* (*am, are, is*), *seem, appear, become,* and is identical with the subject.

Woodrow Wilson was *President* during World War I.

Bill Wood seemed the *man* for the job.

It was *he* whom we sought.

3. In **direct address.**

John, will you please come here?

Freedom, thou art an illusion.

4. In **apposition with a noun in the nominative case.**

Henry, my *brother,* has already been graduated from college.

5. In an **absolute construction,** generally with a participle.

The *ship* having sunk, we began to row away.

The **possessive case** denotes possession. In the singular the possessive of nouns is formed by adding the apostrophe and *s* if the noun does not end in *s;* and by adding the apostrophe and *s,* or the apostrophe only, if the noun ends in *s: captain, captain's; Keats, Keats's* or (less awkward) *Keats'.* In the plural the possessive is formed by adding the apostrophe and *s* if the noun does not end in *s;* and by adding only the apostrophe if the noun ends in *s: men, men's; boys, boys'.*

Indefinite pronouns form the possessive by adding the apostrophe and *s: one's, somebody's, anybody's,* etc. **Personal** and **relative pronouns** do not add the apostrophe to their possessive forms: *its, his, yours, whose,* etc. *It's* is the contraction of *it is,* not the possessive of *it.*

A noun or pronoun may be used in the **objective case** in the following ways:

1. As **direct object** of a transitive verb.

The soldier aimed his *gun* at the target and hit *it.*

2. As **indirect object** of a verb.

Commencement brought *John* and *me* (i.e., *to John and me*) our first thrill (direct object).

3. As **object of a preposition.**

As he threw the ball at *me,* I slipped to the *ground.*

4. As **objective complement.**

The man named his dog (direct object) *Rupert.*

5. As **subject** or **object of an infinitive.**

He asked the *chairman* to open the *meeting.*

He told *me* to sit down.

The following arrangement of the cases of a typical noun and its corresponding pronoun in the singular and plural numbers (an arrangement known as **declension**) will help you to differentiate between the various forms:

Declension

	Singular	Plural
Nominative	boy, he	boys, they
Possessive	boy's, his	boys', their or theirs
Objective	boy, him	boys, them

Clause. A clause is any part of a sentence which includes a subject and predicate.

A clause capable of standing by itself is called a **main** or **independent clause**.

> When I looked through the microscope, *I saw thousands of amazing creatures*.

A clause which is unable to stand alone is called a **subordinate** or **dependent** clause. Such a clause may be used as a noun, an adjective, or an adverb.

> *When I unpacked my knapsack* (subordinate clause used as an adverb modifying *discovered*), I discovered *that my penknife was missing* (subordinate clause used as a noun, the direct object of *discovered*); this was a discovery *which did not disturb me at the time* (subordinate clause used as an adjective to describe *discovery*).

See also **Sentence**.

Comparison, degrees of. See **Adjective** and **Adverb**.

Complex sentence. See **Sentence**.

Compound-complex sentence. See **Sentence**.

Compound sentence. See **Sentence**.

Conjunction. A conjunction is a word that joins words, phrases, or clauses.

A **coordinating conjunction** connects words, phrases, or clauses of equal rank. They are five in number, and you should memorize them: *and, but, for, or, nor*.

> The plane was shot down, *but* the pilot *and* the bombardier escaped unhurt.

A **subordinating conjunction** connects words, phrases, and clauses of unequal rank. The most important subordinating conjunctions are: *after, as, before, since, till, until, although, though, while, when, whenever, if, so that, unless, because, than*.

> *Although* operations in this area were started only yesterday, the attack has already advanced ten miles.

A **conjunctive adverb** may be considered here as a third type of conjunction. It is an adverb which has the force of a conjunction when it joins two coordinate clauses; it is always preceded by a semicolon. The most important ones are: *so, yet, still, then, moreover, however, also, therefore, hence, nevertheless, accordingly, besides, thus.*

> I was unable to recall his name; *however,* I shook his hand warmly.

Correlatives are conjunctions used in pairs; they should always precede parallel constructions. Examples: *both . . . and, either . . . or, neither . . . nor, whether . . . or.*

> I was unable *either* to locate my objective *or* to communicate with headquarters.

A **relative adverb** is a kind of conjunction that introduces a subordinate clause used as an adjective or a noun. Common relative adverbs are: *where, when, why, whence, whither, whereby, whereupon, whether, how.*

> I know of no reason *why you should leave home* (adjective clause modifying *reason*).
> They asked him *where he was going* (noun clause used as the direct object of *asked*).

Conjunctive adverb. See **Conjunction.**

Coordinate, coordinating. Coordinate words, phrases, and clauses are grammatically equal in rank; they are expressed in corresponding, or parallel, constructions.

> An enemy float plane was *damaged* and *driven off by two medium bombers* and *one heavy bomber.*

Coordinating conjunction. See **Conjunction.**

Correlatives. See **Conjunction.**

Demonstrative pronouns. See **Pronoun.**

Dependent clause. See **Clause.**

Direct address. See **Case.**

Direct object. See **Case.**

Elliptical clause. An elliptical clause lacks either an expressed subject or an expressed predicate, or both; these elements, therefore, must be understood before the complete meaning of the sentence is revealed.

> While [supply *he was*] hunting in Kentucky, he shot a Baltimore Oriole.
> You are as tired *as I* [supply *am tired*].

Emphatic form. See **Verb.**

Future perfect tense. See **Verb**.

Future tense. See **Verb**.

Gender. Gender means sex, or the absence of sex, in nouns and pronouns. There are three genders in English: masculine (*boy, lion, he*); feminine (*girl, lioness, she*); neuter (*book, June, it*).

Gerund. See **Verbal**.

Gerund phrase. See **Verbal**.

Imperative mood. See **Verb**.

Indefinite pronouns. See **Pronoun, Case,** and **Person**.

Independent clause. See **Clause**.

Indicative mood. See **Verb**.

Indirect object. See **Case**.

Infinitive. See **Verbal**.

Infinitive phrase. See **Verbal**.

Interjection. An interjection is a word that expresses sudden or strong feeling. It may be followed by a comma or an exclamation mark.

> *Ah,* now I see your meaning.
> *Whew!* That was a close one.

Interrogative pronouns. See **Pronoun**.

Intransitive verb. See **Verb**.

Modifier, modify. A modifier is a word or expression that describes or limits the meaning of a word, phrase, or clause. Thus, in the sentence "He walks quickly," the adverb *quickly* describes the manner of walking. *He walks quickly* has a different meaning from that of *he walks;* hence *quickly* is said to modify *walks*. Notice the italicized modifiers in the following sentence:

> *The courageous* statesman *who expresses his own opinions* has *the* confidence *of his constituents.*

Mood. See **Verb**.

Nominative. See **Case**.

Noun. A noun is a word that names a person, place, thing, quality, act, or idea. Examples: *boy, Dr. Jones, audience, street, Broadway, desk, courage, hunting, democracy*.

For the various properties of nouns see **Case, Gender, Number,** and **Person**.

Noun clause. See **Clause**.

Number. Number, which is a property of nouns and pronouns, indicates either one person, place, or thing (**singular number**), or more than one person, place, or thing (**plural number**). A verb always agrees in number with its subject; that is, a singular noun or pronoun always requires a singular verb, and a plural noun or pronoun always requires a plural verb.

The *farmer says* that the *boys are* trespassing.
You are old enough to understand what *I say.*

Objective. See **Case.**

Objective complement. An objective complement is usually a noun (in the objective case) which is identical with the direct object, and which is used to complete the meaning of the verb.

Colonel Metcalf named Lieutenant Jones (direct object) *liaison officer.*

The objective complement may be an adjective.

They called him (direct object) *unpatriotic.*

Participial phrase. See **Verbal.**
Participle. See **Verbal.**
Parts of speech. The parts of speech are the eight classes into which all the words in our language are divided according to their use in the sentence: noun, pronoun, verb, adjective, adverb, preposition, conjunction, interjection.

There are many words which may be used as different parts of speech, depending upon their use in the sentence.

When I dropped *in* (adverb) last night, he was *in* (preposition) his study.
Like (preposition) all good Irishmen they *like* (verb) applesauce—in small quantities.

Passive voice. See **Verb.**
Past perfect tense. See **Verb.**
Past tense. See **Verb.**
Person. Person is that property of nouns and pronouns which indicates either the person speaking (the **first person**), the person spoken to (the **second person**), or the person, place, or thing spoken of (the **third person**). A subject and its verb always agree in person.

First Person I shall always remember the years I spent in Alaska.
Second Person First you sign your name, and then you receive your textbooks.
Third Person When the sailors saw land once more, they gave a loud groan.

In English the **indefinite pronoun**, used in making a general statement, is the third person *one* (and not *you* or *they*).

One should never underestimate his enemy.

In informal writing, or in writing in which the author is addressing himself directly to his readers, it is permissible, and often desirable, to use the second person (*you*).

> *You men* in the outfield need more practice in chasing flies.

Personal pronouns. See **Pronoun** and **Case**.

Phrase. A phrase is a group of words used as a single part of speech and not containing a subject or predicate.

A **prepositional phrase** consists of a preposition, its object (i.e., the noun or pronoun which immediately follows it), and any modifiers of that object.

> He threw the stone *into the glistening lake*.

A prepositional phrase which is used as an adverb to modify a verb is called an **adverbial phrase**.

> The men marched *with considerable spirit*.

A prepositional phrase which is used as an adjective to modify a noun or pronoun is called an **adjective phrase**.

> The man *with the best record* was chosen.

For verbal phrases—gerund, participial, and infinitive—see **Verbal**.

Possessive. See **Case**.

Predicate. The predicate of a sentence makes an assertion about the subject; it always includes a form of the verb. A simple predicate is the verb alone; a complete predicate includes both the verb and its modifiers.

> He *ran the boat squarely into the dock*. (*Ran* is the simple predicate, and *ran the boat squarely into the dock* is the complete predicate.)

Preposition. A preposition is a word that joins a noun or pronoun to some other word or group of words. The most important prepositions are: *in, into, on, toward, from, for, against, between, among, with, without, behind, over, under, above, at, by, to, around, about, across, through, along, beside, in spite of, like, during, concerning, because of, except*.

> The man *with* the red hair settled back *into* the chair and began reading *from* a book *of* poems.

Prepositional phrase. See **Phrase**.
Present perfect tense. See **Verb**.
Present tense. See **Verb**.
Progressive form. See **Verb**.

Pronoun. A pronoun is a word that takes the place of a noun. Examples: *he, myself, this, anyone, who.*

The noun for which the pronoun is substituted is called the **antecedent** of the pronoun. By **reference of pronouns** is meant the act of a pronoun's referring to its antecedent. A pronoun must agree with its antecedent in gender, number, and person (but not necessarily in case).

A farmer should milk *his* (in the third person, singular number, to agree with *farmer,* the antecedent of *his;* but in the possessive case, as distinct from the nominative case of *farmer*) cows every eight hours if *he* is to obtain a maximum quantity of milk from *them.*

The spirit of our nation's workers, *which* (third person, singular number, nominative case, agreeing with *spirit*) has never flagged, will carry us to victory.

Everyone is responsible for the way in which *he* (third person, singular number, nominative case, agreeing with *everyone*) cleans *his* gun.

The following are the principal classes of pronouns:

1. **Personal pronouns:** *I, you, he, she, it, we, they,* and their forms in the other cases.
2. **Relative pronouns** (used to join clauses as well as to function within their own clauses) : *who, whose, whom, which, what, that;* and their derived forms, *whoever, whomever, whichever,* etc.
3. **Interrogative pronouns** (used to introduce questions) : *who, whose, whom, which, what.*
4. **Demonstrative pronouns** (used to point out a person, place, or thing) : *this, that, these, those.*
5. **Indefinite pronouns** (used to refer to an indefinitely identified person, place, or thing) : *all, another, any, anybody, anyone, anything, both, each, either, everybody, everyone, few, many, neither, nobody, none, no one, nothing, one, other, several, some, somebody,* etc.

The following is an arrangement of the case forms of three classes of pronouns in their proper numbers and persons (an arrangement known as **declension**).

Personal Pronouns

	First Person		Second Person	
	Singular	Plural	Singular	Plural
Nom.	I	we	you	you
Poss.	my, mine	our, ours	your, yours	your, yours
Obj.	me	us	you	you

Third Person

	Singular	Plural
Nom.	he, she, it	they
Poss.	his, her, hers, its	their, theirs
Obj.	him, her, it	them

	Relative Pronouns	Interrogative Pronouns
	Singular and Plural	Singular and Plural
Nom.	who, which, what, that	who, which, what
Poss.	whose	whose
Obj.	whom, which, what, that	whom, which, what

See also **Case, Gender, Number,** and **Person.**

Relative adverbs. See **Conjunction.**

Relative pronouns. See **Pronoun** and **Case.**

Sentence. A sentence is a group of words containing a subject and a predicate and making a grammatically and logically complete statement. Each part of a sentence which includes a subject and a predicate is called a clause. If a clause is able to stand alone and form a sentence by itself, it is called a main or independent clause. If a clause cannot stand by itself, it is called a subordinate or dependent clause.

Kinds of sentences. A sentence containing only one independent clause is called a **simple sentence.**

The boy walked into the room.

A sentence containing two or more independent clauses is called a **compound sentence.**

The wind howled, and the rain fell in torrents.

A sentence containing one independent clause and one or more dependent clauses is called a **complex sentence.**

When the troops landed, the natives began to cheer.

A sentence containing two or more independent clauses and one or more dependent clauses is called a **compound-complex sentence.**

After I had talked with my father, I knew that I was in the wrong; but I was still unable to make a complete confession.

Simple sentence. See **Sentence.**

Subject. The subject of a sentence is a person, place, or thing about which an assertion is made.

The *boy* runs. What does *Bill* want? Here are three *books*.

Subjective complement. See **Case.**
Subjunctive mood. See **Verb.**
Subordinate clause. See **Clause** and **Sentence.**
Subordinate conjunction. See **Conjunction.**
Tense. See **Verb.**
Transitive verb. See **Verb.**
Verb. A verb is a word that asserts action or being about the
    subject of a sentence. Examples: *walks, has cleaned, was,
    will find.* The verb alone is called the **predicate;** the verb
    with its modifiers is called the **complete predicate.**

Kinds of Verbs

Verbals (gerunds, participles, and infinitives) are formed
from verbs but are used as other parts of speech, such as
nouns, adjectives, and adverbs.

A **verb proper** is the simple form of the verb that makes
a statement about the subject without the aid of another
verb: I *am,* she *walks,* he *danced.*

An **auxiliary verb** is used as a helping verb with the verb
proper to show variations in mood, tense, or voice; important auxiliary verbs are: *be, have, do, may, might, can, must,
could, should, would, shall, will, ought.*

A **verb phrase** includes the verb proper and its auxiliary:
she *has replied,* it *could have been prevented,* you *may sit
down.*

A **transitive verb** takes as a direct object the person,
place, or thing which receives the action: The soldier *salutes*
the flag.

An **intransitive verb** takes no direct object because it has
no receiver of the action: he *danced* for joy, she *sang* softly,
they *acceded* to his request.

Properties of Verbs

Voice indicates whether the subject of the verb acts (**active voice**) or is acted upon (**passive voice**).

The man *caught* the horse (active voice).
The horse *was caught* by the man (passive voice).

Mood indicates the manner in which the verb expresses
action or being.

The **indicative mood** states a fact or asks a question.

At noon yesterday our Hurricanes *smashed* a formation
    of enemy fighters.
Were any of our aircraft *missing* from yesterday's opera-
    tions?

The **subjunctive mood** (rarely used today) expresses a wish or a condition contrary to fact.

I wish I *were selected* for the mission.
If he *were* here, he would not hesitate.

The **imperative mood** expresses a command or an entreaty.

Clear the decks immediately!
Let us *give* this matter much thought.

Tense denotes the time of the action or being of the verb: I *take* (**present tense**), I *took* (**past tense**), I *shall take* (**future tense**), I *have taken* (**present perfect tense**), I *had taken* (**past perfect tense**), and I *shall have taken* (**future perfect tense**).

The following is an arrangement of the moods, voices, tenses, numbers, and persons of a regular verb (an arrangement known as **conjugation**):

Conjugation of the Verb *Take*
Indicative Mood

Active Voice		Passive Voice	

Present Tense

Singular	Plural	Singular	Plural
1. I take	we take	I am taken	we are taken
2. you take	you take	you are taken	you are taken
3. he takes	they take	he is taken	they are taken

Past Tense

Singular	Plural	Singular	Plural
1. I took	we took	I was taken	we were taken
2. you took	you took	you were taken	you were taken
3. he took	they took	he was taken	they were taken

Future Tense

Singular	Plural	Singular	Plural
1. I shall take	we shall take	I shall be taken	we shall be taken
2. you will take	you will take	you will be taken	you will be taken
3. he will take	they will take	he will be taken	they will be taken

Present Perfect Tense

Singular	Plural	Singular	Plural
1. I have taken	we have taken	I have been taken	we have been taken
2. you have taken	you have taken	you have been taken	you have been taken
3. he has taken	they have taken	he has been taken	they have been taken

Past Perfect Tense

I, you, he, we, you, they had taken

I, you, he, we, you, they had been taken

Future Perfect Tense

I, we shall have taken
you, he will have taken

I, we shall have been taken
you, they will have been taken

Subjunctive Mood

Active Voice	Passive Voice

Present Tense
- if I, you, he take
- if we, you, they take

if I, you, he were taken
if we, you, they were taken

Past Tense
- if I, you, he took
- if we, you, they took

if I, you, he were taken
if we, you, they were taken

Present Perfect Tense
- if I, you, he have taken
- if we, you, they have taken

if I, you, he have been taken
if we, you, they have been taken

Imperative Mood

Active Voice	Passive Voice
take take	be taken be taken

Participles

Active Voice	Passive Voice

Present taking

being taken

Past

taken

Perfect (Simple) having taken

having been taken

Perfect (Progressive) having been taking

Infinitives

Present (Simple) to take   to be taken
(Progressive) to be taking
Perfect (Simple) to have taken   to have been taken
(Progressive) to have been taking

Note: In addition to this simple form of conjugation there is the **progressive**, formed by combining the proper form of the auxiliary verb *be* with the present participle of the verb concerned; and the **emphatic**, formed by combining the proper form of the auxiliary verb *do* with the present form of the verb concerned.

Progressive form: I am taking, you are taking, etc.
Emphatic form: I do take, you do take, etc.

Verbal. A verbal is a form derived from a verb but used as a noun, adjective, or adverb. There are three kinds of verbals: gerund, participle, and infinitive.

A **gerund** (formed by adding *ing* to the present tense of the verb) may be used in any of the ways in which a noun is used.

> *Walking* is a splendid exercise (subject of the verb).
> I like *walking* in the rain (direct object of the verb).
> The work of *planting* the victory garden was done by the girls (object of the preposition *of*).

A **gerund phrase** consists of a gerund and its modifiers. In the foregoing sentences *walking in the rain* and *planting the victory garden* are examples of gerund phrases.

A **participle** is used as an adjective. The present participle is identical with the gerund in form, e.g., the *walking* doll. For other forms of the participle see **Verb.**

> Dr. Johnson once defined a woman as "a *speaking* cat." The *spoken* word should be as important as the *written* word.

A **participial phrase** consists of a participle and its modifiers.

> *Eating in haste,* he scarcely looked at the food before him.

An **infinitive**, consisting of the so-called sign of the infinitive, *to* (which is sometimes omitted), and the present tense of the verb, may be used as a noun, an adjective, or an adverb.

> *To give* commands clearly is an accomplishment which an officer must learn. (*To give* is used as a noun, the subject of the verb *is*.)
> The way *to attack* the city is not obvious. (*To attack* is used as an adjective describing the noun *way*.)
> The model is easy *to assemble*. (*To assemble* is used as an adverb to modify the adjective *easy*.)

An **infinitive phrase** consists of an infinitive and its modifiers, as *to give commands clearly* and *to attack the city*.

Voice. See **Verb.**

Exercises

1. Study the sections entitled **Parts of Speech, Noun, Pronoun, Verb, Adjective, Adverb, Preposition, Conjunction,** and **Interjection.** In the first paragraph

of reading selection 2 on page 153, identify each word as to part of speech and use in the sentence.

2. Study the sections entitled **Noun, Pronoun, Case, Gender, Number,** and **Person.** In the first three paragraphs of reading selection 3 on page 155, pick out all the nouns and pronouns and identify them as to kind, case, gender, number, and person. Also indicate the antecedent of each pronoun.

3. Study the section entitled **Verb.** In the first two paragraphs of reading selection 5 on page 159, pick out all the verbs and identify them as to kind, voice, tense, and mood.

4. Study the sections entitled **Adjective** and **Adverb.** In reading selection 15 on page 180, pick out all the adjectives and adverbs and identify them as to part of speech and use in the sentence. (Be sure to specify the kind of element each adjective or adverb modifies.)

5. Study the section entitled **Conjunction.** In the first paragraph of reading selection 13 on page 176, pick out all the conjunctions and identify them as to kind and use in the sentence.

6. Study the section entitled **Phrase.** In the first three paragraphs of reading selection 16 on page 181, pick out all the prepositional phrases, name the parts of each phrase, and identify each phrase as to kind and use in the sentence.

7. Study the section entitled **Verbal.** In the first six paragraphs of reading selection 14 on page 178, pick out all verbals and identify them as to kind and use. Also specify which of these verbals are parts of phrases.

8. Study the section entitled **Clause.** In reading selection 8 on page 166, pick out all the subordinate clauses and identify them as to kind and use in the sentence.

9. Study the section entitled **Sentence.** In the first five paragraphs of reading selection 3 on page 155, identify each sentence as to kind. Within each sentence distinguish between independent and dependent clauses.

CHAPTER V

ESSENTIALS OF SENTENCE CONSTRUCTION

A Sentence

Definition of a Sentence. A knowledge of what constitutes a sentence will help you to write sentences that are unified, clear, and emphatic. A sentence is a group of words containing a subject and a predicate and making a grammatically and logically complete statement. A subject is a noun or pronoun about which an assertion is made; a predicate is a verb (or verb phrase) that makes an assertion about a noun or pronoun. Study carefully the following sentences:

> The bomber *formation has* already *located* its target. (*Formation* is the subject, and *has located* the predicate. The other words complete the meaning.)
>
> Then the *enemy* and his *allies massed* their troops and *attacked* our lines. (*Enemy* and *allies* constitute a compound or double subject; *massed* and *attacked* form a compound predicate.)
>
> Our *destroyer fired on* the enemy submarine, and our *planes bombed* it. (Here is a sentence containing two groups of words, each with its separate subject and predicate, and each capable of standing by itself as a sentence.)

You will notice that each of these sentences expresses a thought that is complete within itself; that is to say, each is logically complete. This thought may be further enlarged, of course; but as each sentence stands, it communicates to the reader one complete idea. Notice, too, that each sentence has the necessary grammatical elements, a subject and a predicate, and that each sentence is independent, grammatically, of any other groups of words.

Clauses. Each of the foregoing sentences (and in the last sentence, each group of words) constitutes what is

known as an independent clause. An independent clause
is part of a sentence containing a subject and a predicate
and capable of standing by itself as a complete sentence.
As a further aid to your understanding of a sentence, remember that every sentence must contain at least one independent clause. Opposite to an independent clause is a
dependent clause, which contains a subject and a predicate
but which is not capable of standing by itself as a sentence.
A sentence may contain as many independent and dependent clauses as the thought requires for a complete expression. In the following sentences the dependent clauses are
italicized, and the independent clauses are in regular type:

> *When at last I reached headquarters,* I reported to the
> officer *who was in charge.*
> We knew *that he could be trusted,* and we believed in him;
> but *when he began speaking,* we realized *that he was not
> the man for the job.*

(For a further discussion of clauses and of the various
types of sentences, see **Sentence** in the **Vocabulary of
Grammatical Terms.**)

Sentence Fragments. Not every group of words, however, constitutes a sentence. As we have seen, there are
some groups of words which contain both a subject and a
predicate but are not sentences. Unless you are constantly
on guard in writing and speaking, you will find yourself
using as sentences, elements which are in reality only sentence fragments.

Here are four kinds of fragments that are often written, mistakenly, as sentences.

1. A dependent clause. A dependent clause has been
defined as part of a sentence containing a subject and a
predicate but not capable of standing by itself as a sentence.
You can easily recognize such clauses by remembering that
they are introduced either by subordinating conjunctions
(*if, since, when, although,* etc.), by relative pronouns
(*who, whose, whom, which, what, that*), or by relative adverbs (*where, when, why, how,* etc.).

Dependent clauses like the following should be written only as parts of sentences, attached to independent clauses:

Incorrect: What I like about Bill is his sense of humor. *Particularly when he borrows money from me.*

Correct: What I like about Bill is his sense of humor, *particularly when he borrows money from me.*

Incorrect: We sympathized with his problem. *How he could obtain week-end leave.*

Correct: We sympathized with his problem of *how he could obtain week-end leave.*

2. A gerund phrase. A gerund phrase is a group of words containing a gerund (a type of verbal ending in *ing* and used as a noun) and its modifiers. A gerund phrase can never stand alone; it must be attached to an independent clause.

Incorrect: I like to participate in all kinds of strenuous sports. *Especially sleeping after reveille.*

Correct: I like to participate in all kinds of strenuous sports, *especially sleeping after reveille.*

3. A participial phrase. A participial phrase is a group of words containing a participle (a type of verbal used as an adjective) and its modifiers. Such phrases can never stand alone; they must either be changed into independent clauses, or be attached to independent clauses.

Incorrect: Trucks *rushing past us,* airplanes *screaming overhead,* and thousands and thousands of insignificant infantrymen like myself *marching along the highway.*

Correct: Trucks *rushed past us,* airplanes *screamed overhead,* and thousands and thousands of insignificant infantrymen like myself *marched along the highway.*

Incorrect: The planes went winging into the night. *Plunging into a blackness that seemed impenetrable.*

Correct: The planes went winging into the night, *plunging into a blackness that seemed impenetrable.*

4. An infinitive phrase. An infinitive phrase is a group of words containing an infinitive (a type of verbal used as a noun, an adjective, or an adverb) and its modifiers.

Such a phrase should always be attached to an independent clause as part of a sentence.

Incorrect: Our job is to supply the man behind the man behind the gun with all necessary raw materials. *And to supply him as quickly as possible.*

Correct: Our job is to supply the man behind the man behind the gun with all necessary raw materials, *and to supply him as quickly as possible.*

Incorrect: To apportion one's time. To concentrate on the printed page. To take orderly notes. These are the habits that a good student will cultivate.

Correct: To apportion his time, to concentrate on the printed page, to take orderly notes—these are the habits that a good student will cultivate.

End Punctuation of a Sentence. The mark of punctuation which indicates that a sentence has ended is a period. The only other marks which you may place at the end of a sentence are a question mark, used after a question, and an exclamation mark, used after an exclamatory statement. Failure to place any mark of punctuation after a sentence results in what is called a *fused sentence.* Placing a comma at the end of a sentence results in what is called the *comma fault.*

Incorrect: The man was nervous he could not hold the gun. (Fused sentence.)

Incorrect: The man was nervous, he could not hold the gun. (Comma fault.)

There are several ways in which you can correct this type of error:

Correct: The man was nervous. He could not hold the gun. (This correction is always possible merely from the point of view of punctuation. But it is not always desirable, because, as here, the two clauses are not always of equal importance. Moreover, since they are linked in thought, they should be brought together in the same sentence.)

Correct: The man was nervous, and he could not hold the gun. (This change, secured by the insertion of the proper coordinating conjunction after the comma, is nearly always possible but is sometimes open to the objection that the two clauses are not of equal importance.)

Correct: The man was nervous; he could not hold the gun. (This revision results in a compact sentence, but the objection to the foregoing revision might be considered valid here also.)

Correct: Since the man was nervous, he could not hold the gun.

Correct: The man's nervousness prevented his holding the gun. (These two last revisions, the first of which properly subordinates one clause, and the second of which reduces one clause to a phrase, are the best.)

Exercise A

In the following passages correct all sentence fragments, fused sentences, and comma faults:

1. When I opened the door, I was flabbergasted to see my brother, after I had shaken hands with him, he told me that he had just returned from Shangri-la. A regular hornets' nest, he said.

2. To love one's country above everything else. This is certainly an important part of any definition of *patriotism*.

3. Bill is an amazing boy when he says he is going to do something, he does it.

4. He prefers to settle down in a small village or in the outskirts of a medium-sized city. Although, as a matter of fact, he has lived in such large cities as Paris and New York.

5. When I met Jim for the first time, I thought he was a delightful person it was only when I met him for the third time that he began to bore me.

6. There are many ways in which a woman can serve her country. For example, by not gossiping about the whereabouts of her loved ones.

7. In his *Dictionary* Dr. Johnson defines *dryness* as *siccity,* I wonder if he thought this definition would be useful.

8. What he wanted was a job that would give him a chance to hold up his head and look his fellow men squarely in the face. A job that would allow him to become a decent citizen once more.

9. The Medical Corps provides the trained doctors, nurses, and specialists to care for the sick and the wounded. Operating hospitals, driving ambulances, examining flyers to see if they are fit, and performing a multitude of other duties. The Medical Corps is never idle.

10. A poet once said that it is a man's tragedy that he does not take after his mother. And that it is a woman's tragedy that she does take after her mother. What do these statements really mean?

11. Be sure to lock the door and put out the lights. When you come home, that is.

12. The bombardier is an indispensable member of a combat crew, without a skillful bombardier who can hit his target, a bomber crew might just as well stay home and drink pink tea.

13. In 1934 the Royal Air Force decided upon a remarkable expansion. To increase the production of first-line combat planes tenfold.

14. As the giant cypress crashed to the ground, it brought down with it dozens of smaller trees. All laid low on the floor of the forest.

15. The assault on the fort was to be preceded by a Stuka bombing attack. To be delivered about three o'clock in the afternoon.

16. The Engineer Corps designed these pillboxes chiefly to cover the entrances and dead approaches to the works. Principally by making them rectangular in shape.

17. In the Colmar area, at least, the French were depending upon the Rhine River for their security in this they were sadly disappointed.

18. Hitting the first pitched ball, which was an inside curve, and knocking it into right field, thus bringing home the second run of the game.

19. At the same time the Bible can be read as a supreme work of literature. That will endure as long as the English-speaking race.

20. She drove the car as fast as it would go (nearly twenty-five miles an hour), but she had one difficulty. Slowing up at the corners without using the non-existent brakes.

21. Please write to us as often as you can, write at least twice a week.

22. I was afraid to face him alone. Especially since the details of my recent misconduct were fresh in his mind.

23. The chores were fairly evenly distributed among us. Bill and I mowing the lawns, while the two girls prepared the lunch.

24. We were told that we were to destroy two objectives. One, the bridge near the mill. Second, the munitions dump about two miles down the road.

The Principles of Sentence Construction

After you have learned what constitutes a sentence, your next step is to look within the sentence to see if it is properly constructed. Of each sentence you write or speak, you should ask yourself three questions:

1. Does it express one, and only one, main idea? (**Unity.**)
2. Do its parts (words, phrases, clauses) hold tightly together? (**Clearness.**)
3. Does it express its thought in the most forceful manner possible? (**Emphasis.**)

Only by studying and practicing the principles behind sentence construction will you be able to write unified, clear, and emphatic sentences.

Unity

Singleness of Idea. Since the sentence is the smallest unit which expresses a complete idea, it is wise to insist upon the rule that each sentence should contain only one main idea. An experienced reader will look for only one main idea in a sentence; a careful writer will learn to include only one main idea in a sentence.

> *Incorrect:* Uncle John was an aviator, and stamp collecting is a fascinating hobby. (Two totally separate ideas that have no business in the same sentence.)
> *Correct:* Uncle John was an aviator. Stamp collecting is a fascinating hobby.

> *Incorrect:* Major Dodds is my brother, and he speaks Russian fluently. (Two separate ideas which, unless properly related, should be placed in two separate sentences.)
> *Correct:* Major Dodds is my brother. Major Dodds speaks Russian fluently.

Subordination. In addition to the single main idea, a sentence may contain a number of secondary ideas. These secondary ideas, branches of the main idea, should be carefully related to the main idea and expressed in subordinate words, phrases, or clauses.

> *Correct:* Uncle John, who was an aviator, collects the stamps of those countries over which he once flew. (In this sentence the secondary idea, that John is an aviator, is subordinated to the main idea, that he collects stamps. Notice how skillfully these two thoughts are linked.)
>
> *Correct:* Major Dodds, my brother, speaks Russian fluently. Major Dodds, who is my brother, speaks Russian fluently.

Always be sure that you place your secondary idea in a subordinate element, and your main idea in a main or independent clause.

> *Incorrect:* As I saw the two automobiles collide, I was walking down the street. (The more important idea here, the fact that the writer saw the automobiles collide, is erroneously placed in the subordinate clause; and the less important idea, the fact that he was walking down the street, is erroneously placed in the main clause.)
>
> *Correct:* As I was walking down the street, I saw two automobiles collide.
>
> *Correct:* Walking down the street, I saw two automobiles collide.

Avoid writing a long sentence that contains a great many details, even though they are properly subordinated to the main idea. You can revise such overstuffed sentences by omitting the irrelevant details.

> *Bad:* When we had arrived back at camp that night, and had finished our supper of pork and beans and fresh salad (which tasted delicious), our leader, who was well acquainted with American history, since he had studied this subject and related subjects at the University of Kentucky (this was long before he accepted the directorship of Camp Ohmygosh), squatted before us around the great blazing fire, and, with his pipe in one hand and a mug of tea in the other, told us the simple story of a great American, who, born into poverty and misfortune, climbed the ladder of success through his own efforts.
>
> *Improved:* After supper that night, as we were gathered around the blazing fire, our camp leader told us the story of a self-made American.

Coordination. If the related parts of a single thought are of equal importance, they should be expressed in coordinate constructions.

Incorrect: Tom, who is taking a course in mathematics, is also enrolled in chemistry and physics. (Here the idea that Tom is taking mathematics is erroneously subordinated to the idea that he is studying chemistry and physics. Both ideas are of equal importance.)

Correct: Tom is taking courses in mathematics, chemistry, and physics.

A weak kind of sentence, especially common to the writing of the immature, is the straggling compound sentence, with its excessive coordination. Improve this kind of sentence by breaking it up into shorter, more compact units.

Bad: I came home from the movies, *and* I had supper, *and* afterwards I went to bed, *but* I couldn't sleep, *and so* I began to read the novel which I had bought earlier in the week, *but* I soon lost interest in it *and* fell asleep before I knew what I was doing.

Improved: When I came home from the movies, I had supper and went to bed. Since I couldn't sleep, I tried to read the novel which I had bought earlier in the week. I soon lost interest in it, however, and was asleep before I knew what I was doing.

Exercise B

Correct the following sentences for errors in unity:

1. We piled into the car in helter-skelter fashion, racing along the road at a madcap pace.
2. Finally, give the table three coats of shellac, and then find a place for it in your living room.
3. She satisfied both requirements for the job: she was a registered nurse who did not exceed the maximum weight ceiling of 120 pounds.
4. The field goal, as it turned out later, won the match for the Gamecocks, but this was not the first time that receipts from football paid all the expenses of the Athletic Association.
5. Early that spring we bought several packages of seed, including radishes, carrots, butter beans, and, I believe, cucumbers, and so, when the planting time at last arrived,

we began turning over the soil, and at last had the satisfaction of dropping the tiny seeds into the long rows, but to our dismay we had planted too early, for a late frost nipped our efforts literally in the bud, and we had to begin all over again.

6. After spending a few days in New York, where I visited several old friends of mine, in particular, one Alfred Lumbock, with whom I had gone on a hiking tour, in the late summer of 1939, in the northern part of Ohio (Algonquin county, to be exact), I moved on to Philadelphia, where an elderly relative, Aunt Fanny (on my mother's side), provided me the proverbial bed and board, which turned out to be nothing less than princely in view of the fact that Auntie was eking out a meager existence on Uncle Ben's Spanish-American War pension, a sum which I would guess to be in the neighborhood of $82 a month.

7. Eddy coughed nervously and pulled himself to his feet, making an impromptu speech the like of which no audience had ever heard before in the Lower Basin Street Auditorium.

8. The doorman first of all demanded my card of admission, after which he politely inquired if I were personally acquainted with Mrs. Doublewaste.

9. I arrived in Berlin three hours later and hardly realized that I was in another city.

10. The boy had never seen his grandmother before, so it was with some fear that he walked up to her chair so that he might have a closer view of her gnarled old face, and thus it was that he met Granny Lou, and so passed another milestone in his life.

11. A stormy petrel can walk or run on the water with ease and grace, and trains its young in countless other accomplishments.

12. Proposing that the members of the British Commonwealth of Nations, including Great Britain, Ireland, Canada, Australia, and New Zealand, not to mention the Union of South Africa, join the United States as new states, the Senator gazed at his colleagues with a twinkle in his eye, and, shifting from the left leg to the right (a habit which he had copied from the Right Honorable Edward Blakingham), further remarked that, with all deference to the learning and sagacity of his fellow Senators, here was a plan that would test the sincerity of our allies, if, indeed, it was peace through world union that those allies were seeking.

13. I do not fear for the fate of my country, and so I do not underestimate nor overestimate the struggle which lies ahead, for my faith in her is unbounded, and with God's help I know we shall win.
14. Bill prepared the problems in mathematics, and then he studied the chemistry assignment, after which he wrote his English theme.
15. Mathematics is the language of symbols and is used by Einstein to express some of the most intricate ideas.

Clearness

Your sentences will be clear to the reader if you will observe the following rule of thumb: Make each element in the sentence (word, phrase, or clause) refer unmistakably to the word or words to which it is logically related. In order to determine which elements are logically related to one another, you must be able to think logically. Clearness in the sentence, therefore, may be said to depend almost entirely upon clear, straightforward thinking. As you think, so you will write.

Position of Modifiers. You can most clearly show the relationship between an element and the word or words it modifies in one of two ways: (1) by placing the element as near as possible to the word or words it modifies, or (2) by supplying certain words which will make this relationship unmistakably clear.

Position of Adverbs. Place your adverbs as near as possible to the word or words to which they are logically related.

Possibly correct: John *almost* succeeded in buying two gallons of gasoline. (If the writer of this sentence means that John did not quite *succeed* in buying the gasoline, then his sentence is clear. But does the writer want his sentence to be read in this fashion?)

Possibly correct: John succeeded *almost* in buying two gallons of gasoline. (Here the meaning is that John came only close to *buying* the gasoline. Is this what the writer means to say?)

Correct: John succeeded in buying *almost* two gallons of gasoline. (This sentence means that John bought close to two gallons of gasoline; grammatically speaking, *almost* limits the meaning of *two*. Chances are that this sentence expresses the intended meaning of the author.)

The chief adverbial offender is *only*, which has been called the most misplaced word in the English language. Study the following sentences:

Illogical: We *only* purchased two bonds.
Logical: We purchased *only* two bonds.

Position of Prepositional Phrases. Prepositional phrases should be placed as near as possible to the word or words to which they are logically related.

Incorrect: Everyone looked for a boat rowed by an old woman *with a flat bottom.*
Correct: Everyone looked for a boat *with a flat bottom* rowed by an old woman.
Correct: Everyone looked for a flat-bottomed boat rowed by an old woman.

Position of Clauses. Clauses should be placed as near as possible to the word or words to which they are logically related.

Incorrect: The earthquake knocked down all the cows *that occurred in California.*
Correct: The earthquake *that occurred in California* knocked down all the cows.

Squinting Constructions. Elements must not be so placed as to refer with equal logic to both a preceding word and a following word. Such elements are known as "squinting constructions."

Incorrect: The M.P. told him *when he was inebriated* he was a pain in the neck. (*When he was inebriated* is said to "squint" because the reader does not know whether it modifies *the M.P. told him* or *he was a pain in the neck.*)
Correct: The M.P. told him that *when he was inebriated* he was a pain in the neck.

Position of Correlative Conjunctions (Conjunctions Used in Pairs). Both correlatives should precede elements which are parallel in construction.

Incorrect: I *both* admired his taste in neckties, *and* I praised his choice. (*Both* precedes the verb *admired,* and *and* precedes the clause *I praised his choice.*)

Correct: I *both* admired his taste in neckties *and* praised his choice. (Both correlatives precede verbs.)

Illogical Comparisons. Make your comparisons logical by supplying as many words as are necessary to complete the comparisons.

Illogical: He is as brave, if not braver than I.
Logical: He is as brave as, if not braver than, I.
Best: He is as brave as I, if not braver.

Illogical: Africa is larger than any continent. (Since Africa is a continent, this sentence means that Africa is larger than itself.)
Logical: Africa is larger than any *other* continent.

Illogical: The size of this book is smaller than the one in the window. (Here the *size* of one book is compared to another *book.* Logically, members of different classes cannot be compared to one another.)
Logical: The *size* of this book is smaller than *that* of the one in the window. (Here the size of one book is compared to the size of another book.)

Exercise C

Correct all misplaced modifiers and illogical expressions in the following sentences:

1. The M.P. arrested him as he was tying his shoes with two blondes.
2. Any cadet officer who undertakes to train a group of recruits, even the lowest in rank, will be rewarded with a sense of accomplishment.
3. Although Bill's father has been a member of the legal profession for the last twenty-five years, Bill does not expect to become one.
4. Either you will behave yourself or go home.
5. That man will succeed in all his endeavors who will pay attention to details.
6. The lieutenant shouted to his men when the airplanes appeared to find suitable hiding places.
7. When he bought a loaf of bread and some cheese without any difficulty he found a place in which to eat them.

8. Among the books of poetry, novels, biographies, and works of literature were grouped indiscriminately.
9. The engineers succeeded in capturing more prisoners than any unit in the field.
10. Dumboodle's has the best collection of candle snuffers of any department store in town.
11. The judge only gave him twenty days, because the gun was not loaded which he was carrying.
12. Both in restaurants and public places of entertainment the curfew was strictly enforced.
13. At the same time shouting to Harry in an angry tone of voice the foreman told us to start working immediately.
14. Although I almost found the same number of errors, I don't believe we'll ever find all of them in my opinion.
15. Rhode Island has the fewest number of square miles of any state in New England.
16. I found the manager's attitude to even be more friendly than the other supervisors.
17. Those sections taking freshman English courses which contain less than ten students will be disbanded.
18. A mallet made of lignum vitae will not splinter chisel handles or mar a joint to be driven together beyond repair.
19. The machine gunner not only is a member of the combat crew but also of the ground crew.
20. Since an automobile deteriorates when it stands in the open it should always be parked in a shady place.
21. I stepped into my office as my employer walked down the hall and tried to look busy.

Dangling Modifiers. Four kinds of modifiers—namely, participial phrases, gerund phrases, infinitive phrases, and elliptical clauses—may cause you trouble. Be sure that these modifiers logically relate to the subjects of the independent clauses to which they are attached. Otherwise, these modifiers are said to "dangle," and the sentences of which they are parts become ridiculous.

1. *Dangling Participial Phrases.*

Illogical: Fighting furiously, the objective was soon taken by the soldiers. (The participial phrase *fighting furiously* modifies *objective*, the subject of the independent clause; the sentence means, therefore, that the objective fought furiously!)

There are two ways of correcting a dangling modifier: by supplying the independent clause with a subject with which the participial phrase can logically agree, or by changing the participial phrase into a subordinate clause with its own logical subject.

> *Logical: Fighting furiously,* the soldiers took the objective.
> *Logical: Since the soldiers fought furiously,* the objective was soon taken.
> *Best: Since the soldiers fought furiously,* they soon took the objective.

Note. Avoid ending a sentence with a so-called "trailing" participial phrase which does not modify a preceding noun or pronoun.

> *Illogical:* The championship bout was stopped in the fifth round by the referee, causing the galleryites to boo and whistle. (*Causing* does not modify *referee* or *bout;* rather, it modifies the general idea of the main clause. This practice of employing a participle to refer to an idea instead of to a noun makes for confusion.)
> *Logical:* When the referee stopped the championship bout in the fifth round, the galleryites booed and whistled.

2. *Dangling Gerund Phrases.*

> *Illogical: On sighting the submarine,* our guns opened fire immediately. (This sentence means that our guns sighted the submarine!)
> *Logical: On sighting the submarine,* we immediately opened fire with our guns.
> *Logical: When we sighted the submarine,* our guns opened fire immediately.

3. *Dangling Infinitive Phrases.*

> *Illogical: To fly in the stratosphere,* an oxygen mask is needed. (This sentence means that the oxygen mask does the flying!)
> *Logical: To fly in the stratosphere,* one needs an oxygen mask.
> *Logical: When one flies in the stratosphere,* an oxygen mask is needed.

4. *Dangling Elliptical Clauses.*

An elliptical clause lacks the subject and part or all of the verb; both subject and verb must be understood. The understood subject of an elliptical clause is the same as the subject of the independent clause to which the elliptical clause is attached.

Illogical: While landing on Guadalcanal, his leg was broken.
(This sentence means that his leg landed on Guadalcanal.)
Logical: While landing on Guadalcanal, he broke his leg.
Logical: While he was landing on Guadalcanal, his leg was broken.

Exercise D

Correct all dangling modifiers in the following sentences:

1. Opening the case once more, and discussing all its details, the opinion of the judges was that since there was no *corpus delictus,* the mother cat was scarcely guilty of manslaughter.
2. While at Casablanca, the red fezzes of the men and the veils of the women struck us as being very amusing.
3. To plan the money, a budget should be made.
4. The fire gutted the dwelling house, causing considerable property loss and two deaths.
5. When a mere child, my grandfather told me that he had once killed his man in a duel.
6. After sitting impatiently for fifteen minutes on the hard-bottomed chairs (which, apparently, the manager had bought in order to irritate his patrons), the show finally started.
7. Entering the kitchen, the shock we receive is nothing compared to that when we find ourselves in the living room.
8. To learn how to hold the racket properly, the Continental grip should be first mastered.
9. In writing *Moby Dick,* nobody believes that Melville wanted his book to be used as a manual on whaling.
10. Jim lunged into the tent like an overloaded elephant, giving the impression that all was not well.
11. Crossing the campus, and standing slightly to the right of the Chemistry Building, is the Library.
12. After overcoming the resistance of the enemy's forward line, the progress of our tanks was necessarily slow.
13. Surrounded on all sides, but well supplied with ammunition and food and water, thoughts of surrender were indeed far from the mind of General Montgomery.
14. Strolling down to the Opera House after I had left the café, thousands of Socialists and, I daresay, Communists

were gathered in small groups to discuss the outcome of the plebiscite.

15. Evidently Swift thought that by showing the mistakes of his time in a ridiculous light, the people would correct their errors.

Reference of Pronouns. You need to be especially on the alert in those sentences in which you employ pronouns. Make certain that for every pronoun you use there is a definite noun antecedent, that your pronoun stands as near as possible to that antecedent, and that your pronoun clearly refers to that antecedent.

Vague Reference. Do not use a pronoun to refer to an antecedent which is vague, hidden, or subordinate in construction.

> *Weak:* If you want to master the principles of good writing, you must work long and hard at *it*. (The antecedent of *it* is only vaguely implied.)
>
> *Clear:* If you want to master the principles of good writing, you must study those principles zealously.
>
> *Weak:* Ever since he was a boy, Fred has wanted to take up flying, for *this* is a machine that fascinates him. (The antecedent of *this* is the noun *airplane,* which exists only in the writer's imagination, not in his sentence.)
>
> *Clear:* Ever since he was a boy, Fred has wanted to take up flying, for an airplane fascinates him.
>
> *Weak:* Have you read Thompson's *Engineers in Battle,* which was published in June, 1942, by the Military Service Publishing Company? *He* writes from actual experience. (*He* refers to a noun, *Thompson's,* which is in a subordinate position, the possessive case.)
>
> *Clear:* Have you read Thompson's *Engineers in Battle,* which was published in June, 1942, by the Military Service Publishing Company? Colonel Thompson writes from actual experience.

Ambiguous Reference. A pronoun should clearly refer to one antecedent, and not ambiguously to two or more antecedents.

> *Ambiguous:* The captain requested the orderly to pack *his* belongings before call to quarters. (Does *his* refer to *captain* or to *orderly?* Whose belongings are to be packed?)

Clear: "Pack my belongings before call to quarters," said the captain to the orderly.

Ambiguous: Whispering softly to his horse, the rider slipped a halter around *his* neck and then urged him forward. In a few moments a dead man was hanging from the Pirates' Tree. (It is not until the reader comes to the second sentence that he realizes that the rider slipped the halter around his own neck.)

Clear: Whispering softly to his horse, the rider slipped a halter around his own neck and then urged the horse forward.

General Reference. Do not use a pronoun to refer to the general idea of a preceding clause or sentence. The chief offenders against clear reference in this respect are the relative pronouns *which* and *that* and the demonstrative pronouns *this* and *that.*

Weak: It was suggested that we voluntarily offer our services to the local fire department in the event a fire broke out, *which* we did.

Clear: It was suggested that we voluntarily offer our services to the local fire department in the event a fire broke out. To the suggestion we agreed.

Weak: Temporary workers are required to harvest the crops, but not everybody can do *this.*

Clear: Temporary workers are required to harvest the crops, but not everybody will be able to offer his services for this work.

Faulty Agreement. A pronoun must agree with its antecedent in gender and number.

Incorrect: *Everybody* said that they would agree to the proposal if the profits were equally distributed. (*Everybody* is singular.)

Correct: Everybody said that he would agree to the proposal if the profits were equally distributed.

Incorrect: The platoon was to march to the armory this morning, but *they* did not appear. (At first *platoon* is regarded as singular, to agree with *was;* then it is regarded as plural.)

Correct: The platoon was to march to the armory this morning, but *it* did not appear.

Exercise E

Correct all examples of faulty reference in the following sentences:

1. The diplomat called Senator Wilenski an enemy of his country.

2. The Engineer Commander issued his order in accordance with the plan from headquarters, which was most unsatisfactory at the time.

3. Shakespeare's plays have an advantage over the plays of Shaw in that he wrote primarily to entertain, not to teach.

4. Do not converse with your neighbors during an examination, for it may bring suspicion upon yourself.

5. The Tank Corps is one of the most highly specialized corps in the Army, for it is a machine whose mechanism cannot be mastered overnight.

6. The instructor asked us if we knew the date of the War of 1812. We could not answer that.

7. My mother told Cousin Sue that she was delighted that she was taking us on such a long trip.

8. We were pleased to be stationed in Egypt, for we had heard that their customs were something to write home about.

9. You should not fall into the error (which nearly everyone makes when they play their first game of tennis) of standing in the middle of the court.

10. The police offered to reward John handsomely, but he said that he did not want it.

11. Dr. Jones observed that most children, even those of pre-school age, are fond of telling monstrous stories about their parents' achievements, but I could not agree to this.

12. Tommy's brother wanted to drive to the store with us, but he was late, and so Ed and I went alone.

13. I am always proud of the fact that I was graduated from Dumbnoodle University; what they don't teach there isn't worth learning.

14. She is one of those women who is forever complaining about their ailments.

15. My brother angrily interrupted his uncle to announce that he was old enough to make his own decisions, which caused an uproar.

Consistency. Your sentences will be clear if you consistently employ parallel constructions and the same point of view where logic requires you to use them. Once more, the heavy artillery of logical thinking should clear the way before the sentences are written.

Parallelism. Coordinate ideas should be expressed in parallel constructions. A clause should be followed by a clause, a phrase by a phrase, an adjective by an adjective, and so forth.

> *Illogical:* He asked his brother to write to him often and that he also send him the home paper. (*To write to him often* is an infinitive phrase which the writer illogically makes parallel with the clause *that he also send him the home paper.*)
> *Logical:* He asked his brother to write to him often and also to send him the home paper.
> *Illogical:* The train was slow, dirty, and was far from being comfortable. (*Slow* and *dirty* are adjectives which the author illogically joins with the partial clause *was far from being comfortable.*)
> *Logical:* The train was slow, dirty, and uncomfortable.
> *Illogical:* The landing boat, crowded with sailors, and which also carried the supplies, nearly capsized. (This is an example of the so-called "and which" error. *And* illogically connects the adjective phrase *crowded with sailors* with the adjective clause *which also carried the supplies.* Do not use an "and which" clause unless it is preceded by a "which" clause.)
> *Logical:* The landing boat, which was crowded with sailors and which also carried the supplies, nearly capsized.

Grammatical Consistency. Employ only that part of speech (or word or clause equivalent to it) which is consistent with the demands of grammar. Since this principle is most frequently violated when a writer tries to equate an adverbial *because* clause with a noun, the mistake involved here is often called the "because is" error.

> *Illogical: Because I am ill* is no *reason* for you to stay home. (*Because I am ill,* an adverbial clause, is improperly made equal to another part of speech, *reason,* a noun.)
> *Logical: That I am ill* is no *reason* for you to stay at home. (*That I am ill* is a noun clause which can be equated with the noun *reason.*)
> *Illogical:* I read in this week's *Time where the Senate has passed another anti-inflationary bill.* (The adverbial clause

where the Senate has passed another anti-inflationary bill
cannot be used as the direct object of the verb *read.* Only
a noun or its equivalent can be used in the objective case.)

Logical: I read in this week's *Time that the Senate has
passed another anti-inflationary bill.*

Shift in Point of View. Consistently use the same point
of view unless there is good reason for changing to another.

Illogical: In *Gulliver's Travels* Swift *attacked* the social and
political abuses of the England of George I. In particular
he *singles out* for his scorn the manner in which candi-
dates for office kowtow before the king. (Undesirable
shift from the past tense to the present.)

Logical: In *Gulliver's Travels* Swift *attacks* the social and
political abuses of the England of George I. In particular
he *singles out* for his scorn the manner in which candi-
dates for office *kowtow* before the king.

Illogical: First *we ran* through the obstacle course, and then
the setting-up exercises were done. (Undesirable shift in
subject and voice.)

Logical: First *we ran* through the obstacle course, and then
we did the setting-up exercises.

Illogical: In practice *we* learn not only how we should slide
into a base, but also when *one* needs to do it. (Undesirable
shift in person and number.)

Logical: In practice *we* learn not only how we should slide
into a base, but also when *we* need to do it.

Exercise F

Correct all errors in consistency in the following sentences:

1. As you enter a room in New Barracks, you do not notice
   any broken plaster, mirrors are not scarred, sinks are not
   chipped, and floors are spotless.
2. Arketall was lazy, always late, and did not care how he
   looked.
3. Isn't that what all persons really seek—a life of ease, re-
   laxation, and in which you can enjoy and study nature?
4. Because you show you don't like him is scarcely the way
   to gain his confidence.
5. The inspecting officers went through the trenches, where
   the new guns greatly interest them.

6. Strachey portrays her as an extraordinary woman, doing many things that other women would not dare to do, but always she is being hailed as a queen and receiving attention from everyone.

7. As a final reason, I believe that the arming of these vessels would hold the answer to our problem, in that it would lessen the number of sinkings, make Germany realize that we mean business, and that she had better think twice before taking action.

8. In class today we studied the fauna of South America, and the class made a large colored chart by means of which you can locate important timber areas.

9. If I were a rich man and was to ask you to marry me, what might your answer be?

10. To succeed in banking, one must be honest, capable, and have the respect of the community.

11. Gorillas which were captured full-grown never really become tame; even those which are captured very young develop into ferocious savages.

12. Anyone who desires to acquire a working knowledge of Spanish cannot do better than to spend a vacation in Madrid; there you will have to speak Spanish if you are to obtain the necessities of life and mingle with other human beings.

13. A sacrifice hit is when the batter bunts or hits a fly so that the runner can advance a base.

14. I have traveled extensively in North America, South America, and, perhaps where I have enjoyed myself most, in Australasia.

15. As I studied the plan very carefully, I gathered that the author was an extremely meticulous man and who checked every detail.

Emphasis

After you have learned to write a sentence that expresses a single idea with clarity, your next step is to compel the reader to take notice of what you are saying. Obviously some of your ideas are more important than others. Your problem, then, is to set forth your most important ideas with emphasis. Of the many devices for securing emphasis, the following will prove to be most useful:

1. **Subordination.** Learn to place unimportant ideas in subordinate constructions (single words, phrases, depend-

ent clauses) and important ideas in independent clauses. (Study the foregoing sections on subordination and co-ordination.) Generally speaking, these independent clauses should stand at the end of your sentences.

Unemphatic: In our library there are two reading rooms, and they are a reference room and a periodical room.

Emphatic: In our library there are two reading rooms, a reference room and periodical room. (Reduction of the second independent clause to two nouns and their modifiers, in apposition with *reading rooms.*)

Unemphatic: I noticed the movements of the infantry, and I quickly signaled to headquarters.

Emphatic: Noticing the movements of the infantry, I quickly signaled to headquarters. (Reduction of the first independent clause to a participial phrase.)

Unemphatic: My Uncle John, who is a veteran gardener, has raised his own vegetables for many years.

Emphatic: My Uncle John, a veteran gardener, has raised his own vegetables for many years. (Reduction of a dependent clause to a single word and its modifiers, in apposition with *John.*)

2. Position. Place important words, phrases, and clauses at the beginning or end of the sentence, especially at the end.

Unemphatic: This question has to be considered from another angle, however.

Emphatic: This question has to be considered, however, from another angle. (Learn to bury necessary words of transition, such as *moreover, therefore, in the next place,* etc., in the middle of your sentences.)

Unemphatic: He disliked his fellow workers, whom he found fault with often.

Emphatic: He disliked his fellow workers, with whom he often found fault. (Place the unemphatic preposition *with* and the adverb *often* in the middle of the sentence.)

Unemphatic: I'll pass that course, if I ever find the time.
Emphatic: If I ever find the time, I'll pass that course.

3. Climax. Arrange a series of words, phrases, or clauses in order of ascending importance. Start with the least important and work up to the most important.

Unemphatic: In the fire two houses were destroyed, one life was lost, and much furniture was damaged.

Emphatic: In the fire much furniture was destroyed, two houses were burned, and one life was lost.

4. Repetition. Do not hesitate to repeat important words for emphasis. It is only unintentional repetition that is not effective.

Faulty: In 1926 I worked for an insurance company, working both in the office and in the field.

Better: In 1926 I was employed by an insurance company, working both in the office and in the field.

Emphatic: The only thing we have to *fear* is *fear* itself. (President Roosevelt.)

Emphatic: When I was a *child,* I spake as a *child,* I understood as a *child,* I thought as a *child :* but when I became a man, I put away *childish* things. (St. Paul.)

5. The Active Voice. Unless the doer of the action is unknown, it is usually more emphatic to use the active voice than the passive.

Unemphatic: A pleasant time was spent by the sailors in Alexandria.

Emphatic: The sailors spent a pleasant time in Alexandria.

Exercise G

In the following sentences strengthen all unemphatic constructions :

1. The enemy is not altogether immune to bribery, I would say.
2. The guns were loaded into the boats by the longshoremen, whom we had great difficulty making a contract with.
3. Goodbye, old man, and don't forget to say farewell for me to the rest of the men.
4. I should very much like for you to come to my party, my dear, that is, if you would like to.
5. Schenectady, which is a rather large industrial city located in the State of New York, is the home of the Baldwin Locomotive Works and the General Electric Company, among other things.

6. With his wallet he lost a number of valuable papers—a gasoline coupon book, a list of telephone numbers, and a marriage license.

7. Colonel Waller learned of the situation in the northern part of the country, and he determined to take personal charge of operations.

8. While writing an essay on the need for emphasis in composition, Barrett Wendell gave expression to the following sentence (which afterwards he made more emphatic): "Be sure to end your sentences with words that deserve the distinction you give them."

9. When the fire reached its height, the flame fighters decided that the only way to stop the conflagration was by dynamiting several houses, for otherwise the holocaust would be uncontrollable.

10. He said that liberty must be won anew by each generation —or words to that effect.

11. Butler, who was accompanied by several other officers with a mounted detachment of about forty Marines, made a six-day reconnaissance of nearly 120 miles of rough country, which was exceedingly mountainous.

12. He banged on the table for order, at the same time making a horrible grimace, just as I walked into the room and sat down, loaded down, as usual, with the textbooks which had been prescribed in all my courses.

13. Will you marry me, dear, if I get my promotion?

14. He was shocked by what we had said; indeed, he was so horrified that he failed to conceal his surprise.

15. A magnificent rally was put on by our lads in the ninth inning, in which seven runs were scored.

CHAPTER VI

ESSENTIALS OF PUNCTUATION

Are you a member of the "salt and pepper" school of punctuation? After you have finished writing, do you sprinkle marks of punctuation on your sentences just to please your instructor, who, you imagine, is a "bug" on punctuation? Or are you enrolled in the "iced cake" school, holding that punctuation marks serve as a decoration, an ornament, something that is spread on afterwards to catch the eye, again, of your gullible instructor? Perhaps you belong to a third organization, the "pause and punctuate" squadron, whose members drop punctuation marks, like bombs, at every conceivable place in the sentence where they suppose the reader pauses.

Whatever school of punctuation you may have subscribed to in the past, at present it would be well for you to have a reason for every mark of punctuation you use. You should look upon punctuation as an integral part of your sentence. Further, you should use punctuation marks primarily and uniquely to clarify what you write. A knowledge of the rules governing their use, then, is valuable as an aid to clearness in writing. These marks of punctuation, which you will use deliberately, will help the reader to distinguish between the various units in your sentences; they will prevent him from misreading what you write; and they will aid him in a proper understanding of what you write.

The Period and Other End Marks

The only marks which may be used at the end of a sentence are the period, the exclamation mark, and the question mark.

I am here. What do you want? Listen!

Periods are also used, as everybody knows, after abbreviations: *Mr. Jones, Col. Smith, D.S.C., med.*

Warning: Do not, for purposes of emphasis, place an exclamation mark or question mark in parentheses after a statement the validity of which you question.

Immature: He said he was capable of handling the matter by himself (?)

Immature: She replied that she was still under thirty (!)

The Comma

1. A comma is used to separate words, phrases, or dependent clauses in a series.

A *tall, husky,* and *handsome* soldier said *that we had done our part, that we deserved a rest,* and *that we should have the night off.* (Notice that a comma is placed before the *and* joining the last two members of a series.)

2. A comma is placed after an adverbial clause that precedes the main clause. Such adverbial clauses are also known as dependent or subordinate clauses.

When next we saw Bill, he was sitting in the cockpit of a Mitchell Bomber.

These adverbial clauses are invariably introduced by subordinating conjunctions, a list of which may be found under **Conjunction** in the Vocabulary of Grammatical Terms. The best way to master this rule is to memorize this list.

Note: When an adverbial clause stands at the end of a sentence, it is set off by a comma only if it is non-restrictive. (For the meaning of *non-restrictive* see rule 4 below.)

We were afterwards entertained by the king in his palace, *where we spent a most pleasant evening* (a non-restrictive clause).

The men advanced to a favorable position only *after the enemy retreated* (a restrictive clause).

3. A comma is placed after several types of phrases preceding the main clause: (a) **a long phrase;** (b) **a**

phrase containing a verbal; (c) an adverbial phrase used to modify the thought of the sentence as a whole.

> *Toward the close of a long and sultry night in the middle of an unusually hot August in 1943,* I found myself walking along Piccadilly Circus (a long phrase).
>
> *Upon opening the package and examining the contents,* we were much disappointed (a phrase containing a verbal, that is, a gerund).
>
> *In the first place,* our supplies are inadequate (an adverbial phrase modifying the main clause as a whole).

Note: This rule likewise covers a single adverb which is used to modify the thought of a sentence as a whole.

> *However,* I fancy that we shall soon be over the target.

Warning: This rule does not state that all introductory phrases (or single adverbs) should be set off by commas. The following sentences are correctly punctuated:

> *Last night* we had an abbreviated study period.
> *In this chapter* is found a discussion of the properties of calcium.
> *Jovially* he addressed his men.

4. Commas are used to set off a non-restrictive clause or phrase from the rest of the sentence. (If a clause or phrase can be omitted from a sentence without disturbing the essential meaning of the sentence, it is said to be non-restrictive.)

> A good sailboat, *which costs money,* is a great joy to many a man. (The clause can be omitted without disturbing the essential meaning of the sentence. The clause is therefore non-restrictive and set off by commas.)
>
> A fountain pen *which leaks* is no pen at all. (If the italicized clause is omitted, the sentence becomes nonsense. The clause therefore is said to be restrictive, and is not set off by commas.)
>
> Napoleon, *a nobody from Corsica,* became one of the world's greatest generals. (So-called appositives, which are really elliptical clauses, are almost always non-restrictive. Expanded, this sentence would read: *Napoleon, who was a nobody from Corsica,* became one of the world's greatest generals.)

5. Regardless of rule, a comma is used between sentence parts to prevent misreading.

To Henry, Johnson remarked that there were now only five boats in the harbor.

6. A comma is used before a coordinating conjunction that joins two independent clauses. Memorize the list of coordinating conjunctions: *and, but, for, or, nor.*

A few troops of the 80th Division reached their objective, but the other two divisions were completely thrown back.

Warning: Notice that this rule covers only *independent clauses* joined by a coordinating conjunction. Other kinds of elements joined by coordinating conjunctions are not separated by commas. The following sentences are correctly punctuated:

We anticipated the attack and succeeded in repulsing it. (Here the coordinating conjunction *and* connects two verbs; no comma is necessary.)

The pretty and petite girl is my sister. (Here two adjectives are joined by *and;* no comma is necessary.)

When he saw what was happening and when he heard the firing of the gun, he realized that the enemy was behind him. (*And* connects two subordinate clauses; no comma is necessary.)

7. Commas are used to separate parts of dates and geographical expressions.

On June 26, 1909, our ship sailed into the port of Tobruk, Libya.

Exercise A

Supply commas where they are needed in the following sentences. (Punctuate each numbered unit as a single sentence.)

1. As the air is gradually expelled from the lungs the tube contracts to its original length.
2. This kite is to be raised when a thunder-gust appears and the person who holds the string must stand within a door or window.
3. Take any one of the myriads who read novels and inquire into the grounds of his preference and you will probably receive a hazy answer.

4. Again we have need of poetry for consolation poetry upon which we may call in our hour of need.

5. The tree which stands in the corner of the garden was planted last year.

6. The tree in the corner of the garden which may bloom before long was planted in 1919.

7. We answered the letter just as soon as we received it but to no avail.

8. Glancing around the room he noticed that Mary's fiancé a Dr. Jones and Bill Smith were engaged in what appeared to be an animated discussion.

9. Marry an orphan and the in-law situation will take care of itself.

10. We hoped and prayed and prayed and hoped.

11. We ate our lunch and interviewed the president in his office.

12. This problem on the other hand is misleading to the extent that we believe it to be easy to solve.

13. December 7 1941 bids fair to become a memorable date in American history a date scarcely comparable in significance to any other.

14. When our train reached Aberdeen Maryland and we realized that we were only two miles from home we gave a sigh of relief.

15. From these vats the hides are taken and lie on a platform for twenty-four hours and then are spread on the ground and carefully stretched and staked out with the skin up so that they may dry smooth.

16. "Our everyday life is made up of numerous practical routines," said the little old lady to her handsome overdressed escort.

17. Overseas in the many strange countries of the northwestern and northern parts of Africa there are peoples who do not believe in freedom and justice for all.

18. After we had moored the boats our gunners had sighted the target and we had prepared to land there came up an all-enveloping fog.

19. The one kind of movie which my father enjoys is a comedy-mystery.

20. The Pan-American Highway which we shall complete in 1945 will go through Mexico.

21. The type of highway that engineers like to talk about has six lanes.

22. The highways which are built of macadam last for many years.

23. Shortly before midnight I heard a noise which I was positive was made by no human being.

24. Below Paul was hanging out his wash; all three socks handkerchief and shirt were once more receiving their weekly bath.

25. Although the Navy champion was smaller than his opponent and did not eat spinach he quickly brought the bout to a successful draw.

26. Tunis and Bizerte Tunisia which fell in May 1943 were the enemy's last strongholds in North Africa.

27. In a forced march the Eighth Army had gone ahead for it thought it could reach its destination before night.

28. Solemnly he called on each boy in alphabetical order but no one gave the answer which he wanted.

29. Religion apart the activities of most persons are essentially secular.

30.   "If he mislike
My speech and what is done tell him he has
Hipparchus my enfranchised bondman whom
He may at pleasure whip or hang or torture
As he shall like to quit me. . . ."
Shakespeare, *Antony and Cleopatra,* Act IV.

Exercise B

Compose three sentences illustrating each of the seven rules for the comma. Place a circle around the punctuation mark which you are illustrating.

Exercise C

From books, magazines, or newspapers quote three sentences illustrating each of the seven rules for the comma. Place a circle around the punctuation mark which you are illustrating.

The Semicolon

1. A semicolon is used between two independent clauses not joined by a coordinating conjunction.

On Monday the brigade assembled at Bay Point; two days later it moved against Honey Hill.

The *Hartford* drove off the gunboats; however, it did not escape injury itself. (A conjunctive adverb, such as *however, moreover, therefore, yet, still, so,* etc., is always preceded by a semicolon when it joins two independent clauses.)

On Wednesdays we have our hardest schedule; but it is not a policy of the college for the instructor to lighten our assignments for any reason. (If the writer wishes to indicate a strong break between two coordinate clauses, as in this sentence, it is not incorrect to use both a semicolon and a coordinating conjunction.)

Warning: Generally speaking, whenever you use a semicolon, make sure that it is preceded by at least one independent clause and followed by at least one independent clause.

Incorrect: Although he is not a tall man; he is much taller than any of his brothers.

Incorrect: I suspected that he was wounded; possibly in the right leg. (In both of these sentences use a comma in place of the semicolon.)

2. A semicolon may be substituted for a comma between two independent clauses joined by a coordinating conjunction whenever one or both of these clauses contain subordinate elements separated by commas. The purpose of this rule is to clarify long and intricate sentences.

When we saw the examination questions and realized how difficult they were, we wished we had studied more carefully; but it was too late then, and so we began our three-hour struggle.

Note: This rule can be extended (as an exception to the principle stated in the warning to rule 1) to include the use of semicolons to separate items in a series ordinarily set off by commas.

The box contained an overcoat, which was made of wool; one pair of leggings, evidently designed for a large man; and two pairs of woolen socks, which were much worse for wear.

I registered for courses in physics, with Professor Jones; in chemistry, with Professor Blake; in meteorology, with Professor Star; and in English, with Professor Edwards.

The Colon

1. A colon is used after a formal introduction to a series of items. (A formal introduction consists of a grammatically complete sentence.)

The carpenter purchased the following tools : a combination square, a level, a block plane, and a hack saw.

2. A colon is used after a formal salutation to a letter, and between the hour and minute members of clock time.

Dear Sir : I am not looking forward to seeing you at 12 :29, but I shall be on time.

Anthony Droplegg.

Exercise D

Supply commas, colons, and semicolons where they are needed in the following sentences. (Punctuate each numbered unit as a single sentence.)

1. The troops landed quickly the whole operation took less than twenty-five minutes.
2. The president looked at the matter realistically indeed that was the only way he could have looked at it.
3. All cadets are required to buy these items of clothing two pairs of gray trousers six gray shirts two pairs of black shoes and a raincoat.
4. The last train for Buffalo leaves at 3 56 there won't be another until 8 17.
5. Dear Sir or Madam (as the case may be) I should like to become a member of your Boy Scout troop.

Yours truly, William Peach.
6. Towels should be displayed on the three hooks as follows on the first hook a wash cloth on the second hook a face towel on the third hook a bath towel.
7. I wanted to interview him but however much I tried I failed next year if I should go to Chicago I would have another opportunity.
8. The ceremony required less than twenty minutes however many important details were omitted.
9. The captain asked the supply sergeant to requisition six pairs of work shoes one wheelbarrow and six shovels.
10. Through the half-darkness he was able to make out these things the Beeringen bridge which was partially demol-

ished the canal which was only half full of water the machine guns on the opposite bank.

11. Time and date 10 30 A M June 16 1940.
12. There are many technical flaws in the book thus the reader must be careful not to allow himself to be unduly prejudiced by the style of Burne-Castle.
13. The order of march was thus C Company F Company Engineer Company E Company.
14. The depression was in full swing and the publishing business was slack soon he was looking about to see where he could employ his talents.
15. "And therefore never send to know for whom the bell tolls it tolls for thee." (John Donne.)
16. Throughout the article Mr. Jonson combines two tasks he sums up the medical knowledge of allergy and he writes down to the layman reader.

Exercise E

Compose five sentences illustrating each of the two rules under the semicolon, and five sentences illustrating the first rule under the colon. Place a circle around the punctuation mark which you are illustrating.

Exercise F

From books, magazines, or newspapers quote fifteen sentences governing as many different rules for the semicolon and colon as you can find.

The Apostrophe

1. **An apostrophe is used to form the possessive case of nouns.**

   a. **If a noun, singular or plural, does not end in** *s*, **add the apostrophe and** *s*: boy's; children's; brother-in-law's; Montgomery and Ward's; day's.

   b. **If a singular noun ends in** *s*, **add either an apostrophe and** *s*, **or the apostrophe alone**: Francis's *or* (less awkward) Francis'; Keats's *or* Keats'; Hopkins's *or* Hopkins'; for goodness' sake.

   c. **If a plural noun ends in** *s*, **add the apostrophe alone**: boys'; Byrds'; ladies'.

2. **An apostrophe and** *s* **are used to form the posses-**

sive case of indefinite pronouns: one's, somebody's, nobody's, etc.

Note 1: Personal and relative pronouns do not add the apostrophe to their possessive forms: his, hers, its yours, theirs, whose, etc.

Note 2: It's is the contraction of *it is,* not the possessive of *it.* The form *its'* is non-existent.

3. **An apostrophe is used to show the omission of numbers or letters:** July 1, '43; o'clock; can't; I'll; it's.

4. **An apostrophe and *s* are used to form the plurals of numbers, letters, and words used as words:** 17's; m's; but's. (Remember that numbers, letters, and words used as words are italicized on the printed page; on a typewritten or manuscript page, underlining takes the place of italics.)

Parentheses

Parentheses are used to enclose non-restrictive elements that are loosely connected with the thought of the sentence.

This glazed doorway (see figure 4) shows a treatment that is frequently applied to windows which are extended to the floor.

If you are fortunate enough to get a board 12 inches wide (this should be easy if you choose white pine), the job will be greatly simplified.

Quotation Marks

1. **Double quotation marks, thus ". . . . ," are used to enclose a direct quotation.**

Mary said, "I have cleaned the kitchen."
"What," he asked, "is the meaning of your refusal?"
"This is an outrage!" sputtered the bus conductor; "nobody is allowed to sit on the steering wheel."

Warning: Distinguish between the direct words of a person just as he speaks them (a direct quotation) and the indirect statement of what he says (an indirect quotation). An indirect quotation is not enclosed in quotation marks.

Direct: He said, "I shall go."
Indirect: He said (that) he would go.

2. Single quotation marks, thus '. . . ,' are used to enclose a quotation within a quotation.

The doctor answered, "My colleague says, 'You should operate.' "

3. Begin a new paragraph with every change of speaker. (This rule is not generally observed, but the beginner will do well to follow it in the interests of clarity.)

"What do you want now?" asked Bill.
"I'd like to borrow your bicycle wrench," answered Tom.
"Listen," Henry interrupted. "Do you hear that four-engine bomber coming from over Town Hill way?"

4. A comma and a period are placed inside the quotation marks; the other marks are placed in their logical positions.

"Write your name and address on this card," he directed, "and then come with me."
I said, "I am the supply sergeant"; but all he said to me was, "Is that so?"
"Why did you say, 'This is Mr. and Dr. Jones'?"

5. In a quotation of several paragraphs, quotation marks are placed at the beginning of each paragraph, but at the end of only the last paragraph.

This is the story he told me:
"Several months ago I was hoeing corn on my father's farm in northern Kentucky.
"Then I was drafted, sent to a training camp, and finally ordered abroad.
"And today I am a full-fledged soldier, willing and able to fight for my country."

Exercise G

Supply all the necessary marks of punctuation in each numbered unit (which may be broken up, if desirable, into several sentences).

1. Dickens novels are not the only ones which thoroughly reveal the nineteenth century.
2. A months notice must be given in writing before the tenant vacates the premises see article five of the contract.
3. What is the meaning of that verse in the Bible which reads their foot shall slide in good time.
4. Did you or Paul say to Dick are you going to be busy tonight.
5. I want a months salary in advance he demanded can you give it to me.
6. Unless you dot your *i*s and cross your *t*s I dont know how Ill be able to read your letters.
7. It was reported that the paymaster had said that he was unwilling to issue the checks but what he actually said was I have been ordered not to issue the checks.
8. My answer is no I said however there is nothing to prevent your going to Captain Dumas and presenting your problem to him.
9. The common daisy from the Anglo-Saxon *daeges-eage* meaning days eye daisy is defined by Webster in part as a low scapose carduceous European herb.
10. Bermans and Whiteheads advertisements are always written in good taste that cant be said for Lutkins.
11. Our guns are lighter than theirs but its not merely a question of weight.
12. Your 6s look like your 9s also I wish you would not make your *the*s look like your *then*s.
13. Did you hear Paul say to Dick are you going to be busy tonight.
14. His pomposity or whichever word it was you used is due mainly to what Sigmund Eberts calls the over-inflated non-inflationable.
15. He asked me a simple question was it you who shouted in the middle of the night cant you see Im busy.
16. At seven oclock in the morning the ladies aid society began digging up the lawn in front of the church their leader said we mean business.
17. Fill the tank with what demanded the attendant gas of course Ive plenty of coupons but I havent plenty of gas he barked in reply.
18. The men the captain explained shouted fire and ran for the exits which existed only in their imaginations.
19. Both of my mothers-in-laws automobiles he said were stolen you have two I asked in a hesitating sort of way its all right he replied Im twins.

20. Yes he said its a long story Ill need some refreshment before I continue do you mind.

21. Its *its* when the possessive of *it* is called for its *its* when the contraction of *it is* is the desired form.

22. Twins are a luxury sputtered the expectant father to the nurse as he gazed at the three babies but triplets are a positive extravagance do I have to take them.

Review: All Marks of Punctuation
Exercise H

Supply all the necessary marks of punctuation in each numbered unit (which may be broken up, if desirable, into several sentences).

1. Hitting the ball over the right field fence he trotted slowly around the bases not altogether immune to the applause which came from the grandstand and altogether aware of the sullen looks on his opponents faces.

2. There can be no world peace thundered the speaker unless there is world faith in the principles of democracy freedom and spirituality.

3. We cannot accept all your demands however the ones which seem most important are most acceptable.

4. The final peace must be won in three places said Dick on the battlefield at the peace table and in mans heart.

5. At 7 26 A M Eastern War Time we shall arrive in New York but we shall still be thirty minutes late.

6. Hollywood is full of old men who were never young and young women who are eternally old said Dr. Wentworth thats the best I can do by way of an epigram.

7. Fences which keep out your neighbors cows may likewise keep out your neighbor and thats not all.

8. During the winter which is by all means the dullest season of the year we hibernate said the grandmother bear.

9. If the enemy had attacked us during the night which was cold and black we would have been repulsed as it was we retired almost of our own free will.

10. Just opposite the mill was located down the road aways was my uncles farm the largest in our county or so Uncle Ned always said.

11. In the evenings he would sit and talk but it wasnt what he said that mattered it was his manner.

12. The commanding officer insisted that we take no unnecessary leaves that we stay within limits when we went to

town and that we always conduct ourselves in a manner befitting a United States soldier.

13. General Alexander said that we would begin our attack against Mateur Tunisia at 12 01 on April 13 1943.

14. By April of 1941 Germany had already conquered most of the democracies of Europe including the following France Czechoslovakia Poland and the Baltic states.

15. Jones the commander sighed youre absolutely helpless you cant drill you cant hike you cant obey orders what in the name of Sam Hill am I going to do with you private Jones came to attention rather it was his idea of what constituted attention I have a suggestion sir what is it wearily asked the company commander send me to officer candidate school.

16. He told us we were going on an overnight hike it wont be a picnic either he said.

17. Today Alaskan skies thunder with bombers new bases have taken shape in the wilderness and large numbers of troops have been rushed north from the States.

18. During this trip North talked to admirals and generals to buck privates and ordinary seamen to territorial officials to Aleuts Eskimos and Indians and to the white man-on-the-street.

19. The characters which have no relation whatsoever to human beings include characters like these Noel Thackeray who works in the toy department of a Chicago department store her sister Mimi who sings Christmas carols to entertain the shoppers and Judson Carewe one of the stores many vice-presidents.

20. It is the most informative book yet written on the rise of Hitler the happenings in Spain France Italy and Russia and the defense of Britain it contains nearly all the facts that are known about the men and events that are fashioning the world today.

21. Women once said Uncle Bert think with their hearts may it not also be said that they feel with their minds.

22. Blithely she walked down the street as if she were walking on pneumatic tires but that was when there was a surplus of rubber.

23. To say that Conrad was interested only in technique is to say that he was not a great thinker to say that he was interested only in ideas is to say that he was not a great artist the fact is that he was both.

24. A Fiji farmers philosophy of life says Mr. Coulter can be summed up in the words this is a lovely day why waste it working.

25. Dunkerque has given a new word to the English language it has shown an old quality of the British people.
26. Upon entering the armory the men from Company G were told to stack their guns and prepare for setup exercises although this was not what they had expected to do they quickly carried out the order.

Exercise I

Punctuate the following passage. Make new paragraphs where necessary, but adhere to the indicated sentence divisions.

When Detective Simpson entered the chamber of death six hours later his attention was attracted to three things the body of Mr. Witherspoon lying underneath the library table the rumpled rust-colored tapestry on the floor in the corner and on top of the table the well-thumbed copy of Stevensons *Treasure Island* which was opened at chapter fifteen the man of the island. Silently the police officer examined each but none gave him the clue that he was seeking. Idly he turned the pages of the book nevertheless they yielded him nothing. He fingered the soft tapestry he stared at the dead body and once again he fluttered the pages of the book but he went away empty-handed. Three months later Detective Simpson and Officer Flanagan were seated in the formers office. Although the two men had not spoken for some minutes each knew that the other was thinking of the Witherspoon murder. As queer a case said Flanagan speaking more to himself than to his companion as Ive ever met with. By the way do you know that that copy of *Treasure Island* which we found in Witherspoons library sold at auction today for thirty thousand dollars. But it wasnt a first edition as I remember only a cheap reprint. There were two bidders continued Flanagan yet neither as far as I have been able to find out is a book collector. Both and here he eyed his superior in expectation of the praise that would surely come are relatives of old Witherspoon. By Jove interrupted Simpson I wonder if that book contains a clue to the missing will.

Exercise J

Punctuate the following passage, making the proper divisions into sentences and paragraphs:

Shortly after I had cleaned up the barn and locked the door I went back to the house where Jerry was waiting for me to prepare supper supper was the big meal of the day for we always ate more than we should tonight as I lit the kerosene lamp and placed the few dishes on the table I noticed that Jerry instead of sitting down and watching me nervously padded back and forth between the stove and the kitchen door which you will remember my saying faced the south whats the matter old man I asked are you too hungry to lie down Jerrys only answer was a low growl which he was accustomed to give whenever I spoke to him however he did not wag his tail and for a brief moment I was apprehensive supper was ready now and as usual I gave Jerry his share first not so much from consideration of his wants as from the selfish motive of not having to get up to feed him once I had sat down pulling out his cracked dish from under the stove I filled it with his customary fare hunks of bread scraps of meat and a few pieces of the new potato that he liked so well here you are fellow lets see what you can do with this as he gulped down his food I couldnt help noticing that he kept one eye on the door he seemed to eat his food mechanically as though he were not paying any attention to what he ate I had almost finished my meat pie when there came the first of those three knocks on the door that were to make this evening so memorable Jerry did not look up from his food for both he and I recognized the pattern of that heavy knock come in Hank I said and almost before I had shouted my greeting there shouldered into the room my neighbor who lives in the second house from the highway Hank Kent was a big man what with his broad shoulders long body and oversized feet you can do with a bit of steak pie I asked thanks Joe I dont mind if I do he pulled up a chair to the table and I helped him to some of the pie Jerry paid no attention to Hank nor Hank to Jerry their friendship had long passed the stage where they thought greetings were necessary but the dog must have been wondering as indeed was I why Hank was visiting us that night Hank infrequently left his house after dark both Jerry and I however realized the futility of prodding him he would reveal his mission only when he was ready and it was nearly half an hour later close to nine oclock after Hank had finished his pie and lit his corncob that he opened his mouth what he said surprised me yet his manner of speaking surprised me even more Joe he whined in a voice that was peculiar to him I aint going back home tonight Im goin to stay with you and Jerry awhile youre right welcome to stay as long as you want thanks I thought you wouldnt mind you see I couldnt stay there not tonight at any rate he hesitated a moment but before he could continue there came a second knock at the door a knock which neither Jerry nor I recognized it was only Hank as I remembered later who remained cool come in I said.

CHAPTER VII

CHOICE OF WORDS

In preceding chapters of this book you have learned to think through and to write a composition, or a paragraph, or a sentence that conveys your meaning to the reader with undeniable clearness. We now come to the smallest unit in communication—the word. In order that your words may communicate their meanings to the reader with clearness, they must be the *right* words. The right word is *exact;* it is *in good use;* it is *concrete* and *specific;* and it is *direct.*

As a further aid in your search for the right word, keep beside you, as your constant companion, a copy of a good abridged dictionary, such as the latest edition of *Webster's Collegiate Dictionary.* Refer often to this book as you prepare your studies in your room, and carry it with you into the classroom and the library. This book will with authority help you to distinguish between wrong words and right words. Many times, however, the dictionary will give you several words which are all indicated as properly denoting the thing or idea which you wish to express. The following brief discussion of some of the qualities of the right word will help you to make the correct choice.

The Exact Word

The exact word expresses the meaning that the writer wishes to convey more completely and more accurately than any other word in the language. Just as the romanticist assumes that there is only one woman in the world who will make him a perfect wife, so the seeker after the exact word insists that there is only one word in the English language which will cover the particular meaning that he wants to express. Although you may regard such a criterion as ideal, there are practical considerations to this subject which you, as a prospective officer in our Army or Navy, must not disregard. Suppose that you, a pilot of a bomber plane, have been directed to bomb a certain building in an industrial factory located in an enemy country. As your airplane approaches the factory, you tell the bombardier to locate the "chemistry" building on his map and to bomb this building. The mission successfully completed, you return home and report to your commander that the "chemistry" building was hit and destroyed. To your dismay, you are told that you have hit the wrong objective. And then you remember that you had been ordered to bomb the "chemical" building, not the "chemistry" building. You had assumed that the two words *chemistry* and *chemical* were synonymous; you learn now that the "chemical" building referred to was a warehouse in which chemicals were stored, and that the "chemistry" building was a laboratory in which chemistry experiments were performed. Your carelessness in transmitting the original order to your bombardier resulted in the failure of an important mission. You did not use the exact word.

In your choice of the exact word, be guided by the following suggestions:

1. **Use the exact word, and not one that only approximates your meaning.** Much confusion arises here from words that are similar in form.

> From my *observance* of the terrain, I judged that we were within fifty miles of our *object*. (Supply *observation* and *objective*. *Observance* means *the act of observing a rule or custom;* *observation* means *the act of taking notice.* An *object* is *a concrete thing;* an *objective* is *a point to be hit or reached.*)

2. **Use a fresh and accurate word or phrase rather than one which is overworked.**

Trite: The Hurricane supplied *a long-felt want* in its *field.*

Better: The Hurricane supplied the need for an effective fighter plane.

3. Use the precise word instead of the so-called omnibus word (which is loosely employed to cover a number of widely separated meanings). Some common omnibus words, which you should use only with regard to their exact meanings, are: *case, cute, swell, nice, grand, elegant, lovely, awful.*

Inexact: I had a *grand* time at your party. Those sandwiches you served were *lovely,* and I met such a *nice* boy.

Exact: I had a *pleasant* time at your party. Those sandwiches you served were *delicious,* and I met an *attractive* boy.

4. Use the correct idiom. An idiom is an expression which is peculiar to the language and which cannot be explained by the usual rules of grammar. An example is: "I *had better* not stay here." The choice of the proper preposition may also be considered under idiom.

Incorrect: No soldier has the *privilege to use* the billiard room *in furlough.*

Correct: No soldier has the *privilege of using* the billiard room *during furlough.*

Exercise A

In the following sentences change all words and phrases that are inexact:

1. The instructor brought a swell specie in the classroom and gave us some datum about it.
2. As the soldiers wended their way into the city, at one fell swoop they destroyed the enemy's guns and thus nipped in the bud the incipient uprising.
3. Although he himself seemed a credible person whom anybody might deceive, his report was highly credulous and accepted for the truth by all of us.
4. My uniform is different than yours, but I shall not try and change it, because I am too pleased by it.
5. Use verbal orders only when you are in the field; at headquarters always use written orders.
6. What line of work do you expect to follow when you get assigned to your company?

7. It goes without saying that Jim's case leaves much to be desired; never before was one corporal in such an awful fix.
8. My principle objection of choosing him as principle of the school is that he is without principle.
9. A healthful soldier makes for a healthy condition in any army.
10. You will be excepted by the Army if you can affect your resignation by tomorrow.

The Word in Good Use

Good use includes reputable words and phrases generally employed in speech and writing by educated persons coming from all parts of the United States (or, more broadly, the English-speaking world). These are the words which you will use in your military correspondence, in your written orders, and in your reports. These are the words which you will shout to the members of your company on the field of battle; and whether your men come from Maine, Florida, Indiana, or California, they will understand your orders. These are the words which will be appropriate on nearly every occasion, since they will be largely free from slang, colloquialisms, and undefined technical terms (three groups of words which are appropriate only on special occasions).

Consider, for example, the animal which your dictionary defines as "a large, solid-hoofed, herbivorous mammal domesticated by man . . . [and] . . . used as a beast of burden, a draft animal, or for riding." A homespun person might refer to this creature as a *hoss* or a *nag,* two terms the meaning of which everybody would understand, but terms which not everybody would care to use. Again, a jockey might employ the term *filly* to refer to a particular kind of our animal. A literary or bookish person might say *Pegasus* or *Bucephalus,* terms which would not be clear to the unread. But everybody would understand the word *horse,* a term which would be appropriate on nearly every occasion.

Use sparingly in your speech and writing the following three classes of words:

Slang comprises new words and phrases which are employed for their striking effect. Most slang words are current for only a few years at the most, but a few become accepted into the language. The principal objection to the use of most slang (aside from its often bizarre and forced quality) is that there already exist in the language adequate words to cover the ideas expressed by the slang. In the following sentences the slang expressions are in italics:

> That *drugstore cowboy* gives me a *pain in the neck* when he tries to put me *behind the eight ball*.
> The *skirt* I *dragged* to the *brawl* was a *hot number*.

Slang is sometimes appropriate in very informal or humorous writing and speech, as in discussions of sports or dancing, but even here it should not be used to the exclusion of ordinary English. In official military correspondence and reports there is no place for slang.

Colloquialisms are words and expressions more appropriate to conversations, informal speeches and writing, and familiar letters than to formal English. Colloquialisms are used by the educated and uneducated alike; no stigma is attached to their occasional use in the proper place. The italicized expressions in the following sentences are colloquialisms (notice that they include contractions and abbreviated forms):

> The instructor *made no bones* about the *exam's* being difficult.
> *I'd* be *flabbergasted* if I were asked to drive that *contraption*.

In your official correspondence and reports you should generally avoid the use of colloquialisms. If, however, you find your prose becoming stiff, elbowish, or schoolmarmish instead of being easy and natural, then you should leaven it with colloquial expressions. That picturesque colloquialisms are not entirely absent from the grim business of fighting a war is illustrated by the message which the commander of one of our torpedo-boat destroyers radioed to the world. His ship had just sunk an enemy submarine; his message read: "Sighted sub; blub-blub."

Technical words and phrases may properly be used in technical and scientific works which are written for persons who already are acquainted with most of these terms. They have no place in writings designed for the untrained layman unless their meanings are carefully explained. When Lieutenant General L. J. McNair recently explained to newspaper reporters in Washington that he was hit in the head by a piece of shrapnel in North Africa because he had "miscalculated my defilade," the Associated Press writer was quick to add in his write-up that "The word *defilade* is used to describe protection against enemy fire or observation," and, he might further have explained, it is a word peculiar to the science of fortification. Are you familiar with all the technical words in the following sentences?

> Immunologists of today class anaphylaxis as a form of allergy.
> The momentum of a particle is the vector obtained by multiplying the velocity by the mass m.

Before you write about a technical subject in technical language, make sure that your readers are acquainted with your terms. If you know that your readers are laymen, either define or illustrate your technical terms, or write in non-technical language.

Exercise B

In the following sentences change all words that are not in good use:

1. I guess I've never seen a lousier movie, but I hadn't ought to complain.
2. Our top sarge cussed us for toting a bag of viands into camp.
3. A panda is a plantigrade carnivorous mammal (*Ailurus fulgens*) found in the Himalayas.
4. My old man sure would hate to see me busted out of college.
5. The prof got away with one wisecrack after another yesterday in the chem class.
6. Where a maritime lien has once attached to property, it will continue to attach, unless lost by laches, as long as the thing to which it attaches exists.

7. Jones used to get as mad as a hatter when we told him that he was no great shakes as a leader.
8. It's lots of fun to know a gent like Tom, for he has the singular quality of putting one at his ease under the most trying of circumstances.
9. Tony's is an awful joint alright, but the spaghetti is scrumptious.
10. I suspicioned that he was carrying a gat because he was kind of fresh, but he didn't faze me.

The Concrete and Specific Word

The concrete word makes your reader either see, hear, taste, smell, or touch the object which you are describing. When you use a word that appeals to one of his senses, he comes much closer to your meaning than if you had used an abstract word. The abstract word *beauty,* for example, gives the reader nothing which he can see or touch, nothing tangible which he can take away from your sentence. The word *beauty* in itself will suggest little to him unless he has a strong imagination by means of which he can conjure up a concrete thing which for him is beautiful. But if you translate this word into the phrase *the purple rays of the sun as it sets on the Ashley River* or *the smooth case of a new Colt revolver,* you will be using a concrete expression that the reader can bite into.

The specific word names a particular member of a class or group of related things and therefore claims the interest and attention of the reader. Notice that the second of the following two sentences is much more exciting than the first because it is much more specific:

General: One of our neighbors was hurt last night in an automobile accident.
Specific: Ed Canaday broke his arm last night when he drove his Ford into the big elm at the foot of Naubuc Avenue.

Many writers need to make their verbs more specific.

General: The doctor came into the room.
Specific: The doctor marched jauntily into the room.

Vague: We went downtown to buy a quarter pound of butter.

Specific: We bicycled downtown to buy a quarter pound of butter.

(The immature writer should not hastily conclude that concrete and specific words are always preferable to abstract words. When you wish to name abstract qualities and to make general statements, you will of course use abstract and general words.)

Exercise C

Make the following sentences more concrete and specific:

1. Some airplanes were seen in the sky.
2. An old friend of mine spent several years abroad before he settled down in this part of the country.
3. Our breakfast was most delicious; I have never enjoyed a more tasty meal.
4. Jerry expressed his disapproval of our actions in no uncertain terms.
5. He walked toward the door in a manner that beggared description.
6. There were five or six idle young men in front of the store on the corner.
7. Our captain got mentioned in yesterday's despatch because of his heroism.
8. The loveliness of what lay ahead made an overwhelming impression upon us.
9. I must thank you again for the beautiful present you sent me; I shall always use it.
10. Participation in a sport of this kind will improve one mentally, morally, and physically.

The Direct Word

Words are bullets that must be used sparingly. There must be no random firing into the air for the sake merely of making a noise; each word must speed unerringly to its target. In the practical conduct of the war, whether at home or at the battlefront, you will not have time for ornate and elaborate diction. You will need to be economical in your choice of words, to make every word count.

Do not allow your ideas to overlap. Avoid expressing your thought in one group of words and then repeating the same thought in different words.

> *Overlapping:* The two firms combined together to fight their rival. (Strike out *together,* which only repeats the meaning present in *combined.*)
>
> *Overlapping:* Although our foes were many in number, they lacked the important essential of an armored division. (Strike out the overlapping words *in number* and *important.*)

Do not use roundabout expressions. The shortest distance between a thought and its expression is the fewest number of words possible.

> *Roundabout:* It is my personal opinion that if we are to approach the matter of a second front, that is, if we are to face the matter and not shy away from it, we must be prepared to bend all our energies toward the solution of that problem with unflagging and untiring zeal. (52 words.)
>
> *Direct:* I believe that we must consider the opening of a second front with energy. (14 words.)
>
> *Roundabout:* There were three boys who were waiting for the bus. (10 words.)
>
> *Direct:* Three boys were waiting for the bus. (7 words.)

Exercise D

Rewrite the following sentences, making the language as direct as possible:

1. The good benefits of my proposal are many in number.
2. When they returned back to the hotel, there were two more new arrivals who had just checked in.
3. In regard to the matter of admission, which you apply for in your letter of July 1, it gives me great pleasure to inform you that the committee on admissions has acted favorably on your request and has instructed me, as its secretary, to communicate its sentiments to you.
4. Boswell's biography of the life of Johnson is not a book that should be read completely from cover to cover.
5. In the case of a policeman who has a definite beat to walk, he should know the names and business occupations of all persons on his beat.

6. Others may indulge in the participation of sports, such as football, basketball, swimming, polo, and the like, or many other sports which they may enjoy.

7. In the field of insurance, along the lines of which I have personally labored for seventeen years, I have come to know many interesting characters and personalities.

8. His remarks fully prepared me for what was to come, and therefore I was ready with an answer when Bill questioned me.

9. When he put in an appearance at headquarters, he was really alarmed, and was in considerable doubt as to what action would be taken concerning the disposition of his case.

10. In your sentences use the direct word, and, above all, aim at conciseness in everything you write.

Exercise E: Review

Improve the wording of the following sentences:

1. For a soldier who trains hard all day, the one game for him is pool.

2. A knowledge of this here book is a necessary requisite to a complete and full understanding of what I am about to say.

3. There is many a phenomena in nature that rarely ever can be explained by reference to known facts.

4. When we finally got to the restaurant, we had really a nice meal; the main dish in particular was quite good.

5. In regard to your proposition, Mr. Jones, allow me to state that I am of the opinion that my company would be ill advised to except your offer at this time; in a word, I'm afraid that my answer must continue to be in the negative.

6. My father's situation is such that he no longer finds himself in a position to do the physical feats which he was accustomed to performing in the palmy days of his youth.

7. As the vehicle passed him, he went behind a clump of bushes and remained there for several minutes.

8. I was not fazed by his remarks about the enormousness of my conduct; but I did resent his references to my lady friend.

9. Henry wanted to throw in the sponge before his client really began taking the count.

10. The moving van had several articles of furniture piled promiscuously in a helter-skelter fashion.

11. He won his promotion through a signal act of bravery under circumstances that reflect upon both his courage and skill.

12. "It isn't cricket," said the Britisher as the lead-off man poled a line drive just inside the hot corner.

13. Punctured pneumatic tires repaired on the premises.

14. Brazil is different than United States in more ways than this South American country is similar with ours.

15. Percy is a swell egg in many respects, but I don't think he would make a sufficiently hard-boiled top sergeant.

16. As the conversation continued along the lines of food rationing and gradually assumed the character of a general debate, I am afraid my remarks were conspicuous by their absence.

17. Montalembert's tenaille system consisted of redans, with salient angles of 60° or more, flanking each other at right angles.

18. My principle objection for your plan is that you stray too far from the basic principals as laid by leading strategists.

19. The total _effect_ of all this maneuvering was that the enemy had to ascend up the mountain to regain its position once more.

20. For once I agree with your proposal, although I do not often agree with you.

21. The merchant vessel had only one gun, and that was stationery, but it was superior than anything the enemy had.

22. Count Fleet is one hot number among the bangtails this year.

23. My sister showed her temper in a way that left little to be desired from a pyrotechnic standpoint.

24. He was a funny specimen of humanity as he sat in the bathtub smoking his pipe; but that he was a budding genius, I beg leave to doubt.

25. Carl Hubbell, the Giants' meal-ticket, once whiffed five American leaguers in a row; but the old southpaw is not what he used to be.

CHAPTER VIII

EFFECTIVE SPEAKING

Your Aim in Speaking

The aim of speaking, as it will be presented in this chapter, is simple and practical. You have a job to do, and that job demands effective speaking. In doing it you will not need oratory, the subtleties of persuasion, or the fine art of after-dinner speaking. But before your job is done, your life and the lives of others may depend upon your success in telling other men what you know and in making them hear and understand you. If that statement seems a bit exaggerated, just recall the suggested situations in Chapter I in which English is a constantly used and vital tool; mostly they called for an effective use of English in speech. Such situations make it an absolute necessity that an officer speak so that he can be heard and understood.

The duties and responsibilities of a young officer in training his men reveal the aim he must set for himself in his speaking. The aim of speaking must be the simple one of conveying information about things and processes, communicating ideas and problems, from the speaker to the listener, whether the listener be one or many. And this aim will remain the same, effective communication through speech, wherever the speaking takes place, in the quiet of the classroom or during the haste of impending attack.

The Officers' Guide, although it does not have "official" War Department standing, has all the force of law and gospel for Army officers; they will tell you that it is their constant friend and counselor. The following is a statement of what the Army expects of its officers as speakers:

"It can be stated with confidence that the government does not expect all of its military officers to become orators of distinction just as it cannot hope that each will develop the leadership qualities of a Pershing, a Lee, a Grant, or a Washington. . . . The Army has no pressing need for great orators, nor has it any need whatever for spellbinders and rabble-rousers. But it has a great need for officers who have knowledge, logical conclusions based upon it, and ability to impart it to others." [1]

Establishing Right Attitudes

Your problems in the attainment of effective communication will be of two general kinds, those of speech composition and those of speech delivery. These two general types of problems will be considered in the order in which they have been mentioned, because this is the order in which you will face them. First you decide what you are going to say; then comes the problem of delivery, or how you are going to say it. There is no suggestion that either is more important than the other, for the truth is that neglect of either one may cause a speaker to fail in his job.

But the average student is not ready to approach the problems of speaking until he has cleared his mind of some common misconceptions about the nature of speechmaking. Like the dub golfer who finally decides to take lessons, the average student of speechmaking has to unlearn bad habits before he is ready to progress.

Speechmaking Is not an Unnatural Act. The painful embarrassment most youngsters have suffered while reciting "a few choice lines" should not be taken as an indication that there is anything unnatural in a person's standing before a group and speaking to them. Either reading or speaking to a group is only a natural extension of conversation to meet an enlarged situation.

You feel no unnaturalness in carrying on a conversation with a member of your family or even with a small group of your friends. One reason why you feel no strain in these situations is that you have been long accustomed to such speaking, but the more important reason is that you are not thinking about yourself or your appearance.

[1] *The Officers' Guide,* 7th Edition (Feb., 1942), Harrisburg, Pa., The Military Service Publishing Company.

You want to tell about something you have seen or heard, or about an idea that has occurred to you. You have a job to do; so you do it as well as you know how. An increase in the number of persons listening to you—an increase from five to ten, to a hundred or more—should not change your attitude toward your listeners, for your task is still the same—to communicate your meaning to them.

Speechmaking Is not a Fine Art but a Useful Art. The fine arts, such as painting or acting or elocution or oratory, have value because they give pleasure. On the other hand, speechmaking, one of the practical or useful arts like cabinetmaking or knitting or operating a telegraph key, has value because of its usefulness in the ordinary daily affairs of men. The speechmaker is not like the actor or orator, either of whom puts on a performance; the speechmaker must learn to think of himself as only one of three elements in the speechmaking process: the speaker, the speech, the audience. Two of these elements are his to control; over the third control must be gained.

Speechmaking at Its Best. Now that your mind has been cleared of false conceptions of the nature of speechmaking, you are ready for a definition. Speechmaking is at its best when a speaker has a strong conviction that he should talk with a particular audience about a topic to which he brings both interest and knowledge. But that definition might apply to any speechmaker and his choice of subject. You will have an even stronger motive for your speechmaking—a sense of duty will make you do your best to put your subjects over to your audiences. In fact, the nature of the work for which you are preparing limits somewhat the problems you will have to consider. For instance, you will not have to bother much about the choice of subjects for your speeches; mostly your subjects will be chosen for you by your superior officers or by the circumstances that confront you.

Furthermore, you will not have to give attention to the niceties of audience adaptation in your choice of subjects, because your audiences, as well as your subjects, will be chosen for you. Your subjects will be decided by the nature of the work in hand, and your listeners will be nearly as eager to gain information as you are to impart it. You have a job to do; your listeners know they have a job to do. With that understanding between you and your audience, you may be sure that your listeners will be with you if you play fair with them. All they will ask of you is that you present your material in such a manner that they can understand and that you use your voice so that they can hear distinctly the words you utter.

Because your audiences will be relatively homogeneous, your problem in adjusting your speeches to them will be the simple one of discovering their average intelligence and adjusting your speechmaking to that level. However, there may be urgent times when you will have to speak plainly enough, bluntly enough, to reach the lowest intelligence in your audience. When a patrol is going out, you must make sure that every member understands his assigned task, that he understands it beyond the shadow of a doubt. Or you may be called upon to explain to a group how to adjust gas masks or how to prepare to take to lifeboats. In such situations it is not good enough if nearly every listener understands you; every man listening to you must understand perfectly.

You may have harbored for a long time a secret ambition to be an oratorical spellbinder or to have the wit to charm your friends at a banquet. Unfortunately, such ambitions will have to remain unsatisfied for the present; there is no time for the lace trimmings. For now you will be concerned only with how you can most successfully impart information to your listeners. You will be required to explain to others what you have learned about an object, a process, or an idea. In explanatory speaking, as in the writing of the paragraph or the complete explanatory composition, you must have a thorough knowledge of your subject, you must work out a plan of presentation, and you must compose the parts carefully.

The special problems of speechmaking, as distinguished from written composition, will be considered under two headings: those of composition and those of delivery. Before proceeding to the problems of speech preparation, you should realize that the methods which you will find in the following sections constitute the ideal. Limitations of time or other circumstances will often prevent your adherence to the ideal. But it may reasonably be expected that a man will not be thrust into emergency speaking before he has had some experience in more nearly normal speaking. Furthermore, if you have thoroughly mastered the methods of speech preparation, you will find that you can do the hasty job when the need arises better than you could if you had never thoroughly prepared any speech. A gun crew puts in hours of practice so that they will do the right thing by habit when time is all important. Likewise, you must by practice acquire the speaker's mental habits.

Problems of Speech Composition

Principles of Writing and Speaking. Some of the principles of writing that have been stated in preceding chapters apply equally to speaking. Both spoken and written composition must have a single topic which is completely developed and presented in an orderly manner; both must have carefully organized paragraphs, good sentence structure, and carefully chosen words.

Know Your Exact Purpose in Each Speech. In speaking it is even more important than in writing that you have a firm grasp of what you are trying to do in a particular speech to a particular audience. If you do not quite know this yourself, it is hardly likely that the audience will find out. You may sometimes wish only to make an explanation. Thus, if you are telling a group of enlisted men how to make application for furlough, simple explanation will suffice; the desirability of such a a procedure speaks for itself. Occasionally, however, you may need to convince an audience that they should accept an idea or an explanation that you have given. The same group of men that applied for furlough will need to be convinced of the importance of keeping a neat appearance while they are away from their post. The veteran sergeant not only will tell recruits how to clean a rifle; he also will miss no opportunity to convince them, by both speech and other ways sergeants have, that they must keep their rifles clean. At other times you may need to stir the emotions of an audience to lead them to do as you wish them to. For instance, a leader is often able to get the final perfection of technique from his men by a simple appeal to their pride.

Whichever purpose or combination of these purposes is the motive for your speech, you must know absolutely beforehand. So important is sureness of purpose that, if opportunity allows, you should write a statement of your purpose in black and white in complete sentence form. Haziness of purpose can be eliminated by putting pen to paper; if you cannot express your purpose in a compact sentence, you need to do some more thinking.

Know Your Subject Matter. Nothing short of complete mastery of the materials of your speech will suffice. A writer who lacks this mastery may escape detection and produce a reasonably clear composition if he does a little "boning up" as he progresses from one topic to another. Such a hack writer can hardly be regarded as an authority, although he may deceive many readers. But the speaker must do all of his studying on his materials before he starts speaking, for he cannot take all his source books or experimental apparatus with him to the platform. He must assimilate his materials, make them his own, in order to earn the right to take the time of an audience.

As a speaker you must know your subject even more thoroughly than you would need to for your own use; you must have such a complete understanding of its ins and outs that you can make it clear to others. There are those writers who apparently assume that their readers will be sufficiently patient or industrious to ferret out the meaning of what they have written. The speaker, on the contrary, cannot rely upon the patience or industry of his audience. At the best, he can hope for no more than thoughtful attentiveness, and he will receive that as long as he makes himself clear. You can see that you will have to make your message clear as you speak, or it will never reach your audience. As you well know from your experience as a listener, a speaker who is obviously uncertain about his material or vague in his presentation of it is sure to lose your respect and confidence.

If time and circumstances permit, you will do well to test your grasp of your material by talking your subject over with a friend or colleague upon whose honesty and judgment you can rely. This practice will be especially valuable to you during the preparation of your first few attempts at public speaking. Of course, such conferences will often be out of the question; then the duty of critically examining your own assimilation of material will devolve upon you.

Have a Plan for Your Speech. You should outline your speeches if you have the opportunity. For your first few speeches you must make the opportunity. The methods of outlining presented in Chapter III, "The Complete Explanatory Composition," will suffice. If circumstances make it impossible for you to work out a written outline, then you will have to do some careful mental planning; for you are under an obligation, both to yourself and to your audience, to speak from some sort of plan. It is only through planning that you can keep your speeches from rambling and digressing. As an absolute minimum of planning, you must make provision for the beginning and ending of your speech.

Methods of Speech Preparation. There are two general methods of speech preparation: (1) that of the written and memorized speech, and (2) that of the extemporaneous speech. Although the memorized speech has some advantages, its use is confined mostly to more formal speaking occasions; it is assumed that you will not often have time for this method of preparation. Therefore only the extemporaneous method will be considered here. You must not confuse extemporaneous speaking with impromptu speaking, which is on the spur of the moment and completely unprepared. Impromptu speeches should never be made except when they are absolutely necessary.

Extemporaneous Speaking. The advantage of extemporaneous speaking is that the speaker's mind is not tied up with his effort to recall the precise words that he has committed to memory. The speaker who memorizes word for word may be thrown off balance if he forgets a single word or phrase. The extemporaneous speaker, on the other hand, has memorized only a train of thought; most people find it easier to recall a step in the development of a thought than to recall a precise word in a chain of several hundred or more. The extemporaneous speaker is more nearly free to give his attention to his audience, to talk with them, to observe their reactions to what he says, and even to modify his speech to meet reactions or situations which he has been unable to foresee.

You must be under no illusion that the extemporaneous method is an easy way out of speech preparation. On the contrary, the successful extemporaneous speech is a result of thorough mastery of material, careful planning, and practice in "saying the speech over aloud" before it is delivered. For extemporaneous speaking you must prepare so thoroughly that you will not digress from your main topic or give an undue amount of time to minor matters within your topic. Either of these faults may cause you to run over your time limit or to have your speech cut off before your message is completed. As you know, the President of the United States is about the only speaker who cannot be cut off the radio when the time is up. So save your long-winded, rambling speeches for the time when you are President—then you will know better than to make such speeches.

By going over your speech aloud and thus getting practice in the phrasing of your ideas, you can avoid the awkward and hesitant manner that results from the poorly prepared speaker's efforts to find the right words. Practice aloud gives you a further check on your grasp of your subject, for what you really know you can express in your own words. If in this practicing you find that you are at a great loss for words, you may be sure that you don't really know what you are talking about.

There are some speakers who are slow and hesitant starters, and others who are hard to stop once they are started. If you are one of these, then probably you should, at least for the longer more formal speeches, write out and memorize the opening and closing remarks of your speech.

Use of Notes in Extemporaneous Speaking. Brief notes, if they are properly used, will not detract from the extemporaneous speaker's presentation of his subject. Speaking notes should, however, be limited to brief statements, hardly more than phrases, of the main points of your speech or of difficult transitions from one point to another. They should be written neatly and compactly on small slips of paper, or preferably on small cards, such as 3 x 5 filing cards. You need not try to hide the fact that you are using note cards; but you will find it disconcerting both to you and to your audience if you have to scramble through a sheaf of loose papers on which you have scrawled your notes. Furthermore, you must never neglect your listeners while you submerge yourself in your notes to discover what comes next; in other words, speaking notes must not be regarded as a substitute for good hard thinking during the preparation of the speech.

One exception to the rule of brevity for notes must be mentioned. If your speech is to contain material that must be given with perfect accuracy, such as quotations, statistics, or formulas, you should write out this material completely and correctly and then read it to your audience.

Differences Between Eye Perception and Ear Perception. The speaker must realize that to a large extent he reaches the understanding of his listeners through their ears. Because auditory perception is somewhat less efficient and stable than visual perception, he must face and overcome problems which do not trouble the writer. Auditory perception and attention are slower, less constant, and more easily distracted than visual perception and attention. The wise speaker recognizes these differences between eye and ear capacities and makes the necessary adjustments. The inexperienced speaker often fails because he has not realized that what may be perfectly clear on the printed page may cause only confusion when presented from a platform. There follow some of the concessions which skillful speakers make for their listeners.

The topics or ideas in a speech must be a little more slowly developed than they are in writing. Speaking cannot have the same concentration, the same compression, as some explanatory compositions. For instance, the speaker must slow up enough to make certain that his definitions and terminology are understood by his audience. The reader can puzzle over a definition until he does understand it. The listener must be given the same opportunity to stay with a definition until he has mastered it and is ready for the material of the speech which depends upon the definition.

The speaker may feel more at liberty than the writer to use repetition, although even he must use it judiciously if he hopes to avoid monotony. Nevertheless, it is his duty to hammer at a point until he is certain that it is driven home. The repetition may involve the use of the same words more than once, especially when they are complex or unfamiliar to the audience. Or it may be a restatement of an idea in different words or from a different point of view. The speaker will freely use example and illustration, comparison and contrast.

A subject can often be clarified by a speaker for his

audience if he will make them aware of the structure of his speech. Audiences appreciate the thoughtfulness of the speaker who gives them the impression that they are progressing with him step by step. Such an impression can be created by the use of connective words and phrases (see connective expressions, pages 16–17) and by the speaker's announcement of the topics he intends to cover. Such an announcement sometimes makes a satisfactory introduction for a speech, but once this promise has been made, it must be fulfilled in the speech.

A speaker should use visual aids when they are available. The armed forces have prepared great masses of material for visual aid in instruction because they know that a man has a better understanding of what he has seen than he has of what he has heard about. You know that a purely oral presentation of the construction of a water tower is a poor makeshift. For a better presentation you would supplement your speech with diagrams and drawings. But for the best results you would take your audience to a water tower. The little tricks that make for the most effective use of visual aids you will have to work out for yourself, but you should realize that there are right and wrong ways of using charts and samples and drawings.

Finally, you must make an effort to win the undivided attention of your audiences, and you must remember that it is easier to hold attention than to regain it.

Problems of Speech Delivery

A study of the problems of delivery must be based on a firm understanding of the aims of public speaking as they were stated in the opening of this chapter, for through reference to these general aims the speaker can usually decide whether or not any particular practice in delivery is good. Any practice that promotes effective communication between speaker and listener is good; any practice that detracts from such communication is bad.

There is your yardstick for determining what is good delivery.

Since speaking in public should be regarded not as an unnatural activity but as a normal function, it follows that delivery should be natural, that it should have the same qualities as good, vigorous conversation, plus the necessary adaptation to the changed conditions under which you are speaking. The first and most obvious step in this adaptation is to raise or put more force into your voice. The essence of good public speaking being communication between speaker and audience, it follows that clarity of utterance, making yourself heard, is the foundation of good speech delivery.

Making Yourself Heard. You must remember that an audience which is under no particular restraint will probably "walk out on" the speaker who does not make himself heard. Although the side-show barker is hardly a model for the study of speech delivery, he has learned in a hard school the necessity of making his voice reach his listeners. The more conventional speaker has no right to impose upon his audience with unintelligible mumbling when they are restrained from leaving either by politeness or by sterner necessity. Thus the teacher who stands before his class, apparently talking only to himself or at most to the front row, is taking an unfair advantage of his students; certainly they cannot be blamed if they go to sleep, and they can hardly be expected to tell him that he is not making himself heard.

Equally or even more at fault is the officer who will not or cannot make his voice reach his men. It is not too much to suggest that an important mission might fail because of the inefficiency of such an officer. The least harmful effect of speaking which cannot be heard is the loss of valuable time spent in repeating, in a louder voice, what has already been said. Unfortunately, an officer cannot count upon his men telling him when they fail to hear him. The reticence of audiences to tell a speaker that they are unable to hear him imposes upon every speaker the duty of watching his listeners for signs that he is not being heard. If he is still uncertain, because of bad acoustical and other unfavorable conditions, he should ask if he is making himself heard.

This first necessity of satisfactory delivery requires that, in speaking as in conversation, you produce a sufficient volume of sound. Conversing with a friend in the quiet of your own living room, you would use only a moderate volume; but if you met a friend at a busy street corner, you would raise your voice (increase the volume) enough to make yourself heard in spite of the noise of traffic. In speaking you will make the same adjustments, according to the number in the audience, the size and acoustic qualities of the place where you are speaking, and the disturbing noises that you have to overcome. With experience you will learn to adjust your voice to rooms of different shapes, to indoor and outdoor speaking.

If at first you seem unable to hit the correct volume, then risk being too loud. With experience and observation, however, you should be able to gauge volume very closely and learn to vary the volume of your voice, occasionally raising your voice to give emphasis to some particular points of your speech.

Because of the rapid increase in the number of public address systems it seems advisable to say a word about their use. First of all, dispense with them whenever possible, for none of those in general use have yet succeeded in reproducing the human voice accurately. However, public address systems are sometimes a great help to the speaker, and he should learn how to speak into one. In talking into the microphone, you can afford to neglect the volume of your voice because the system will amplify your voice as much as necessary; but because of the reproduction deficiencies of most systems, you will have to be more than ordinarily careful about enunciation. One more thing you must remember: you will need to remain in a reasonably fixed position in relation to the microphone

—at least most pickups are noticeably affected when a speaker increases his distance from the microphone or changes the direction in which he is talking.

Making Your Words Clear. A speaker may put enough force into his voice so that his audience can hear the noise he is making, and yet fail to make his audience hear *what* he has to say because he fails to make his words clear. Such a failure is due to faulty articulation, which may reduce a speaker's words to a mere blur of sounds.

Faulty articulation may be due to a speaker's not knowing the correct individual speech sounds; but most faults of articulation are caused not by a lack of knowledge but by the speaker's failure to use vigorously, precisely, or correctly the organs of articulation. A speaker can avoid most faults of articulation if he will allow his jaws some freedom of movement, if he will open his mouth, and if he will use his tongue, teeth, and lips more vigorously.

A too precise articulation of speech sounds may attract attention to how you are forming your words and consequently distract attention from what the words mean, from your message. You may be certain, though, that between slovenly articulation and overly careful articulation, the latter is by all odds the lesser of two evils.

Pronouncing Your Words Correctly. Almost as essential to good delivery as clear, sharp articulation is correct pronunciation of your words. Whether or not audiences are justified in their severe judgments upon mispronunciations cannot be settled here, but the fact remains that many a man has done more damage to his reputation as a speaker by two or three scattered slips in pronunciation than he can counteract by a whole speech based on sound and well-organized thinking.

Since listeners will be alert to pick up your errors in pronunciation and judge you harshly because of them, you must endeavor to eliminate them from your speaking. This means that you will need to become better acquainted with your dictionary, for it is the authority on matters of correct pronunciation. It will help you, however, only if you are willing to help yourself to the extent of mastering its symbols and guides to pronunciation.

Before making a speech, you should look up and learn the correct pronunciation of any new or unusual words which you expect to use. For your speaking, both public and otherwise, you should not try to "put on," to affect, a manner of pronunciation which is foreign to your background and training. But neither should you be stubborn in your adherence to the gross peculiarities of pronunciation that you have been accustomed to "back home."

Attaining a Satisfactory Rate of Delivery. If you speak too rapidly, you suggest to your listeners that you are insincere, that you are dashing off words without any sense of their meaning. An even more serious result of your speaking too rapidly is that your audience may not be able to follow your thought. Also, a rate of speaking that is too slow or is jerky will seriously detract from your speaking effectiveness. You must avoid uttering a few words and then hesitating, uttering another two or three words and then pausing again, and so on throughout your speech. In order to determine what is a good speaking rate, listen to successful speakers. Try to develop variety of rate and thereby avoid monotonous delivery. Furthermore, by slowing down from a prevailing rate, you can focus attention on those parts of your speech which you wish to emphasize.

Posture and Movement in Speechmaking. Posture and movement are considered together because both are parts of the speaker's physical appearance before his audience. The ideal in these, as in the use of the voice, is naturalness and ease, plus alertness.

Although a generally useful and desirable posture can be described, it must be understood that a speaker would seriously curtail his effectiveness if he held himself in any one posture continuously throughout a speech. The speaker who rigidly maintains one posture is in danger of suggesting monotony of delivery, and he is certainly neglecting an appeal to the more alert visual perceptions of his audience. For there will undoubtedly be one or more points in every speech that call for some movement of the body. Thus any posture the speaker takes will be interrupted from time to time. Nevertheless, persistent questions indicate that young speakers want to know what to do with themselves between those points that call for movement. What they want is a generally suitable posture.

Such a posture needs to be appropriate to the most common speech situations; it should be neither too relaxed nor too stiff; it should be a good starting point for those movements which will be necessary at some points in every speech. Such a posture can be best described in military parlance. The "At Ease" posture is too relaxed; the "Attention" posture is much too stiff. The in-between posture, "Parade Rest," is a good general posture for the soldier and the speaker. It is relaxed but alert, easy and yet dignified. From this posture the speaker can move easily into other positions.

Movement is here intended to include somewhat more than the motions of a speaker's hands and arms commonly known as gestures—usually the great bugaboo of small boys reciting "pieces" in the classroom and at Sunday school. Movement here includes any modification or change of the speaker's posture or position on the platform, or even facial expression. The underlying principle of movement before an audience is that any movement which facilitates the communication of your meaning is good. Any movement which attracts attention to itself is bad, because the attention of the audience has been partially or temporarily drawn away from what you are saying. Some motivated movement is highly desirable because it helps to break monotonousness of delivery.

You will be able to improve your use of motivated movement if you will apply three tests to the motions you use in speechmaking: (1) Is the movement appropriate? Does it supplement your words in expressing your meaning? (2) Is it properly timed in relation to the words which it is intended to supplement? (3) Have you allowed yourself complete freedom of movement by overcoming any restraints upon muscular action? As a starter, you might well apply these tests to the movement you make in pointing. This particular application is suggested because pointing is obviously one of the movements that everyone has occasion to use. Certainly you, as a leader of men, will have to point; you might as well learn to do it properly.

Holding the Attention of Your Audience. To win and hold the attention of your audience will usually demand a positive and energetic effort on your part. You may be able to sit back and relax while you are talking things over with an old friend, but holding the attention of all the members of an audience is somewhat more difficult than holding the attention of an individual in a conversation. In speaking to a group you must reach and hold many and varied personalities, and the distribution of your efforts to hold attention necessarily spreads more thinly the effects of those efforts. Furthermore, an individual in a group is more easily distracted than he would be in a conversation with another individual. Inattention is contagious; so nip in the bud any signs of wavering attention.

You can decrease the effect of distractions and the danger of inattention by avoiding monotony in your delivery. Break up any tendency toward monotony by variations in the volume, the rate, and the pitch of your voice; by changes in posture, by the use of movement, and by liveliness of facial expression. You must never make the mistake of allowing your attention to remain centered on one part of your audience or, worst of all, on one remote corner of the room where you are speaking. Face your audience squarely and try to make every one of your listeners feel that you are talking to him alone. Finally, remember that people in groups are more susceptible to suggestion than they are singly. The speaker who can suggest by his own bearing that he is alert and ready to do a job usually finds that his audience is willing to accept the suggestion.

Overcoming Nervousness and Developing Confidence. The best antidotes for nervousness are a realization of the true nature of public speaking and thorough preparation for each speech. If you are full of your subject and thinking about the best way of "putting it over" to your audience, your mind will not be able to do much worrying about your appearing foolish on the platform. It will be fully occupied with the job you have to do.

You should not, however, confuse nervousness and the natural tenseness you experience as you approach any important task; in fact, you should neither expect nor desire a complete absence of tenseness, for some mental and muscular tenseness is good for both speaker and athlete. Such tenseness, within control, helps either one to rise a little above his usual level of performance.

The old adage that practice makes perfect is as true for speaking as it is for any other skill. Seize every opportunity for putting into practice what you have learned about speechmaking. Practice good speaking in classroom recitations, take an active part in club and association meetings, and make a self-imposed rule to accept all opportunities for speaking to groups, large or small.

A short time after the end of World War I, Philip Gibbs, an English war correspondent, came to the United States to make a lecture tour. He had made a great reputation by his splended news stories written from the front lines. He had suffered as many hardships and dangers as any soldier, and been exposed to the same shocks; yet he had come through with no more fear or flinching than any man would feel. But he had had so little experience as a speaker that he spent the entire Atlantic crossing in dreading his first appearance. He was so nerved up by the time he reached Carnegie Hall in New York for the first lecture that he was, by his own admission, unable to recall what he had planned to talk

about. Nor had his fears left him by the time he rose
to speak. He was afraid that Americans would not understand his British accent; he was afraid that he would
be dull; in fact, he was afraid of a great many things,
mostly imaginary. Finally he looked out over his audience,
and gradually he realized that the people out there had
come because they wanted to hear him. They were no
longer enemies to be feared. The thought amused him
and he smiled; the audience smiled back. Then and there
he knew that he was among friends and that all he had
to do was tell them about the things he had seen and
done. He knew that he would be able to complete the tour
that had been arranged.

Suggested Plan for Practice in Speaking

Correlation of Speaking and Writing. It is the belief
of the authors that students using this book should study
and progress in speaking simultaneously as they study
and progress in writing. This belief is based on the
knowledge that those responsible for the war training
programs are not so much interested in writing or speaking as they are in communication, whether it be written
or oral. The belief is fortified by the realization that if
either one is given precedence, the other one will almost
certainly suffer partial neglect.

Main Units in Practice Speaking

1. Each student should make several short explanatory talks (2 to 3 minutes).
2. Each student should at several times prepare in
   advance to read to the group a short passage of
   standard prose.
3. Each student should prepare at least one longer
   speech (about 10 minutes).
4. Every student should join in the discussion and
   criticism of the speaking and reading of others.

Short Explanatory Talks. The first of these might well
follow and be simply an oral presentation of the topic

the student has presented in his first exercise on paragraph writing. He should, however, begin his speechmaking only after he has studied at least the first two parts of this chapter, "Your Aim in Speaking" and "Establishing Right Attitudes." These first talks should deal with relatively simple things and processes such as he will be using in his written paragraphs. Actual topics which he might use are suggested at the end of Chapter II. These talks should last from two to three minutes.

Reading to the Group. Reading aloud must be taken seriously; that means careful preparation in advance for oral reading, because good oral reading is neither a gift nor an easy acquirement. The student must have the right attitude toward reading aloud because he will likely be called upon to read to groups. A much more important reason for his taking oral reading seriously is that it gives him an opportunity to concentrate on delivery; he does not have to concentrate on the creation of meaning, as he does in his speaking. The skill he gains in the delivery of the words of others he should take back to his own speaking. However, the reader should not assume that he does not need to give close attention to the meaning of what he reads aloud, both in its parts and as a whole. Oral reading which has not been prepared in advance tends to become a mere babble of words or even muffled sounds because the reader has not learned beforehand the import of the words he utters.

For practice in delivery the student should select passages of about paragraph length for oral presentation before his group. Suitable passages for oral reading (approximately 150 to 200 words) can be found in the illustrative paragraphs in Chapter II, in the illustrative compositions in Chapter III, or among the reading selections in Chapter IX. Appropriate passages may be found in printed speeches, famous plays, or well-known historical documents; the Bible is, of course, a rich storehouse of material for oral reading. The student may even wish to try himself out on passages which he anticipates being called on to read aloud and thereby profit both by practice and by the criticisms of his listeners.

The Longer Speech. The interpretation of *longer* will, of course, be decided by the instructor, but the term is used here to indicate a speech which either presents a larger topic or presents it in more detail than did the short explanatory talks which were given earlier. These longer speeches should not, however, run over ten minutes; generally the speaker will learn more of speaking in three ten-minute speeches than he would in one of thirty minutes. These later speeches should probably be correlated with the study of Chapter III, which contains several lists of suggestive topics for longer speeches.

However, the longer speech is really the occasion for the speaker to put away crutches, to strike out into topics of his own selection, topics that he really knows about, topics in which he has a genuine interest. Likewise, the longer speech offers him a chance to try his hand in practice on topics which he may reasonably expect to use later when he cannot afford to make mistakes.

Audience Discussion and Criticism. Certainly not the least valuable instruction a student speaker receives is the criticism which his fellow students give him. Of course, students should not need the reminder that criticism may be either favorable or unfavorable, or both; nevertheless, experience reveals that they sometimes need to be reminded that *criticism* is not synonymous with *tearing down* or *pulling apart*. By being an alert listener and a ready critic of each speech, the student is doing his part toward audience participation in speaking. Each student in a group should try to be fair and intelligent in his criticisms. He should try to avoid an undue concern with trifling matters, such as a slight slip of the tongue or minor mannerisms that do not especially distract attention. He will be generous in praise for a job well done, but he will hit hard and clean when he criticizes a speaker who has obviously not done his best. If each student in a group will strive for such standards of speech discussion and criticism, not only will the class sessions be lively and instructive, but each member of the group will receive a great boost toward speaking skill. Each speaker gets back about what he puts into the game.

CHAPTER IX

EFFICIENT READING

Speed Not a Main Issue

You should fix in your mind at once that speed in reading explanatory material, the type that you will increasingly be called upon to read, is not necessarily a mark of efficient reading. Although it is well to develop as much speed as sound understanding will allow, sound understanding must ever be your primary objective. Too many people become discouraged, think themselves stupid, and stop trying if they cannot intelligently read difficult explanations at the same speed at which they read fiction. You must not be one of these. Remember that the absorbing of information is always a gradual process.

The Need for Concentration

Efficient reading is first of all a matter of concentration. What is concentration? It is a gluing of the mind to the matter at hand. It arises mainly from interest or firm purpose. If you can bring to your reading the interest with which you patched your first bicycle inner tube or the firmness of purpose with which you charged for that last touchdown in the final game of the season, you are well on the way to being an efficient reader.

Four Important Steps Toward Efficient Reading

In your effort to become an efficient reader you will find the following steps helpful. In the first place, you should make sure that you **understand the words** of a passage; for unless you know the words, all the interest or firmness of purpose in the world will do you no good. For example, how well could you master the following paragraph without knowing the meaning of such words as *propagation, conduction, radiation, deflagration, propellant, primer,* and *ignition?*

Explosions are usefully divided into two classes depending upon the manner of propagation of the explosive reaction from one part of the explosive substance to the other. The explosion may be propagated relatively slowly by the conduction or radiation of heat from the burnt part to the unburnt part. This is called deflagration or more simply burning. Such an explosion occurs in the burning of propellant powders in a gun. The outside surfaces of the solid grains are heated by the primer gases to a temperature of some 400° C, at which temperature a reaction occurs producing hot gases. These hot gases in turn raise the newly exposed surfaces to the ignition point and they are transformed in turn into gas. The rate of propagation of such a burning or deflagration is relatively slow. Even at the high pressure of 100,000 lb./in.^{2}, the rate is only, approximately, 2 ft./sec.[1]

In much of your general reading you may be able to determine the meaning of an unfamiliar word by a scrutiny of the words around it, that is, of the context. In reading technical material, however, you should rely heavily upon your dictionary, selecting that meaning of a word that best fits into the particular context. Always remember that the dictionary and a good reader are close friends.

In the second place, you should **note the organization** of the passage. That is, you should note the main idea, which will usually be expressed at the beginning, and each successive subordinate idea, with its most significant details. In other words, you should reconstruct the outline from which the passage was written. By so doing you will bring into focus, in their proper order, the essentials of the writer's thought. Some readers underline this significant material, and so have it marked for future reference and review. This would be a helpful custom for you to adopt, if you use it conscientiously. Still other readers reconstruct the outline in brief notes written in the margin of the book.

[1] From "Explosives and Their Military Applications" by R. H. Kent, *Journal of Applied Physics,* Vol. XIII, No. 6 (June, 1942). Reprinted by permission.

In the following passage you will find an example of the reconstruction of the outline by underlining:

Main idea { Explosions are usefully divided into two classes depending upon the manner of propagation of the explosive reaction from one part of the explosive substance to the other.

First subordinate idea { The explosion may be propagated relatively slowly by the conduction or radiation of heat from the burnt part to the unburnt part. This is called deflagration or more simply burning.

Important example { Such an explosion occurs in the burning of propellant powders in a gun.

Significant details of process { The outside surfaces of the solid grains are heated by the primer gases to a temperature of some 400° C, at which temperature a reaction occurs producing hot gases. These hot gases in turn raise the newly exposed surfaces to the ignition point and they are transformed in turn into gas. The rate of propagation of such a burning or deflagration is relatively slow. Even at the high pressure of 100,000 lb./in.^{2}, the rate is only, approximately, 2 ft./sec.

Second subordinate idea { If a sufficiently powerful blow or impact is imparted to certain explosives, they will detonate instead of burn. In a detonation the reaction is propagated not by heat conduction but by wave action.

Significant details of process { A pressure wave of great violence is produced which travels at high speed through the explosive substance compressing and heating each layer of the substance it reaches. Under the influence of the wave, the unstable explosive breaks down into a gas. The successive layers are thus suddenly converted into more stable compounds, mostly gaseous. The rate of propagation in a detonation in nitroglycerin by wave action is sometimes as great as 5 mi./sec. Because of the much greater suddenness with which the explosive is converted into gases in a detonation than in a deflagration, the effects of a detonation on nearby structures and on personnel are much greater than the effects produced by a deflagration or burning.

Important contrast { Twenty-five lb. of powder burning in a 155-mm G.P.F. gun will impart a velocity of 2400 ft./sec. to the 95-lb. projectile but will leave the gun unharmed. Twenty-five lb. of powder detonated in the G.P.F. gun would smash the gun and projectile into thousands of pieces.[2]

Of course, outlining such a difficult passage as this will always require more than one reading. It will also require some sweat and eraser work. But the job well done will pay high dividends in understanding.

In the third place, you should **make a précis**. A précis is a concise statement of the essential thought of a passage in one's own words. The length varies with the compression or looseness of the wording in the original passage, but should usually not exceed one-half the number of words in the original. The précis of a long or difficult passage should always be preceded by an outline of the passage. When you have made the outline in accordance with the suggestions above, you will have the materials for the précis. Also you will have them in the order in which you will normally want to present them: (1) the main idea, (2) each successive subordinate idea with its significant supporting material. You must compose the précis with such care that a listener or reader unfamiliar with the original might readily grasp the essential thought of it. There follows a précis of the passage on explosions, made from the underlined outline of that passage:

In accordance with the manner of propagation of the explosive reaction, explosions are divided into deflagrations and detonations. In a deflagration or burning (which occurs in propellant powders in guns) the heat is propagated by conduction or radiation. Exposed solid grains of the explosive substance are heated by primer gases until the substance is transformed into hot gases, which, in turn, will heat and transform newly exposed solid surfaces. The rate of this relatively slow propagation, even at a pressure of 100,000 lb./in.^{2}, is only about 2 ft./sec. In a detonation the explosive reaction is propagated by wave action produced by impact. A violent pressure wave at

[2] *Ibid.* Reprinted by permission.

high speed compresses and heats each successive layer of the explosive substance, which suddenly breaks down into a gas. The rate of propagation is much greater than in deflagration, 5 mi./sec. in nitroglycerin. While a deflagration of 25 lbs. of powder in a 155-mm G.P.F. gun imparts to the projectile a velocity of 2400 ft./sec., leaving the gun unharmed, a detonation of 25 lbs. of powder would smash gun and projectile to bits. (About 175 words, reduced from about 350 words.)

In this instance the original passage is a difficult one to précis. Check whether the précis is correct. Find the sentence in the original that is not represented in the précis and try to decide why it is not. Note how in many instances one word in the précis is made to do the work of two or three in the original.

Making a careful précis, in your mind or in writing, will prove invaluable in your reading, because it will assure you of correct understanding of the writer's thought and because the repetition involved will be likely to fix the thought on your memory. Efficient readers always use the device when they are are engaged in mastering important and difficult material.

In the fourth place, when the materials read are at all within the range of your experience or study, you should **undertake to discover some details and examples of your own in support of the writer's ideas.** This act will prove of value in your reading because finding your own examples that support or do not support the writer's ideas will bring you to a keener understanding of those ideas and will tend, as a result of your close work with them, to fix them in your mind.

If you will diligently follow these four steps in your reading of explanatory material, not only will you improve your understanding of what you read but you will increase your speed in reading.

Exercises

The following exercises have been designed for practice in reading. They are mainly of a semi-technical nature and are arranged roughly in an ascending order of difficulty.

The questions at the end of each passage will not always check you on the application of the four steps presented above. Asking the same questions each time would be too monotonous. Nevertheless, you must always follow these four steps. If you do conscientiously, you will probably find easy any other questions that may be asked.

1.

Air tactics concern the employment of aviation units in battle. Air strategy involves all the methods by which a nation impresses its will through the employment of air forces. Strategy normally is precedent to tactics. There will be no confusion in the military mind as to the compartments or bins which we label strategy and tactics, and all the bolts, parts, and pieces will be stored in their proper places if the military students but remember that strategy is the precursor, that it is the overlord, that it is the label for the national effort, aim and purpose. Strategic factors are the playthings of the statesmen and legislators. Tactics on the other hand are the tools of the generals on the battlefield.[3]

Questions

1. What is the main purpose behind the writing of this paragraph?
2. State the idea in a sentence of no more than thirty words.
3. Pick out at least three figures of speech and comment on their effectiveness.
4. Explain the derivation of the following words: *employment, involves, impresses, precedent, confusion, compartments, remember, precursor.* Are these words specific or general? Concrete or abstract?

2.

Barrage balloons may be classified into three general types: high altitude balloons; low altitude balloons; and small barrage balloons which have certain special uses. With respect to their internal functional design, barrage balloons of any of the above three classifications may be either of the dilatable or

[3] From *Army Flyer* by Lieutenant General H. H. Arnold and Brigadier General Ira C. Eaker, Harper & Brothers, p. 255. Reprinted by permission.

the ballonet type. The dilatable balloon is entirely filled with gas, and has elastic cords placed internally or externally to retain the shape during expansion and contraction of the gas. The ballonet balloon has a horizontal diaphragm which divides it into two compartments, the upper of which contains gas and the lower part is filled with air by means of a wind scoop at the bottom of the balloon.

A barrage balloon consists essentially of a gas filled bag of woven fabric impregnated with rubber or a synthetic substitute, flown attached by means of rigging to a steel cable paid out from a winch. Hydrogen is the most suitable gas which can be made available in the quantity required, but several substitute gases may be used in emergency. The hydrogen may be obtained from conveniently located commercial factories, or it may be manufactured locally by portable field generators with which balloon units are equipped. A rip panel is built into the balloon and a rip link is attached to the upper end of the cable. The rip link is designed weaker than the cable, so that a rip cord, attached to the cable and the panel, will deflate the balloon when the shear pin fails. The hydrogen gas is stored in steel cylinders, and is hauled to the balloon site on trucks or trailers. Numerous items of auxiliary equipment are required.

High altitude balloons should be capable of being flown up to such altitudes as would preclude precision bombing. Such altitudes can be reached by large single balloons, by connecting two balloons in tandem, or by attaching kites to the cables to assist the lift of the balloon. The single large balloon has an advantage in that it can be flown or hauled down more quickly than the tandem or kite assisted balloons, a very important consideration when operating in conjunction with friendly aviation and antiaircraft artillery, or when hauling down the balloons to protect them from sudden storms.

A possible use of high altitude balloons appears to be their joint employment with low altitude balloons, the high balloons being disposed around the outer perimeter of a barrage where they would be more effective against horizontal flight bombardment. In some cases, such as an extensive barrage defending large multiple areas, a more uniform distribution throughout the barrage might be desirable. Another possible use is the establishment of a surprise barrage put up during periods of low visibility to intercept hostile aircraft on a frequently used avenue of approach.

The low altitude balloon is the type having the most universal application. They are flown within the cloud layer, whenever it is practicable to do so, for several reasons: (1)

to deny the use of the cloud layer by hostile aircraft as a means of concealment; (2) to conceal the balloons in order to render them less vulnerable; (3) to render the dispositions of the balloons less visible from hostile aircraft; (4) to prevent the dispositions of the balloons from disclosing the location of defended areas on the ground; (5) to prevent the superheating of the balloons by direct rays from the sun.

Small barrage balloons are effective only against low-flying aircraft employing hedge-hopping or dive-bombing tactics. They have principally been attached by cables to the masts of ships, or used for the protection of small installations which offer only precision targets. Mobile units, equipped with small balloons, could be used to accompany armies in the field, and employed in the protection of vital routes, defiles, or installations against any form of low-flying air attack.[4]

Questions

1. Define the following words as they are used in the selection: *dilatory, ballonet, diaphragm, impregnated, synthetic, auxiliary, preclude, tandem, perimeter, vulnerable, disposition, mobile, defile*.

2. Noting that the material here is organized on the basis of the *use* and *design* of the barrage balloon, make a brief outline of the passage.

3. Why does the author order his discussion of the three kinds of barrage balloons as he does?

3.

Much has been said about the use of planes and blimps against the submarine menace; and a few words here are pertinent.

Once a submarine is submerged, the plane's chances of spotting the boat are practically nil. The pilot of the ordinary plane sent out on a submarine patrol is unable to look straight down from his plane to the water without exposing his head to a wind rushing at him at a minimum of about 200 miles per hour. He would be lucky to keep his head connected to his shoulders in such a case. To look out ahead in the two-seaters is not an easy task as the engine rises in front to obstruct his view.

His only clear field is to either side, and even then he must look out for some distance to see the water. Unless the sub-

[4] Colonel R. E. Turley, Jr., "Barrage Balloons," *Coast Artillery Journal*, Vol. LXXXV, No. 1 (January-February, 1942), pp. 20–21. Reprinted by permission.

marine is traveling at a high rate of speed with the periscope exposed, and the sea is glassy calm, the pilot's chances of sighting it would again be zero. Patrol bombers have an aperture at the lower part of the fuselage for looking out, and this is practicable for sighting a submarine if the plane is directly overhead the submarine. With this lower lookout post the field of vision is extremely limited. Considering the vastness of the ocean under which the submarine can lurk, the chances are again quite remote.

The question arises: Why have planes out searching for submarines? The planes have a great value in ferreting out the submarine. Under ordinary conditions the submarine spends the great majority of its time on the surface. It only dives when forced as a surface craft bears down on it, or a plane suddenly appears out of the skies. In the latter case the plane has its greatest value.

If a plane is conducting a submarine search patrol, and the skies are overcast enough to permit it to hide behind the clouds, and yet keep low enough to the water to spot any craft on the surface, it is a dangerous anti-submarine weapon. Even supposing that the submarine is able to dive in less than a minute, the plane with its great speed can swoop down and lay a string of depth bombs on it before it gets completely under. The plane then has only one dimension to contend with. If it can only put its string of bombs across the submarine, another undersea raider will be ripped wide open. A number of submarines, both Allied and Axis, have been destroyed in this manner so far in World War II.

Another aircraft is being developed in this war that will make a name for itself in anti-submarine defense. I refer to those ungraceful, sausagelike bags called blimps. The plane must travel at a high rate of speed and covers the ground so fast that it is difficult to watch the waters below, but the blimp suffers none of these disadvantages.

With a speed to suit the nature of the hunt, the blimp cruises along leisurely back and forth along the coast line where submarines may be hiding out during the day. For our East coast they are particularly efficient because of the gradually shelving bottom that drops off very gently for many miles out.

If an enemy submarine tries to lie in wait during the day in order to be in an attacking position for the evening's work, the blimp stands an excellent chance of sighting the dark spot that the submarine makes on the bottom. The submarine may even obligingly release a few air bubbles. Once the submarine is located, only a few minutes are required to have a squadron of patrol bombers rushing to its lair with racks of large depth bombs. The blimp itself may be carrying a few of the bombs. It is my opinion that our blimp coastal patrol will make the sport of sinking our ships close to land a very perilous one.[5]

Questions

1. Define the following words as they are used in this selection: *submarine* (What is the derivation of this word?), *periscope, aperture, fuselage, dimension.* What is the probable origin of the word *blimp?*
2. State the central idea in a short sentence of your own.
3. What is the function of the first sentence in Paragraph 6?
4. Describe the organization of this selection and make a brief outline of it.
5. In addition to the use of airplanes and blimps, what other means are there of combating the submarine menace?

4.

Mr. Webster tosses off a little definition of the word "portable" to mean capable of being easily transported. Now leaving out all question of that adverb "easily," it's still safe to say Mr. Webster is right—even to the point of transporting a liquid that is not stowed in portable containers. All right, suppose it does sound a bit out of the ordinary in a temporary installation, it's been done.

It was done by the Quartermaster Corps on the recent Carolina maneuvers. The liquid was that volatile stuff known as gasoline. Four separate tests were made, pumping gasoline for use in Army trucks through a portable pipeline that was laid directly on the ground. These tests showed that the use of portable gasoline pipelines for military operations is feasible and that such lines have several very practicable applications.

Gasoline has long been pumped through commercial pipelines across hundreds and even thousands of miles. Such pipelines are buried, however, and are permanent installations requiring a considerable period of time to lay. In war, and especially in a theater of operations, time is of the essence. Therefore the Army's portable gas line, made up of sections of 3-inch steel pipe quickly coupled together in the field with

[5] From *Serpent of the Seas* by Commander Harley F. Cope, Funk & Wagnalls Company, pp. 147–150. Reprinted by permission of the author and the publisher.

leak-proof couplings, is literally portable. It is laid as needed, centrifugal pumps pumping the gasoline through the line. On level ground one pump is sufficient for about every mile, in hilly country one every ½ mile, in mountain country one every ⅓ mile or less. Also lying on the ground and running beside the pipeline from one end to the other is a telephone line encased in a rubber-covered, lead sheathing for pliability. This telephone line is a vital adjunct to the pipeline project.

There are valves along the pipeline, three or four to the half mile, to cut off the flow. A "milker" can be cut into the pipeline at any coupling to drain off gasoline where needed. This is done by installing a "T" in the line fastening the "milker" to the valved opening. The "milker" installation can be made while the line is operating—provided previous arrangements were made to install "T's" at probable dispensing locations. Then three men, one working on each of the three hoses, can fill five-gallon cans.

The portable pipeline project was assigned to First Army Headquarters for the purpose of determining the feasibility of using such a system for distributing gasoline. The pipeline unit was composed of one truck company and about one hundred men from a maintenance company, the pipe being carried on 2½-ton trucks. Colonel Douglas C. Cordiner, Q.M.C., Assistant to the First Army Quartermaster, was charged with coordinating pipeline activities.

The first pipeline installation was made from a railroad siding at Pine Bluff, North Carolina, to a dispensing point located about 4,900 feet distant. The installation was handled as follows:

A truck, ¼-ton ("jeep" to you), was used for reconnaissance of the area in order to determine pump locations and possible positions of the pipe trucks so that the line could be laid simultaneously from three points. Although the terrain was comparatively flat, considerable difficulty was encountered in passing through swampy, heavy underbrush to cut a path sufficiently wide to carry in the pipe. In spite of the time involved in cutting through the swamp, carrying the pipe for several hundred yards and making an installation across a pond, the entire system was installed in about 4½ hours by a section of 19 men.

For that part of the line installed across the pond, Neoprene-lined fire hose was used for this installation, supported by rubber pontoons. The line was installed by coupling 50-foot sections, fastening the pontoons on the shore, and drawing the one end of the hose across the pond in a boat while men carried the hose from the ground to the edge of the lake as the boat moved forward. Two pumps were used in this line. After the line was completed, it was thoroughly checked before the pumping was started. When it was filled with gasoline and under pressure, it was again checked and only two small leaks were found. These were quickly remedied by tightening the coupling.

This particular installation was capable of pumping 94 gallons of gasoline per minute with one pump. With both pumps operating, it was possible to pump 124 gallons of gasoline per minute. By redesigning the pump it will be possible to increase the quantity to 200–225 gallons per minute. This installation was used for ten days without operating difficulty, and, although it was not an official gasoline dispensing point, about 60,000 gallons of gasoline were dispensed during the ten-day period. After several experiences it was determined that the best way of draining the line is flushing it with water. The line was uncoupled and loaded on trucks in about two hours.[6]

Questions

1. What are the reasons for your interest in this selection and your ready understanding of it?
2. Underline ten of the most difficult words and come to class prepared to define them.
3. Explain a "milker" installation.
4. How would you describe the choice of words in this selection?
5. What are the main divisions into which this selection falls?

5.

Dawn was behind a riot of grays, all tints from dirt to pearl. The skipper came out of the little room behind the charthouse, where a shakedown had been arranged for him, took a cup of coffee, and pronounced it would be clear enough to fly in spite of the low opinion of the day's weather expressed by the meteorologists (whom he called "mythologists"). It had better be clear enough to fly; the convoy was deep in the U-boat zone, a British tanker had been sunk three hundred miles north on the day before, and half the night the radio shack had been clamorous with high-pitched German code.

[6] Captain E. P. Hogan, "Gas on the Ground," *The Quartermaster Review*, Vol. XXI, No. 6 (May-June, 1942), pp. 48–49. Reprinted by permission.

The weather would be clear enough to fly if the skipper said so, anyway, no matter if to other eyes the vials of tempest seem to have been opened. The first tale every new flier aboard heard, was how, on a previous cruise, a brass-bound admiral brought up in the days before the Navy had wings, signaled across thick mist and heavy swells that it was perhaps too dangerous for the young men to fly. He was right by the book but—"Mph," said the skipper, "didn't say anything about old men, did he?" ordered out a fighter and took her aloft. His story was that, like everyone in Naval Air, he had to have a certain number of flying hours to keep his wings, and as he got no chance in port he might as well take them at sea at a time when the business would not interrupt tactical operations.

Someone shook to wakefulness the operations officer, who had been keeping himself going on benzedrine sulfate for the last three days, extracted from him the sheaf of carefully-calculated orders, and took them into the air plot in the island, where there was already written on the blackboard the permanent heading—"*Objective—Enemy Submarines.*" Underneath he wrote: "Course—28 true . . ." Down in the wardroom the pilots of the second squadron were arguing, over that last cup of coffee, whether a certain hand should have produced a small slam instead of the three tricks set that had been the actual result. The loud speakers summoned them; they trooped up companionways where the first sickly daylight could not yet rival the intense blue glow of the night condition lights. In the air plot the flight officer was waiting with a pointer in his hand, like a college professor. He claimed to be the homeliest man in the service.

On deck, dawn had given light enough to show color in the thin cotton jerseys and close-fitting cloth helmets the deck crew were pulling on—red, blue, and yellow, classifying them by function; the reds crash and repair men, the blues handling the planes while static, the yellows directing their movements. Seen from the height of the bridge they looked like grotesque and busy fairy-tale gnomes, with the fire-watch stalking through their midst in his furry asbestos suit, like a white teddy bear. Forward and aft, the sky-guns moved ceaselessly and uneasily, to and fro, up and down, always ready with steel helmeted gunners in the bucket-seats.

The carrier stepped up her speed till the thin plume of vapor above her funnel lay flat; out ahead, a destroyer charged into position with spray flying over No. 1 turret and a long, lashing wake spinning out behind. The cruisers sheared away, signal flags flying and blinkers flashing energetic conversation.

Over the flight deck from the bridge a red flag was hung,

not in honor of the Soviet allies, but to show that the ship was about to launch planes. A bo'sun's pipe shrilled, its sound magnified to a factory whistle by the loud-speaker system, and a voice whose tones would have suited admirably the reference in Gen. 3:9 shouted, "Pilots, man your planes!"

Even in a navy where steam power has replaced the muscles of the iron men, the tradition of obeying orders on the run is still preserved. The pilots burst from the island like a football team going onto the field, their helmets and life jackets increasing the resemblance. They climbed in with the precise ordered motion of a group of Rockettes and the speaker bellowed, "Pilots, start your engines!" Every propeller on the deck began to revolve, with a terrific machine-gun beat of engines. The blue gnomes had disappeared, all but the pair who stood at the chocks of the squadron leader's plane; the yellows formed a line across the deck.

"Prepare to launch planes!" thundered the voice above the motors' roar. The chocks were whipped from beneath the squadron leader's plane, he cut in his gun, and she trundled down to a position midway of the deck, with a yellow gnome walking backward just ahead of her, making come-on motions with uplifted hands. He dropped them and the machine stopped; the pilot's head turned to watch another yellow gnome, who held a checkered flag uplifted, just forward of the island.

The skipper's frosty profile came out of the door from the navigating bridge in interruption of this ordered procedure. "Walters!" he bellowed to the chief signalman. "Signal the stupid monkey on that destroyer that if he doesn't keep station, I'll break out the after guns and give him a salvo!" Not a muscle moved in any face presented to the world, but there was a sound of subdued chuckles, and an under-breath remark that the Old Man must be feeling all right, was in his best form that morning.

Down on the flight deck there had been suspended animation. Now "Launch planes!" cried the loud-speaker, with a note of that excitement the moment holds, no matter how often it be repeated. The man with the checkered flag turned his free hand in a grinding motion, and the lead plane's motor speeded up; increased his pace and was imitated by the engine, then suddenly flung down the flag. The plane moved up the deck, gathered speed and soared away into the wind, turning slightly to the right as it did so. One after another the others followed into the growing light from the east. On the signal bridge a young boot fresh from Newport, gazed after them. "They all take off different," he observed.

The chief signalman, who had done ten years in the *Lexington,* looked at him, astounded by such ignorance of the facts of life. "Why, of course," he said. "Those pilots are all individualists. It's the only job in this war where a man can be. Nobody's going to make up your mind for you out there on the scouting line." [7]

Questions

1. Define the following words and phrases as they are used in this selection: *charthouse, shakedown, operations officer, benzedrine sulfate, wardroom, gnomes, bucketseats, bo'sun's pipe, Gen. 3:9, Rockettes, chocks.*

2. Select at least three examples of figurative or picturesque language that add to the effectiveness of this selection.

3. Choose an appropriate title for this selection.

4. What type of ship provides the setting for this sketch? On what kind of duty is this ship?

5. To what extent is this selection an explanation and to what extent a narrative?

6. In about 300 to 400 words write a précis of this selection, omitting all the narrative elements.

6.

Used in springs and in diaphragms of delicate instruments, heat-treated beryllium alloys stick to their job even under fiercely corrosive conditions. In tests made under a salt spray, springs of beryllium copper have gone on functioning long after their spring-steel rivals have broken.

"Hope springs eternal and so does beryllium," might be this metal's slogan.

Such Spartan refusal to quit in the pinches has given beryllium a small but crucial part in the vitals of today's mechanical armies, air fleets, and navies. It serves in the sensitive fire-control apparatus which aims big guns and in other military equipment so secret that details cannot be given here.

But beryllium's biggest use now is in airplanes, for parts whose failure would mean disaster. The metal plays its life-or-death role in the motor and instrument panel of every American warplane and those of every other major power—provided they can get it. . . .

[7] From *The Navy Has Wings* by Fletcher Pratt, Harper & Brothers, pp. 163–167. Reprinted by permission.

As a commercial metal, beryllium is young—little over sweet sixteen. Although it was discovered more than a century ago, up to 1925 few dreamed of a practical use for it.

Today its uses are steadily widening. Its lightness (two-thirds the weight of aluminum), and the astonishing strength it gives its alloys, stamp it as a metal with a brilliant future.

Beryllium comes from stones known as beryl crystals, which are always six-sided. Usually pale green, yellowish, or grayish white, common beryl is a poor relation of the fabulously valuable emerald, which is actually a kind of beryl.

The Roman Emperor Nero viewed gladiatorial gore through a monocle made of a choice bit of beryl.

In the world there are probably enough beryl crystals to last for several generations at any foreseeable rate of consumption. The ore is found on all continents, but Europe has comparatively little. Hitler acquired a limited amount of beryl in Austria, and if he had conquered Russia he would have gotten the beryl of the Urals.

Virtually all of the beryllium now produced in the United States comes from Brazilian and Argentine ores, though beryl in several of our States could be worked in an emergency. Beryl crystals are being imported today in vastly increased quantities.[8]

Questions

1. What is the particular quality of beryllium that makes it so important to the war effort?

2. Suppose that you have been asked to write a research article on beryllium. Prepare an outline of this proposed article in the form of section headings.

3. Explain the significance of the following phrases and point out their effectiveness: *Hope springs eternal and so does beryllium; Spartan refusal; crucial part; vitals of today's mechanical armies; sweet sixteen; a poor relation; Nero viewed gladiatorial gore through a monocle; the beryl of the Urals.*

7.

Aluminum went up in the air with the Wright brothers in 1903 and has been there ever since. The new light metal

[8] Frederick G. Vosburgh, "Metal Sinews of Strength," *The National Geographic Magazine,* Vol. LXXXI, No. 4 (April, 1942), pp. 457–458. Copyright, National Geographic Society. Used by Special Permission.

helped make possible that first of all heavier-than-air flights, for an aluminum-copper alloy crankcase and water jacket aided in bringing down the weight of the 12-horsepower motor to the then phenomenal figure of 12.7 pounds per horsepower.

About a decade later, aluminum gave up one of its strangest and most significant secrets. A German scientist, Alfred Wilm, discovered that if aluminum was mixed with about four percent of copper, one-half percent of magnesium, and one-half percent of manganese—and if the resulting alloy was heated, quenched, then allowed to "age" several days at room temperature—this light and relatively soft, weak metal increased its strength fourfold. It became as strong as steel.

He called the alloy "duralumin."

From that metallurgical miracle were born the Zeppelins and the world's armadas of modern all-metal planes, for all consist largely of improved varieties of duralumin.

But duralumin had an Achilles' heel: it was vulnerable to corrosion. Pure aluminum, on the other hand, is highly resistant to corrosion, since it immediately acquires a virtually invisible coating of oxide which protects it from further attack.

Scientists of the National Bureau of Standards pondered the problem—and came up with the answer: "Coat the strong alloy with pure aluminum." Metallurgists of the Aluminum Company of America, after much experimentation, then developed a practical commercial method of producing "Alclad sheet." This is a duplex skin; the strong alloy wears, as a part of itself, a thin layer of high-purity aluminum.

Even if this epidermis is broken or marred, the underlying alloy is not attacked, for the pure aluminum has a higher electrical solution potential, and corrosive forces prefer it.

Wings and other surfaces of most big modern planes are made of this twofold metal skin, which serves their needs almost as well as our human skin serves ours.

Nearly four-fifths of the weight of today's all-metal plane is aluminum—enough in a four-motored bomber to make 30,-000 skillets.

In warplanes virgin aluminum is used. Hence your old coffeepot or frying pan will probably never be reincarnated as part of a 400-mile-an-hour fighter, or roar through the blue with a load of bombs. But by filling more humdrum needs and freeing virgin metal for planes, it will have the same effect.

Aluminum rivets are used by the millions—some 277,500 in a typical patrol bomber. In the aircraft factories the visitor notes that the freshly heat-treated rivets are kept "on ice" like milk or butter until used. The reason is that they remain soft when kept cold, but at room temperature they get hard and tough.

One ingenious rivet, developed by Du Pont, locks itself into place by explosion.

But many a rivet is now losing its job to a newcomer known as the spot welder. Put two pieces of aluminum together, apply an electrode on each side, and turn on a powerful current for a fraction of a second—it's as simple as that. The metal between the electrodes fuses, stiffens, and the two pieces henceforth are one.

Already some specially designed planes have been assembled almost entirely by spot welding. One of the Glenn L. Martin production experts recently predicted that with improvement of this device it will be possible to put parts into a form and turn out half a plane at the touch of a button.

At the Aluminum Company's Research Laboratories, I saw aluminum being tested to the breaking point in elaborate "torture chambers." Parts must be strong enough but no stronger, for warplanes can carry no excess weight. On the walls of aircraft designing rooms is the query, "Have you saved your ounce today?"

Many aluminum products are made by extrusion, the metal being squeezed like toothpaste through openings that give the desired shape. The metal of a whole store front can be squeezed out in a few simple pieces.

Powdered aluminum, plus iron oxide, forms the dread thermite used in incendiary bombs. When ignited, this mixture turns to molten iron, which will burn its way through a house from roof to cellar in a trice.

Some incendiaries are filled entirely with thermite. In others it merely serves to ignite magnesium. In peace thermite is used for welding steel.[9]

Questions

1. Why is duralumin superior to aluminum?
2. Explain the formation of the words *duralumin* and *Alclad*.
3. Explain the process known as *spot welding*.
4. Define the following words and phrases as they are used in this selection: *alloy, corrosion, electrode, extrusion, iron oxide, thermite, incendiary, ignited.*

[9] *Ibid.*, pp. 463–469. Copyright, National Geographic Society. Used by Special Permission.

5. Pick out three examples of picturesque or figurative phrases and comment on their effectiveness.

8.

The torpedo shoot is divided into two parts, the *approach*, and the *firing*. For a successful firing, a good approach is necessary. However it does not necessarily follow that a good approach insures a successful firing—it merely puts the submarine in a favorable position for the shot.

Before discussing the approach, it will be well to mention several other factors necessary to round out a successful shoot.

Torpedoes have been bettered through the years by continual toil and experimentation. At the torpedo stations, submarine bases, and on board the ships carrying torpedoes, the personnel is constantly on the lookout for means of simplifying this engine of destruction and making it as mechanically perfect as possible. Thanks to the many hundreds of shots which have been fired each gunnery year, our torpedoes can be depended upon. There will always remain the personnel factor, however. A slight slip-up in making the final adjustments on the torpedo by the personnel and the best approach in the world will be of no avail. For that reason the check-off lists are double checked.

The Diving Officer has his bad days, and sometimes the submarine becomes as tricky and stubborn as a mule. The task of keeping the submarine at the required depth during the approach and the attack becomes a veritable nightmare. If too much speed is needed to maintain the depth during the later stages of the approach, the resultant wake left on the surface may easily disclose the presence of the submarine to surface ships or patrol planes. Then the approach is abruptly terminated, often fatally.

Assuming that all factors within the submarine are functioning properly, the commanding officer, from his station on the bridge while the submarine is on the surface, scans the horizon for the smoke or masts of his intended target. The skies also come in for careful search, not only from the captain but from the other bridge lookouts. A plane suddenly screaming down with open throttle, and unloading bombs, can do much to upset the planned attack on the surface ship.

When the masts of the target ship come in plain sight, the submarine captain makes an estimate as to its course, then submerges his boat well before the lookouts on the surface ship can possibly see him.

The skipper then allows his Diving Officer enough time to check the diving trim of the boat and get the submarine under control. He slows down to a low speed. It is bad practice to raise the periscope while the submarine is making much speed because the wake caused by the periscope can be seen for miles around.

After the boat has settled down, the skipper takes a look at the target and makes his first estimate of the problem before him. The target at this period is perhaps 12,000 to 14,000 yards away. In this brief look the skipper estimates what is termed the "angle on the bow"—the angle between the line from the submarine to the target, and the line straight out through the target's bow. The skipper obtains a true bearing of the target from the submarine, and notes how many marks on the periscope lens the target subtends for the range. His estimates are given to the officer assisting in the approach. By means of his instruments the latter officer is able to inform the captain of the course of the target and the range to it. He suggests the course to be steered to place the submarine on a tentative firing course.

The target's position is plotted, which is also set up on the range machine. The listener carefully counts its propeller turns, and after a few more observations and estimates by the skipper, the speed of the target is fairly well established. This important item is checked throughout the approach to detect any changes which may occur.

The captain is aware that the target will zigzag, also that destroyers will have formed an anti-submarine screen about it.

About five minutes after the first observation the skipper takes another look through his periscope to see whether the enemy has changed course.

If it has, another set of estimates is made and the submarine is placed on a new firing course. The position of the destroyer screen in relation to the target is noted. Upon their location depends the captain's decision to make his firing position either the bow, beam, or quarter of the target, and whether he will try and get inside the screen or remain out for a longer shot. Over a period of years submarine officers have reported the positions they like least for destroyer screens to occupy, and of course these positions are fully covered by the destroyers.

By the time the target has reached a position about 3,000 yards from the submarine, the skipper of the latter realizes that the crucial moment has arrived and that the success or failure of the whole show will depend on the next few minutes. To allow himself the best chance for success with a medium range, when the zigzag takes place, he endeavors to place his submarine as nearly ahead of the enemy as possible.

When the target makes the next change of course, the submarine must immediately come to the firing position and get off the torpedoes as quickly as possible—before the target changes course again.

If this ideal condition exists, and it often does, the experienced skipper of the submarine has a good shoot.[10]

Questions

1. Comment on the way in which the various parts of the body of this selection are held together by the *place* (or *space*) element. Draw a simple diagram to make your discussion clear.

2. What does the author accomplish in the opening paragraph?

3. What is the function of the first sentence in Paragraph 5? Of the final sentence in this selection?

4. What are the two divisions of this article as it stands? What third aspect of the general topic is left undiscussed here?

5. In about 300 words write a précis of this selection.

9.

It is difficult to imagine military operations across the vast global distances of the present war being carried out, or even adequately planned, without the facilities of instantaneous communication made possible by the electron tube and all the radio apparatus that has been built upon and around it. The Signal Corps, the agency of the Army which procures all communication apparatus and coordinates its tactical use, is ever conscious of the significant contribution of electronic science to the tools which are used in modern war.

Communications have always been a matter of prime concern to the military commander. The factors which distinguish modern war from the campaigns recorded in history are greatly multiplied fire-power, armor, mobility, and communications. All military leaders from the most ancient times until

[10] From *Serpent of the Seas* by Commander Harley F. Cope, Funk & Wagnalls Company, pp. 91–95. Reprinted by permission of the author and the publisher.

a century ago had to rely for communication on couriers afoot or mounted and on such visual signals as beacon fires and flags. Napoleon improved upon the visual signal system by employing Galileo's invention, the telescope, in a chain of semaphore stations to form what was then known as a "telegraph." It remained for the American Civil War, in which the Signal Corps had its baptism of fire, for the electric telegraph to prove itself in a major role as an instrument of military communication. The pioneering discoveries and inventions in electricity were made in the nineteenth century, and they gave us telegraphy and telephony. The great discoveries in electronics in the twentieth century have given us the art of radio communication. This had its military try-out in the first World War and has affected in many ways the strategic and tactical maneuvers which are being used in the present conflict.

Radio plays a crucial role in coordinating our operations in this global war at every stage of the way, from the powerful fixed transmitters of the War Department Signal Center in Washington to the man on the front line reporting the effects of artillery fire over his back-transported walkie-talkie, and to the bomber winging hundreds of miles beyond the enemy's lines. At every stage of the way, armies of electrons pulsating between cathodes and anodes of evacuated tubes, setting up magnetic fields in coils and electric fields in the dielectric of capacitors, serve to speed onward vital messages of military importance to the men waiting upon them for the signal to action.[11]

Questions

1. Define *electron tube* and *electronic science*.
2. In your own words explain the work of the Signal Corps of the Army.
3. Select a sentence which states the main idea of this selection, and paraphrase it in your own words.
4. Paraphrase the final sentence in this selection.
5. In no more than 200 words write a précis of this selection.

[11] Lieutenant Colonel C. J. McIntyre, "Military Communications . . . ," *Electronics*, Vol. 16, No. 3 (March, 1943), pp. 100–101. Reprinted by permission.

10.

THE POLAR ROUTE TO VICTORY [12]

Are you aware that investigations by competent engineers and explorers over a period of many years have shown that the Arctic route is not only the shortest but in many ways the most practicable air route between the United States and Russia and Siberia? The flying distance from north Greenland across the Arctic Sea to Murmansk is only about thirteen hundred miles. Compare this with the flying distance between Newfoundland and Ireland—two thousand miles!

The Arctic route is completely protected and is not threatened by the Axis, unless possibly from Spitsbergen—of which more later. Sir Hubert Wilkins proved that a light plane —and the Russians proved that heavy freight planes—can land and take off successfully from moving polar ice. It has also been proved that "ground" organization for air transport can be maintained on the ice. It was known long ago that landing fields could be constructed on the northern tip of Greenland and elsewhere in the Arctic and that the Greenland ice cap is one vast natural landing field. "The Arctic Sea," says Captain Ashley McKinley of the Byrd Antarctic Expedition, "is the only sea left on earth of which the United Nations still have complete and unchallenged control; it is too bad that we are not doing anything about using it."

If all these things are true, why isn't this Arctic shortcut extensively used?

1. Because only a handful of men in our Army and Navy seem fully aware of these facts. (A high Admiral is reported to have written within the year that ships must not be used in the Arctic if they are needed for war work!) This attitude springs, in turn, from

2. Distorted teaching of geography in our schools. Children are taught that the earth is round, but their knowledge of geography comes almost entirely from the distorted Mercator Projection, used in school texts, which depicts the world as a cylinder, cut open along one meridian and spread out flat. Millions of Americans and citizens of other nations have been schooled in the false perspective of this map, an invention of the 16th century and still used in a supposedly scientific age! Few children, or grown people for that matter, know how to

[12] Earl Parker Hanson, "The Polar Route to Victory," *Harper's Magazine*, Vol. 185, No. 1110 (November, 1942), pp. 639–641. Reprinted by permission.

use a globe. Another reason for ignorance about the Arctic is

3. The belief, fostered for a hundred years by explorers in their books, lectures, and films, that the Arctic is a frozen, desolate land of the dead. Thirty years ago Vilhjalmur Stefansson and others began the labor of breaking down this belief in order to show that *by adapting oneself to Arctic conditions one could live there with ease.* Stefansson did this by living for eleven years with the Eskimos, by living for months on the ice pack and feeding himself by hunting and fishing. Through these years a great quantity of practical information on weather, food, and living conditions has been accumulated. In addition to these reasons, there is always

4. The dead weight of habit and inertia, the dislike of using a new way, even though the new way lies straight and clear ahead. "It was never done that way before."

The map that accompanies this article, known as a Polar Equidistant Projection, shows the Northern Hemisphere, down to the 30th Parallel. It is drawn as though the reader were looking straight down at the Pole. This map has its distortions also—south of 60° the areas are stretched in an east-west direction—but it is sufficiently accurate to demonstrate the availability of the Arctic routes.

Study this map and you will see that Germany, Italy, and Japan are at the edge of the earth, separated by a great swath that reaches clear across the world. This swath is the territory of the United Nations. It begins on one side with China, India, and Iran, moves north through Russia and Siberia, over the Arctic Sea—our own Mediterranean—and south through Alaska and Canada to the United States and Mexico. Only the edges of this gigantic territory have been penetrated so far, except at one point—Norway.

The ice of this polar Mediterranean is, to be sure, a barrier to surface transport, but the Russians—using ice breakers, adequate meteorological service, and scouting planes along Siberia's north coast—have shown that the ice is not nearly as much of a barrier as was believed. Fringe navigation by steamer, carrying munitions, from Nome through Bering Strait direct to Soviet Arctic ports is perfectly feasible now for two or three summer months of the year. The completion of the Alaskan highway will make such a connection even easier. Air freight from the United States to Alaska is another way of making such a connection. Recently a twenty-four-bed demountable hospital with all its equipment was air-freighted to Alaska in thirty-six hours.

The survey of the Arctic by Americans for practical occupational purposes goes back at least seventy-five years to

1867, when Seward, wanting to acquire Greenland, had information on the big island gathered and published in a State Department report. The record in recent years includes the following:

1925–28 Amundsen, Byrd and Nobile all flew over the Pole.

1927   Wilkins demonstrated the feasibility of airplane landings on polar ice.

1928   Wilkins made his survey flight from Point Barrow to Spitsbergen.

1932   Beginning in this year, Pan American Airways sent four land expeditions to Greenland to lay out an air route. Lindbergh flew this route for Pan American Airways. Juan Trippe of Pan American said in 1937 that "it isn't because of anything found along the route that we aren't flying it today." The implication was that actual use of the route was prevented by the world politics of those days.

1937   The Russians landed a party on the ice at the Pole to make observations. The party stayed on a drifting floe for eight months, doing invaluable scientific work, and finally emerged in the open sea off N.E. Greenland.

1937   Russians made two non-stop flights from Moscow to California via the North Pole.

1937   Wilkins proved, in the search for Levanevsky, that flying conditions by full moon in the "long dark winter night" are better than in the constant daylight of the summer.

In addition to all this, Wilkins has shown that submarines in the Arctic Sea never have to dive deeper than fifteen feet or travel submerged for more than fifty miles from one lead to another. There are no icebergs in the Arctic Sea. The ones that harass Atlantic shipping break off the Greenland glaciers, drift south, and never touch the Arctic Sea. It is now known that the Arctic Sea is one of the calmest large areas on earth and is far warmer than is generally supposed.

The tremendous importance of Spitsbergen becomes clear from the map. It is the half-way point between Greenland and Murmansk. For the most part Spitsbergen is mountainous. But we know that in 1926 Byrd took off his heavily loaded plane from King's Bay. In 1928 Wilkins, arriving from Alaska, made a blind landing on uninhabited Dead Man's Island and later put his plane down at King's Bay. The attitude of the United Nations, as reported in the papers, is a baffling mystery to civilian observers. At this writing the United Nations have only raided—not occupied—the islands. At the time of this raid the Axis did not occupy this highly strategic position, but friendly Norwegian and Russian coal miners did. The raiders took these miners away and destroyed the coal that might have had great value in operations in the Arctic Sea or on the now-traveled route to Murmansk. As far as can be told from the newspapers, nobody now knows for certain whether the Germans are occupying Spitsbergen or not, though it is believed at this writing that they are not there. Wrangel Island is straight over the Pole from Spitsbergen. Wrangel has fully developed aviation facilities, excellent meteorological services, and is tied by the Soviet transportation system to Vladivostok and all the rest of the Soviet Union.

From New York to Vladivostok by way of San Francisco is about 8,000 miles, and about 5,000 of those miles are across the enemy-infested Pacific. But from New York to Vladivostok by way of either north Greenland or Spitsbergen and Wrangel Island is about 6,000 miles.

Use the Arctic route!

Questions

1. Define the following words and phrases as they are used in this selection: *Mercator Projection, meridian, perspective, inertia, a Polar Equidistant Projection, meteorological, demountable, feasibility, implication, harass, strategic.*

2. As you read this article, keep beside you a map of the Arctic regions (or, better, a globe) and locate the places mentioned.

3. In the biographical section of your dictionary look up the names of the persons mentioned in this article.

4. This selection is an argument. What is the subject of this argument? Pick out a sentence which states the subject of the argument. On which side—affirmative or negative—is the author?

5. Summarize in outline form the main reasons which the author brings forward to support his side of the argument.

6. What kinds of evidence does the author employ to substantiate his main reasons? Which parts of this evidence seem most impressive?

7. Does the author present the other side of the argument?

What might be some of the main reasons for supporting the other side?

II.

The Zero—it is called that because Jap planes are designated by the final digit of the year in which they go into service, which was 1940, in the case of the Zero (or the year 2600, in the Japanese calendar)—is a single-seater, low-wing monoplane. Its fuselage is a good quality of duralumin, although thinner than that used for American planes. An interesting feature of the fuselage design is that the wings and fuselage are in one piece. This means that there is no interchangeability of damaged wings in the case of the Zero. If a wing-tip is damaged, for instance, there's no such thing as slapping a new wing into its place. The whole fuselage of the Zero must be discarded.

Use of the one-piece design has the advantage of weighing less than the demountable wing type and it also can be manufactured faster. The weight factor probably was controlling in the Japs' decision to use the one-piece type because it contributed directly to the attainment of the two characteristics at which they evidently were aiming—climb and maneuverability.

The fly in the ointment—the hole in the Zero, so to speak—is its structural weakness and lack of protection for the pilot and gas tanks. American flyers repeatedly have found that a burst of .50 caliber fire will break the back of any Zero if it hits just behind the wings. It causes the fuselage to crumple at that point. On the other hand, American fighter planes consistently get back to their bases or carriers even though riddled with Jap machine gun and cannon fire. In that connection, it is pretty generally agreed that the Zero's inferior firepower is another of its major weaknesses.

Instead of the heavier .50 caliber machine guns upon which American airmen place their greatest dependence, the Japs use two 20 mm. cannon, mounted one in each wing, and a pair of 7.7 mm. machine guns, mounted in grooves atop the engine cowling and synchronized to fire through the propeller. That system is a holdover from World War I and had been discarded by most other air forces a long time ago, primarily because synchronization of fire with the propeller necessarily slows down the rate of fire.

The cannon used in the Zero is probably the Swiss Oerlikon gun, which both we and the British belatedly decided to adopt after it was found that the Nazis were wrecking British planes with a similar weapon. An ironical thing about this particular gun is that it was offered to the United States Army and Navy as far back as 1927—but they weren't interested, so the salesman went on to Japan where he had better luck!

Like the U.S. Navy's carrier-based fighter planes, the Zero is powered by a radial engine—a twin-row, 14-cylinder job which is very similar to a well-known American engine. It is somewhat less powerful, however, probably turning up between 950 and 1,000 h.p.

The plane weighs between 4,500 and 5,100 pounds loaded, and at normal flying weight it can do about 315 m.p.h. at 10,000 feet altitude. It has a service ceiling, however, of about 36,000 feet.[13]

Questions

1. Define the following terms (all connected with an airplane): *monoplane, fuselage, wing-tip, engine cowling, propeller, radial engine, cylinder.* What essential parts of an airplane are not included in this list?
2. Define the following terms as they are used in this selection: *duralumin, synchronization, ironical, service ceiling, caliber.*
3. What is the author's purpose in writing this selection? Does he state any conclusions? Does he imply any?
4. How is the central idea developed? Make a brief outline of this selection.

12.

By the sensitiveness of an explosive is meant the ease with which it can be detonated by a shock or blow. Some explosives like lead azide or mercury fulminate can be easily detonated by a light blow from a hammer or firing pin. Such a sensitive explosive, while very useful in fuzes to set off other less sensitive explosives, would be extremely hazardous if used as a bomb or shell filler. There would not only be a likelihood of an explosion during transportation, but a shell filled with such an explosive would certainly burst in the gun. Other explosives like T.N.T. and ammonium picrate are extremely insensitive and require a most violent blow or shock to detonate them, especially if they are pressed to a high density. Ammonium picrate is commonly used as a filler of armor

[13] Rex Sydney, "The Zero," *Flying*, Vol. XXXI, No. 5 (November, 1942), p. 90. Reprinted by permission.

piercing projectiles. Even the violent shock of impact against armor 12″ thick or more is insufficient to set it off. However many other desirable properties an explosive may possess, unless it is distinctly insensitive it should not be used as a bomb or shell filler because fatal nerve and morale shattering accidents will result from its use.[14]

Questions

1. What is the topic sentence of this paragraph?
2. By what method does the author develop his topic sentence?
3. How would you define the *insensitiveness* of an explosive?
4. Briefly define the following terms in non-technical language: *lead azide, mercury fulminate, T.N.T., ammonium picrate.*
5. Distinguish between the two words *morale* and *moral.*
6. Write a précis of this paragraph in about 75 words.

13.

Some of the important military characteristics of explosives such as insensitiveness, blasting power, and shattering power have been discussed. An attempt will now be made to describe in a general way what happens when an explosive explodes. Suppose a 2000-lb. bomb with a booster and a quick-acting, point-detonating fuze hits the deck of a battleship or an airdrome. The fuze is so constructed that as its firing pin hits the target, it is pushed back, striking some sensitive priming mixture. The friction of the sharp point causes it to detonate. The wave from the priming mixture then hits the explosive in the booster. The booster explosive is less sensitive than the priming mixture but more sensitive as a rule than the T.N.T. or other explosive which constitutes the main charge of the bomb. The wave from the priming mixture initiates a more powerful detonating wave in the explosive charge of the booster which soon reaches the T.N.T. or other explosive of the bomb and causes it to detonate in turn. If the bomb is six feet in length and the rate of detonation is, for example, 18,000 ft./sec., it will require only about $\frac{1}{3000}$ of a second for the solid T.N.T. to be converted into a dense gas at a

[14] R. H. Kent, "Explosives and Their Military Applications," *Journal of Applied Physics,* Vol. 13, No. 6 (June, 1942), pp. 348–349. Reprinted by permission.

pressure of the order of a million lb./in.^{2} Under the influence of this enormous pressure, the steel case of the bomb is shattered into thousands of fragments, and the gas, somewhat retarded by the atmospheric inertia, begins to expand rapidly. Within a distance of a few feet, the velocity of the outer envelope of the explosive gas mass attains a magnitude of some 10,000 or 15,000 ft./sec., while a velocity of about 3000 ft./sec. is imparted to the fragments. The fragments thus become lethal missiles and remain so until they have lost a good part of their velocity because of air resistance. As the velocity of the gas envelope increases, the pressure within the gas decreases to such an extent that at a distance of a few feet from the bomb it is only a small fraction of the original pressure. Although the pressure at say 10 ft. from the bomb is relatively low, the gases by virtue of their velocity of 10,000 ft./sec. or more are enormously destructive. A wind of 100 or 150 mi./hr. is considered as very destructive. How much more destructive is a wind of 7000 mi./hr.! The blast effect often referred to is truly the effect of a blast in the original meaning of the word, a violent wind, but not in the sense sometimes associated with explosives, that is, a shattering effect. The blast is indeed a wind of terrific force.

As the gas continues to expand, it does work on the surrounding atmosphere and loses its kinetic energy until at a distance of approximately 50 ft. the velocity of the envelope of the gas becomes zero. By this time, however, the pressure within the gas mass has fallen to a point appreciably below atmospheric, and the surrounding air rushes in to fill the partial vacuum. Previous to this, however, the expanding gas compresses the air surrounding it, producing pressures in excess of atmospheric and velocities of the order of that of the gaseous envelope. This excess of pressure and air velocity is transmitted as a wave of gradually decreasing amplitude to great distances.

The ensuing flow of the air into the partial vacuum surrounding the point of explosion causes a rarefaction of the air which is also transmitted as a wave. Thus at a point somewhat remote from the explosion there will arrive a wave of compression followed by one of rarefaction of smaller amplitude. The compressional wave will tend to push in roofs and windows, etc., while the wave of rarefaction will tend to suck them outwards. If the structure is strong enough to withstand the compression, it is frequently so weakened that it cannot withstand the effects of the rarefaction and will burst outward, a tendency which may be reinforced by the rebound from the previous wave of compression. Depending upon the violence of the explosion, the distance, and the type of construction, some structures will be crushed in and others will burst outward. According to eyewitnesses of the Lake Denmark explosion, this is what happened in that tremendous explosion.[15]

Questions

1. Explain the following words and phrases as they are used in this selection: *booster, fuze, priming mixture, friction, detonate, T.N.T., atmospheric inertia, lethal missile, velocity, kinetic energy, vacuum, amplitude, refraction, transmitted, compression.*

2. Draw a rough sketch of a bomb and label the parts which are described in this article.

3. Which sentence best sums up the central idea of this selection?

4. By what method does the author develop the central idea? Briefly outline the principal steps in that development.

14.

This method of attack [surface night attack] had many advantages over that of the daylight submerged attack. Assuming that the submarine has succeeded in reaching a desirable firing position without being observed by the surface patrols, which is more than likely, it fires its spread of torpedoes. In daylight the wakes of the torpedoes can often be seen well before the target is reached. This immediately discloses the position of the submarine to the escorting destroyers who waste no time in placing themselves in a position to depth charge the undersea raider. There is not much the latter can do about it except hope that the destroyer is not very adept at plotting in its position from sound bearings. In these days of very exact sound devices this is too much to hope for or to depend on. It has cost the Germans many submarines to become convinced of the fact.

A night surface attack has practically all the advantages of the daylight submerged attack plus some of its own, with hardly any of the daylight disadvantages. During the dark of the night the submarine, running along in an awash condition, is as hard or even more difficult to spot than a submarine in daylight with periscope exposed.

When making a daylight submerged attack the submarine, because of its low submerged speed, must take the first chance

[15] *Ibid.*, pp. 353–354. Reprinted by permission.

offered to get in a thrust. If it doesn't, the chance may not happen again, for a convoy with any speed at all will soon be beyond its reach. The storage battery gives the submarine only a limited submerged range, about 80 miles at a low speed. If it employs much speed it is good for about 15 miles. Besides, the consequent ebullition of water on the surface will expose its position to the sharp-eyed submarine lookouts in the surface ships and to patrolling planes.

This condition does not hold, however, at night. With its engines the submarine can run indefinitely at a speed of between 18 and 20 knots, faster than any convoy. With this great asset the submarine is able to trail the convoy on the surface during the night, probe its flanks for an opening between destroyers and, when satisfied with its position, launch the torpedoes.

With a great amount of luck, and if the night is not too dark, the ship being fired at may sight the wake immediately before the torpedo strikes it. The chances of the destroyer doing so are very small.

The position of the submarine after such an attack is not immediately disclosed. In all probability its skipper has made careful note regarding the location of the destroyers and, even before his torpedoes reach their targets, the submarine is heading out to sea at full speed and is soon swallowed up by the darkness. The U-boat, too, is equipped with an excellent listening device and can detect the approach of a destroyer. Running as it does at 20 knots on the surface, it becomes as difficult to locate in the dark as the proverbial needle in the haystack.

The more daring of the U-boat captains have often turned back to the attack as soon as they have reloaded their torpedo tubes. If the torpedoed ship is burning, as is often the case with tankers, the U-boat's favorite target, the glare thrown up reveals additional ships of the convoy, while the flanks are left in darkness. The other members of the submarine pack can now come into the outer ring of darkness, and in comparative safety fire their torpedoes at the brilliantly illuminated targets.

For a while the U-boats working against the convoys adopted a very clever ruse that paid them excellent dividends. One submarine was placed on one side of the convoy, the rest of the pack on the other. The lone submarine purposely created a diversion, causing the destroyers to leave their assigned stations and go charging after it. This left huge exposed and unprotected gaps in the convoys. Before the destroyers could detect the trickery, the rest of the submarine pack had closed in at full speed and taken a terrific toll of the convoy, and were away before they could be fired upon or even sighted by the destroyers. But escorting destroyers can no longer be lured away by such trickery.

Even when the lines about the convoys have been tightly drawn, some of the more daring of the U-boat captains have broken through and sent off their torpedoes. Instead of attempting to break out of the encirclement on the surface, they have submerged and remained in the midst of the convoy, firing other torpedoes by using their efficient sound gear. The confusion that must exist to some extent when a number of ships have been torpedoed has permitted the convoy to pass over the now submerged position of the U-boat. When the sound gear indicates that it is safe to do so, the U-boat emerges and again trails the convoy until another opportune moment arrives.

The most skilful of U-boat captains cannot always attain success in this dangerous game, however. Our destroyers continue to take a steady toll of their more experienced ones, and whenever the losses exceed the replacement of such people, the convoys will go through with lessening interference, until they will be able to cross the ocean with the comparative safety of the 1918 convoy.[16]

Questions

1. Underline five to ten of the most difficult words in this selection and come to class prepared to define them.
2. Choose a sentence which contains the central idea of this selection.
3. How does the author develop his central idea? What other methods of development might he have employed?
4. In about 300 words write a précis of this selection.

15.

The claims for this type of all-metal ship [such as the *ZMC-2*, which the Navy had for a number of years] were tremendously impressive. Structurally—that is, internally— she was like the Zeppelins; a succession of main transverse frames connected by longitudinals; but the likeness practically ended there. She was duralumin throughout, except for some wires which were aircraft steel, and the ballonets, or helium cells, which were of doped rubberized cloth. Her skin was sheet aluminum alloy 8/1000 of an inch thick, the plates sewn together by automatic riveting machines. It is claimed that this

[16] From *Serpent of the Seas* by Commander Harley F. Cope, Funk & Wagnalls Company, pp. 80–84. Reprinted by permission of the author and the publisher.

material would not tear, soak up rain water, or catch on fire as fabric will; and its use, curiously enough, made the all-metal dirigible, size for size, lighter than the cloth-clad. This is because the fabric ship's external covering merely resists the outer air pressure and performs no strengthening function at all. Under the fabric it is necessary to put an elaborate system of metal wiring, netting, and cordage. This, all heavy stuff, takes care of the gas cells, the pressure, and the stress factor known as shear. In the metal-clad, the aluminum envelope is claimed to carry the tensile and shear stresses itself supporting and reinforcing the members of the frame. It thus reduces the necessary extra inner strengthening to practically nothing.[17]

Questions

1. What is a dirigible? Does the derivation of *dirigible* help you to define it?
2. What is the origin of the word *Zeppelin?*
3. Translate "a succession of main transverse frames connected by longitudinals" into the language of a twelve-year-old boy.
4. Define the following words and phrases as they are used in this selection: *duralumin, ballonets, helium cells, doped rubberized cloth, cordage, shear stress, tensile stress.*
5. Are there any superfluous words or phrases in this paragraph? Would it be easy to make a précis of it?
6. What is the most striking feature about the dirigible described here?

16.

DAS STURZKAMPFFLUGZEUG [18]

Military air tactics have gone through a great revolution since the days of the first World War. Then, air fighting was directed almost entirely against other flying machines, and the

[17] From "Don't Forget The Dirigible!" by C. Lester Walker, *Harper's Magazine,* Vol. 185, No. 1110 (November, 1942), p. 613. Reprinted by permission.

[18] David C. Cooke, *War Planes of the Axis,* Robert M. McBride and Company, pp. 44-46. Reprinted by permission of the publisher.

most potent of all war craft was the fighter. All of this has now been changed, however, by the strategy employed by the Axis in the current war.

The now famous "workhorse" of the German *Luftwaffe* is the dreaded Stuka. (Stuka, as you have probably gathered from the chapter heading, is a contraction of the word *Sturzkampf-flugzeug* which simply means fighter dive bomber.) The battle operations of these craft are to cooperate with infantry troops in destroying ground objectives, to penetrate where other and heavier bombers cannot reach, and to demoralize civilians and troops by use of their hideously screaming bombs. And it can never be said that these ships were not utterly effective in Poland, Norway, Holland, Belgium, and France. In Rotterdam, for instance, Stuka planes destroyed 26,000 buildings and killed 25,000 civilians in an attack which lasted only two and one-half hours. Those figures constitute the greatest mass destruction ever witnessed in warfare.

Stukas are not only effective against land objectives, but they have proved to a skeptical world that they can also be used with great success against merchant marine and seapower as a whole. In the rôle of commerce raiders, however, dive bombers are not as effective in one way as submarines, because their aim with heavy bombs must be accurate on the first dive, and because they cannot shell surface vessels as U-boats can; in another way, they are better suited to this duty than submarines, because they are inexpensive in comparison, because they can attack swiftly and elude attack on themselves, and because they can return to bases for more bombs if necessary.

In dive bombing the bombs are released as the machine is pulled out of a dive and not, as is commonly believed, while it is being aimed directly at the target. The reason for this is the fact that the bomb does not travel in a straight line after release. Penetration is as great as that of a bomb dropped from a machine flying straight and level at a greater height, since the dive gives additional velocity to the projectile. This, of course, does not hold true for heights above which the terminal velocity of the bomb is attained.

As far as is known, German dive-bombing tactics are generally the same as those of the other Powers. When an individual machine is attacking on its own, the usual system, if conditions are suitable, is to dive out of the sun to handicap the aim and visibility of antiaircraft gunners who are likely to be concentrated around the military objectives which are the targets of the dive bombers. The element of surprise may also be possible in cloudy or poor flying weather. Specialized dive bomber squadrons practice converging attacks in order to confuse ground defenses.

Attacks are usually started from a considerable height—about 10,000 feet—and the pilot may "corkscrew" his machine on its ailerons on the way down to baffle further the gunners on the ground. The final aiming dive is made at an angle of 60 to 90 degrees and the bomb is released at a height of from 1,000 to 3,000 feet, after which the pilot makes his plane as inconspicuous as possible to evade ground fire.

Since the introduction of monoplanes as dive bombers, it has been found necessary to fit some form of air brake to limit the diving speed (and consequently the pull-out stresses on machine and pilot) and to permit a closer approach to the target. The diving speed may also be limited by the use of a reversible-pitch propeller of the type which has been developed in Germany by the V.D.M. concern. Before these devices became available, it is said that German dive-bombing pilots used to tuck their heads between their knees to minimize the effect of gravity during the pull-out. A special transparent port, at that time, was fitted in the floor of the cockpit for sighting purposes.

The most widely employed and effective dive bombers in service with the *Luftwaffe* are the Junkers Ju. 87 (pronounced Yoonkers) two seaters. A standard single seater is the Henschel Hs. 123 biplane. In addition, the single-seat Blohm and Voss Ha. 137 and the two-seat Heinkel machines are used extensively.

According to a statement issued from the Junkers works late in June, 1939: "It is no longer a secret that Germany had taken up the construction of military aircraft quite some time before she recovered her liberty of armament, and in this connection we should mention the activities of Junkers *Flugzeug-und-Motorenwerke* (Junkers airplane and motor works) which had never neglected the development of such craft (dive bombers) in their Swedish branch works before 1933." The Swedish machine referred to was the K–47, a two seater with a 600-h.p. B.M.W. engine. Bombing trials conducted with this craft by the Swedish government are said to have given results which have not been surpassed up to the present.

The Ju. 87, which is a direct descendant of the K–47, is exceptionally easy to recognize because of its sharply cranked wing and fixed undercarriage. It was first seen in public at Nuremberg in September, 1938, and was used effectively in the Spanish Civil War. It saw much service in Poland, Norway, Holland, Belgium, France, Greece, and all other countries in which German operations were carried on. Currently, this craft is being operated against Russian and English land objectives and shipping.

Questions

1. Define the following words and phrases as they are used in this selection: *demoralize, skeptical, elude, terminal velocity, converging, ailerons, reversible-pitch, minimize.*

2. Comment on the amount of information which the author imparts. Under what general headings would you classify this information?

3. Does the second paragraph suggest the way in which the article is organized as a whole?

4. What is the function of the first sentence of the third paragraph?

5. Explain the comparison in the first sentence of the sixth paragraph. Is it apt?

6. Write a précis of this selection in about 300 words.

17.

The most picturesque of these modern meteorological "tools" is the radiosonde, which explores the atmosphere vertically for data on pressure, temperature, and humidity, which it reports to the ground by means of a small radio transmitter. At the ground, the message is recorded and is plotted as a function of the time of flight. A counterpart of the radiosonde is the aerometeorograph which is borne aloft by a plane. The data which it records are evaluated upon the return of the plane to the ground.

The radiosonde is regarded as preferable to the aerograph for several reasons. It can go up and report on weather conditions high aloft on days of low ceilings, when the airplane remains grounded. These days, notably, are the ones when ascents are most needed. Of course, no hazard to personnel is involved when the radiosonde is used. Savings in time and cost—a matter of considerable importance as the demand for knowledge of the weather has so widely expanded—are produced by the use of it. Since readings are made automatically as the radiosonde climbs, no time is lost. The ground station equipment which receives data from the minute light-weight transmitter during its lofty journey is a permanent installation, the cost and upkeep of which are very low in comparison to these costs for airplanes. The radiosonde travels upward until it reaches atmosphere so rarefied that the balloon bursts. Then the meteorograph drops earthward, its return journey being eased by a parachute. A large proportion of meteorographs sent into the upper atmosphere in this fashion are recovered and used again.[19]

Questions

1. Give a non-technical definition of the science of meteorology.
2. Distinguish between *meteorograph, radiosonde,* and *aerometeorograph (aerograph).* (The derivations of these words will help you to define them.)
3. Drawing your information from this selection alone, how would you describe a radiosonde?
4. Which sentence contains the best statement of the central idea? Does this sentence reveal the purpose of the author in writing this selection?
5. Write a précis of this selection in about 125 words.

18.

The scientific concepts of television are not new as judged in relation to the pace of modern engineering developments, but it has been only within the last 15 years that rapid progress in the field of electronics has made possible the development of a television system adequate for a commercial service. During this period the electronics art and the television art have been extensively interlocked, many electronic developments having resulted directly or indirectly from the search for better television. Modern television is electronic television, and the electronics art in turn owes much to television.

The television principle of breaking a picture up into elementary areas and transmitting the information in sequence to a distant point where the scene is re-assembled, was suggested in 1884 by Nipkow.

This operation is necessary because the electrical circuits and the radio channel associated with the television system are incapable of transmitting at once all of the information contained in the usual scene. Instead, this information is sent for one elementary area at a time, the scanning rate being made high enough so that many complete pictures are transmitted in

[19] Lieutenant Colonel Oscar C. Maier, "Meteorology," *Radio News,* Vol. 28, No. 5 (November, 1942), pp. 96–97. Reprinted by permission.

a second (30 per second is standard), and the eye, due to the phenomenon of persistence of vision, sees a complete picture on the reproducing screen in spite of the fact that only an elementary area is actually being presented at any given instant.[20]

Questions

1. How does the derivation of *television* help you to define that word?
2. What is a *scientific concept?*
3. What are the nature and the scope of the science of electronics?
4. The purpose of this selection is to state the relationship between television and electronics. Using as many of your own words as possible, define that relationship in one or two sentences.

19.

Here's an example of a submarine hunt. A destroyer makes positive contact on what it thinks is a submarine, and immediately moves in for a depth charge attack. The destroyer is confronted with two problems. To locate the submarine in two planes—the horizontal and the vertical. The listening device will inform the hunter where the submarine is crawling along; but there is still the problem of wondering or guessing at what depth the submarine is traveling—and the listening device does not tell that. Assuming that the destroyer has had perfect bearings and that the range is similarly correct, the destroyer's skipper still has to decide upon the submarine's depth.

If we accept the supposition that the depth charge destroys at a distance of 40 yards, what will be the destroyer's chances of getting the submarine? It really resolves itself as to what dimension the destroyer's skipper proposes to put the most faith in. If he figures that his distance from the submarine, as given by his sound device, is very accurate, he must then drop his depth charges at varying depths in order to gain the maximum chance in the vertical field of winging his prey.

In a 120-foot danger space he would have to give his charges a series of depths from 75 to 600 feet. This would then spread out his other dimension, and even if his estimate in that direction had been absolutely correct he would not necessarily wreck the submarine. Despite the excellent depth charges we have,

[20] Robert E. Shelby, "Television," *Electronics*, March, 1943, p. 96. Reprinted by permission.

plus the listening devices for locating the submarine, it may be seen that it is no easy matter to bag one. Actually a number of submarines reported to have been destroyed returned safely to port. Others, for which no claims were made at all, were unable to regain control of the boat once it had started its downward plunge during the crash dive.[21]

Questions

1. Using your own words, state clearly the two problems which confront the captain of a destroyer when he tries to locate the exact position of a submarine.
2. Come to class prepared (a) to draw on the blackboard a diagram showing the two planes in which a submarine moves, and (b) to explain orally how a submarine may easily elude the depth charge attacks of a destroyer.

20.

Geography is the study of the earth, its regions, and, more particularly, the relationship of one region to another. Maps are tools for the study of geography.

If the earth were flat as a tabletop, there would be few problems in mapmaking. Each item of geographical interest could be shown in true relationship to any other item since the map, like a tabletop, is a plane and, hence, two-dimensional. The earth, unfortunately, is a round solid. Mapmaking is mainly concerned with the problem of representing three dimensions on a two-dimensional piece of paper. Consider a globe—it represents the world in all respects, distances, areas, directions, shapes; this it does because it is a three-dimensional scale model. If a globe had a skin, it would be impossible to peel it off and flatten it into any single shape without splitting or stretching it. How to perform this operation is the dilemma of mapmaking. The greater the extent of the sphere's surface depicted by the map, the greater is the distortion, and the smaller the extent of the surface the smaller the distortion. In large-scale tactical maps it shrinks almost to the vanishing point, but it is present, nevertheless. In an area large enough to show a perceptible curvature of the earth, the distortion becomes an appreciable factor. It reaches a maximum when we attempt to depict the whole earth on one map.

[21] From *Serpent of the Seas* by Commander Harley F. Cope, Funk & Wagnalls Company, pp. 144–146. Reprinted by permission of the author and the publisher.

This difficult art of trying to represent the impossible is called cartography, and the devices by which cartographers attempt to show a round surface on a flat and generally rectangular piece of paper are called projections. Mapmaking through the ages has necessarily limited itself to controlling distortion, so that one of the four properties—distance, direction, shape, or area—is shown correctly at the expense of the others, or to achieve the best compromise among them without any one being mathematically true. For example, a map on which all areas are shown in true relative size (called equal area) is bound to have distortions in shape, distance, and direction. In some, two properties can be satisfactorily combined, as for example in the azimuthal equidistant map. This is so constructed that from its central point, direction and distance are true to any other point, but a non-radial distance is more or less seriously out of scale. (The term "azimuthal" is typical of the obscure terminology of cartography. In the case of maps it simply means radial, or as the spoke of a wheel.) The well-known Mercator map has the remarkable property of showing both true compass directions (but not the great circle directions) and true shape. The size of areas and distances, however, are highly misleading.

Perhaps the question most frequently asked of cartographers is, "What is the best world map?" The question goes to the heart of the cartographer's problem, for the answer is, "There is no such thing as the perfect map." One can pick out a "best" map for a given purpose, but that map will not satisfy other requirements. For example: the density of population is measured by the number of people inhabiting a specific area and should be shown on an equal area map, for to show it on a map where unit areas differ would introduce another variable making the study of relative density valueless. Where true compass direction between points is required (as in navigation), we must use Mercator; where great circles (the shortest distance between two points on the globe) is the object of study, we must use the gnomonic projection, which is unfortunately limited in scope to less than a hemisphere. To measure distances accurately we must have recourse to the globe or use cumbersome methods for translating these distances from different projections. In fact, all of these questions can best be studied on a scale model of the earth. Only a scale model is proportionately accurate in all respects—provided it is accurately made. Unfortunately the globe has disadvantages too. One can see less than half of it at a given moment; it is bulky; it is expensive. A fine collection of good detailed maps or a first-class atlas can be purchased for the price of an eighteen-inch globe. But a globe is the one and only corrective for the distortion present in all maps.[22]

Questions

1. Carefully distinguish between these terms: *geography, cartography, projection, Mercator's projection, gnomonic projection.*

2. What is the chief problem connected with mapmaking? What seems to be the solution to this problem? Do these two questions suggest to you the organization of this selection?

3. In about 250 words write a précis of this selection.

[22] From "Maps, Strategy, and World Politics" by Richard Edes Harrison and Robert Strausz-Hupé, *Infantry Journal*, Vol. LI, No. 5 (November, 1942), p. 38. Copyright by The Infantry Journal, Inc. Reprinted by permission.

Appendix

MILITARY ORDERS
and
MILITARY CORRESPONDENCE

When you are ill, you go to the doctor for advice; when you want legal advice, you go to a lawyer; when you want to know about military writing, the man to go to is the Adjutant General.

To Brigadier General H. C. Holdridge, U.S. Army, Commandant of the Adjutant General's School, the authors wish to express their gratitude for his generous permission to reprint the following portions of two publications of the Adjutant General's School, Fort Washington, Maryland.

MILITARY CORRESPONDENCE
A CHECK LIST [1]

MILITARY LETTERS

DEFINITIONS AND LIMITATIONS

1. **Communication**

   Regulations define the term "communication" as official letters, memoranda, reports, indorsements, telegrams, radiograms, and cablegrams. *Par 2, AR 340–15.*

2. **Limiting Correspondence**

   Is it really necessary to write this letter? Could the matter be handled more expeditiously by informal con-

[1] *Military Correspondence, A Check List,* Published by the Book Service, Adjutant General's School, Fort Washington, Maryland, Fifth Edition, March, 1943. Reprinted by permission.

ference, telephone, or informal action sheet ("buck slip")? *Par 1, AR 340–15.*

3. Limiting Contents

Refer to one subject only in each military letter. *Par 18, AR 340–15.*

STANDARDS

4. Abbreviations

Maximum use will be made of authorized abbreviations as given in AR 850–150 and FM 21–30. *Par 23, AR 340–15.*

5. Paper

Use only standard letter-size paper (8″ x 10½″). Use bond paper for first sheet and onion skin or tissue paper for carbon copies. *Par 25, AR 340–15.*

6. One Side of Sheet

Use only one side of sheet in all communications, except for prescribed forms and mimeographed or other reproduced matter. *Par 24, AR 340–15.*

7. Copies

Unless instructed otherwise (see Par 21d), make two carbon copies of both letter and indorsements. More copies are required under special conditions. *Par 38, AR 340–15.*

LAY-OUT

8. Margins

On the first page, always leave an unused margin of not less than one inch at the top; one and one-quarter inches on the left of the page; one inch at the bottom (exclusive of the page number); and three quarters of an inch at the right. The second and succeeding pages should have not less than a one and one-quarter inch unused margin at the top of the page. *Par 26, AR 340–15.*

9. Numbering Pages

Number each page in the center of the sheet, one-half inch from the bottom edge. A single-page letter *will* be numbered. *Par 27, AR 340–15.*

10. Folding

Communications will be folded in thirds, the lower third being folded over the face of the communication and the upper third folded toward the back of the communication. (Exception—See Par 15.) *Par 40, AR 340–15.*

11. Fastening

Fasten securely with paper clips or similar devices so that the communication may be taken apart without mutilating the pages. Avoid using pins or staples wherever possible. *Par 30c, AR 340–15.*

12. Arrangement

a. Except for filing, arrange the several parts of military letters in the following order:

(1) Original letter with pages in numerical sequence, followed by originals of indorsements in numerical sequence, *except* that the last indorsement together with its copies will be on top with pages in numerical sequence.

(2) Carbon copies, if any, of the basic letter, followed by all copies of indorsements, except the last, in numerical sequence.

(3) Inclosures, together with all copies, in numerical sequence.

b. For filing purposes the several parts will be arranged in the same manner and fastened together, except that the original of the last indorsement will follow immediately the originals of the other indorsements, and the copies of the last indorsement, if any, will follow immediately the copies of the other indorsements. *Par 30, AR 340–15.*

HANDLING

13. Prompt Reply

a. When a communication requires a reply, answer it promptly. The reply should be mailed within 24 hours.

If reply cannot be made within the 24 hour period, notify the party concerned of the delay, the reason thereof, and when the reply can be expected, either by separate letter or in an informal manner (see Par 2).

b. When immediate action is desired, state so in the text of the communication and give the date on which the reply is required (see Par 17f). *Par 3, AR 340–15, as changed by C2.*

14. Messageform Communications

a. Messageform blanks and envelopes will be used when matters require prompt attention but the use of electrical means of communication is not justified. These messageforms will also be used for messages transmitted by electrical means.

b. Messages prepared on these blanks will be prepared in the same manner (see Par 25) as telegrams, radiograms, and cablegrams. *Par 31, AR 340–15, as changed by C2.*

15. Letter Mail

When several communications are being mailed to the same address, inclose them in one envelope, unfolded, and mark the envelope "Letter Mail." *Par 40b, AR 340–15.*

16. Letter of Transmittal

This form of letter is used to transmit papers and refers only to the matter being transmitted. (Used in place of Wrapper Indorsement now discontinued.) *Par 19, AR 340–15.*

FORM OF MILITARY LETTER

17. Heading

a. Letterhead: It will be placed immediately below the top margin and centered between the left and right margins. It will consist of the designation of the headquarters or office and will be typed or printed in upper case letters. On the next line or lines below, and centered, will be placed the designation of the office within the headquarters, if any, and this will be typed or printed with only the first letters of words in upper case. *Par 32, AR 340–15.*

b. Identifying initials: Identifying initials will be typed on the file copy on the same line as the first line of the letterhead and will be typed so as to end at the right margin. The initials of the signer of the letter are usually typed in upper case letters, those of the typist in lower case; the two sets of initials separated by a diagonal (/). *Par 32, AR 340–15.*

c. Post Office Address: Typed in the fourth space below the last line of the letterhead so as to end at the right margin. *Par 32, AR 340–15.*

d. Date: Typed in the space below the post office address. *Par 32, AR 340–15.*

It is usual practice to have the first letter of the date typed directly under the first letter of the post office address. (The month will not be expressed by a number, but will be expressed by spelling out or abbreviating the name of the month. See Sec IV, Cir No 23, WD, 1943.)

e. File number: Typed on the same line as the date, starting from the left unused margin. In the space immediately above the file number the words "In reply refer to:" may be typed or printed. *Par 32, AR 340–15.*

f. Suspense date: This date, signifying when a reply is due at the requesting headquarters, is usually typed in parentheses, using an upper case S followed by a colon, the month, the day, and the year. Example: (S: Aug 15, 1943).

This suspense date will be typed in the space directly above the post office address and the first parenthesis will be directly over the first letter of the post office address.

g. Subject: In the fourth space below the file number and beginning at the left margin, the word *Subject* will be typed or printed, followed by a colon and a brief (10 words or less) statement of the subject matter contained in the letter. If there are several letters on the same general subject, the same subject designation should be used on all, for convenience in filing. *Par 32, AR 340–15.*

h. Address: Type the word *To,* followed by a colon, in the second space below the subject. Then type the official designation or grade, name, organization or arm or service of the person addressed on the same line, directly under the subject of the letter. Preferably on the next line, type the location of the addressee. The first letter of the address should be written directly under the first letter of the subject. *Par 32, AR 340–15.*

1. If it is desired to indicate that a communication is to pass through other than normal administrative channels, type the word *Through,* followed by a colon, in the second space below the subject. On the same line type the official designation of the commander to whom the letter is to be sent. The word *To,* followed by a colon, and the address will be typed in the second space below. Example:

> Subject: Leave of Absence.
>
> (1 space)
>
> Through: Commanding Officer, First Battalion 1000th Infantry.
>
> (1 space)

To: Commanding Officer, 1000th
           Infantry,
           Fort Washington, Maryland.

An alternate form is:

Subject: Leave of Absence.
           (1 space)
To: Commanding Officer, 1000th
           Infantry,
           Fort Washington, Maryland.
           (Through: Commanding Officer,
           1st Bn)

The expression "Thru channels" is an indefinite and inappropriate remark.

2. If a letter report or communication is to be directed to a staff officer, it should be addressed to the commanding officer, the word *To* and the address being typed in the second space below the subject. Then in the second space below the address should be typed *Attention of,* followed by a colon and the official designation of the officer or section for whose attention the communication has been prepared. Example:

Subject: Quarantine.
           (1 space)
To: Commanding Officer, 1000th Infantry,
           Fort Washington, Maryland.
           (1 space)
Attention of: Regimental Surgeon.

18. Body

a. Numbering of Paragraphs:

(1) Main paragraphs, if more than one, will be numbered in a single series of Arabic numerals, followed by periods.

(2) Subparagraphs of main paragraphs will be lettered, using lower case letters, followed by periods.

(3) Subdivisions of subparagraphs will be numbered with Arabic numerals enclosed in parentheses.

(4) Subdivisions of subdivisions will be lettered in lower case letters, enclosed in parentheses.

(5) Further subdivisions will be avoided, but if used, will be numbered with Arabic numerals, underscored, and followed by periods. *Par 29, AR 340–15,* as changed by C4.

b. Indenting of Paragraphs:

(1) Main paragraphs will be indented five spaces from the left margin. The second and subsequent lines of these divisions will begin at the left margin.

(2) The letter designations of subparagraphs will fall directly beneath the first letter of the first word of the main paragraph. The second and subsequent lines of subparagraphs will maintain the same margin as the first letter of the first word of the subparagraphs.

(3) The first parentheses of the designations of subdivisions of subparagraphs will fall directly beneath the first letter of the first word of the subparagraph, and second and subsequent lines of these subdivisions will maintain the same margin as the first letter of the first word of the subdivision.

(4) Further subdivisions will follow the style of subdivisions of subparagraphs. *Par 29, AR 340–15,* as changed by C4.

c. Spacing:

(1) Communications will be single spaced except that there will be double spacing between paragraphs and between all subdivisions of paragraphs.

(2) Communications of eight lines or less may be double spaced. *Par 28, AR 340–15,* as changed by C4.

d. References:

(1) In referring to Army Regulations, general orders, bulletins, circulars, etc., state the reference to include the following in that order: paragraph number, section number, title number, and date. Example: Par 3, Sec II, AR 605–5, March 7, 1942.

(2) In referring to letters or indorsements include enough of the following to insure easy identification: symbol, file number, subject, and date of the communication. Example: SPXAD AG 314.56 Survey Reports Jan 3, 1943. *Pars 21 and 22, AR 340–15,* and *Par 6, AR 310–10, Feb 27, 1943.*

e. Continuation on second and subsequent pages:

(1) On each page after the first page of a basic letter place the file number, the date, and the word *continued* directly under the top margin and beginning at the left margin.

(2) On each page after the first page of an indorsement follow the procedure indicated in Par 18e(1) above except that you should put the number of the indorsement between the file designation and the date.

(3) The complete references outlined in (1) and (2) above should not be typed so as to extend beyond the middle of the page. If necessary use more than one line.

(4) When letters or indorsements cannot be completed on the first page, divide the text of the body so that at least a portion of the last paragraph will appear on the final page.

f. The Command Line:

(1) The command line is the statement of authority used by an officer (usually the Adjutant) when signing a communication for the commander of the originating headquarters. It is typed in the second space below the last line of the body of the communication and it will be followed by a colon. The first letter of this line should be indented so as to place it directly under the first letters of the subject and the address. Abbreviations will *not* be used in the Command Line in military correspondence.

(2) When writing to subordinate headquarters from a headquarters commanded by a general officer use this form:

By command of Major General KAY:

(3) When writing to other than subordinate headquarters from a headquarters commanded by a general officer use this form:

For the Commanding General:

(4) When writing to a subordinate headquarters from a headquarters commanded by other than a general officer use this form:

By order of Colonel JONES:

(5) When writing to other than a subordinate headquarters from a headquarters commanded by other than a general officer use this form:

For the Commanding Officer:
Par 36, AR 340–15.

19. Signature

a. Typed signature:

(1) Component parts:

(*a*) *First Line:* First name, middle initial, and last name of the signator, or his customary signature, typed in capital letters. This will be followed by the Army Serial Number whenever an enlisted man is signing. Also if an officer is signing an official letter pertaining to personal matters, it is desirable to add to the typewritten signature the Army Serial Number for purposes of identification.

(*b*) *Second Line:* Grade and organization or arm or service in the case of an Officer. Grade and specific organization in the case of an enlisted man.

(*c*) *Third Line:* Title of position or, when applicable, the word "Commanding," or a designation of special capacity as for example "Inspector," or "Summary Court."

(2) Placement: Type the first line in the fifth space below the "Command Line" or the last line of the final paragraph, beginning to the right of the center of the sheet. Begin the second and third lines under the first letter of the first line, or center the second and third lines on the first line. *Par 37, AR 340–15.*

b. Written Signature: Write signature plainly and legibly with pen, or when necessary, with indelible pencil, but *never* use facsimile, except in printed, mimeographed, or other types of reproductions. *Par 37 a1, AR 340–15.*

20. Inclosures

a. Definition: An inclosure is a separate piece of correspondence or other matter that accompanies a communication. Carbons of communications or inclosures which accompany the original are *not* separate inclosures. *Par 47, AR 340–15.*

b. Placement of notation: It will be placed below the body of the communication, beginning at the left margin, and beginning on the same line as the last line in the typewritten signature. *Par 51, AR 340–15.*

c. The first line of the notation, beginning at the left margin, will contain the remark of the total number of inclosures being forwarded. Thereafter all remarks will begin five spaces from the left margin. *Par 51, AR 340–15.*

d. The original notation will include the total number of inclosures and a listing of each inclosure separately, giving assigned number, title or brief description, number of copies if more than one, number of indorsements to inclosures if any, and number of inclosures to inclosures if any. *Pars 51 and 52, AR 340–15.*

e. The second and subsequent notations will be a part of the indorsements to a basic letter. These subsequent notations of inclosures will include, in this order, the total number of inclosures, the assigned numbers of inclosures forwarded without change so listed, the assigned numbers of inclosures or copies of inclosures so listed giving the number of copies withdrawn and the number forwarded, and a statement of inclosures added together with proper identification. *Pars 51, 52, and 53, AR 340–15.*

f. Inclosures will be numbered in a single series of Arabic numerals, and the serial number of an inclosure which has been withdrawn from a communication will not be given to any other inclosure to that communication. If an inclosure is withdrawn and later replaced it will be designated by its former number at the time of replacement. *Par 49, AR 340–15.*

g. Notation will be made in pencil in the lower left hand corner, on the face of each copy, of the number of each inclosure. If an inclosure is in duplicate, triplicate, etc., the original, duplicate, etc., will be marked in a single series of Arabic numerals written small and to the upper right of the basic number. Example: 1^1, 1^2, 1^3. *Par 50, AR 340–15.*

21. Indorsements

a. Definition: An indorsement is a form of correspondence used when further action is required on a military communication. It is appended to and remains a part of the communication.

b. Indorsements are numbered in a single series of ordinals.

c. Arrangement:

(1) An indorsement will be placed on the page one-half inch below the last line of the preceding letter or indorsement.

(2) The file number will be typed on the first line beginning at the left margin. The serial number and title (Example: 2d Ind) will be typed on the first line centered on the typed sheet. The identifying

initials will be typed on the first line (See Par 17b.) so as to end at the right margin.

(3) On the second line of the indorsement, in the space below the first line and starting at the left margin, will be typed the address of the originating headquarters together with the date of the indorsement.

(4) The address to which the indorsement is being sent will be typed on the second line below the last line of the address of the originating headquarters. It will be typed starting at the left margin beginning with the word *To* followed by a colon and then the address.

(5) The body of the indorsement, if any, will be typed beginning in the second space below the last line of the address to which it is being sent. The rules applying to the body of letters will apply. (See Par 18.)

(6) The signature and command line will be governed by the rules applying to letters. (See Pars 18f and 19.)

(7) The form for continuing an indorsement on a second page will be governed by the same rules applying to letters (See Par 18e (2).). *Pars 41, 42, 43, 44, AR 340–15.*

d. Stamped indorsements are prepared rubber stamps arranged in the manner of regular indorsements with appropriate blanks left for changeable information. They will not be larger in size than $3\frac{1}{2}$ inches by $1\frac{1}{2}$ inches and will include in the stamp a rectangular border enclosing the indorsement. They may be used where appropriate but *never in disciplinary cases.* They will be placed on the sheet, two to a line from left to right, in numerical sequence. Stamped indorsements will be made on correspondence in duplicate. *Par 43, AR 340–15.*

e. A "check" or "initial" indorsement is used when a communication passes through a headquarters but requires no comments. "Check" or "initial" indorsements are the same as regular written indorsements except that they will have no body and will be signed with the initials of the signer only. *Par 37 a (2) (c), AR 340–15.*

22. Inspection Check List

Inspect the finished communication, checking the following points:

    a. Margins.

    b. Numbering and indentation of paragraphs.

    c. Page numbering.

    d. Correct spelling and punctuation.

    e. Correct names and serial numbers.

    f. Correct references.

    g. Inclosures noted and properly listed on letter.

    h. Inclosures properly marked as such.

    i. Original communications, indorsements, carbon copies, and inclosures arranged in proper sequence.

SPECIMEN MILITARY LETTERS

(1 inch margin)

ADJUTANT GENERAL'S SCHOOL LSC/mbw

Fort Washington, Maryland,

January 15, 1943.

In reply refer to:

312.4

SUBJECT: Military Letters.

TO: Students of the Adjutant General's School.

    1. It is apparent at a glance that the typewritten matter on the first fold of this letter is properly spaced.

    2. You will note that a margin of approximately one inch has been left at the top edge and one and one-quarter inches at the left edge of the paper and a margin of three-fourths of an inch at the right edge.

    (¾ inch margin)

    3. You will also note that the paragraph numerals are indented five spaces and that the writing is single

spaced within the paragraphs, with double spacing between paragraphs.

4. Care in the following things will aid you in turning out good military letters :

    a. Correct spelling

    b. Proper punctuation

    c. Proper spacing

    d. Neatness. Special care should be devoted to the following points :

        (1) Keep your type clean. Satisfactory work cannot be done if letters are clogged with lint and dirt.

        (2) Erasures must be made carefully.

5. Incidentally, paragraph 4 has shown you how the subparagraphs are spaced and indented.

By command of Brigadier General HOLDRIDGE :

/s/ R. E. Masters
/t/ R. E. MASTERS
Major, AGD
Adjutant

(1 inch margin)

Camp Hitchcock, Texas
November 10, 1941

SUBJECT : Leave of Absence.

TO :   Commanding Officer, 998th Coast Artillery Training Battalion, Camp Hitchcock, Texas.

1. I request that I be granted ten (10) days ordinary leave of absence effective on or about November 15, 1941, for the purpose of attending to urgent personal business.

2. If leave is granted, my address while on leave will be :

901 N. College Place,
Newark, N.J.

3. The following information is submitted regarding leave status :

    a. I have twenty-eight (28) days accrued leave.

201—Jones, Howard T. (O)
1st Ind, Nov 10, 1941, contd.

     b. I am not a member of a general or special court martial, or of a board of officers.

     c. Present duty: Battery Executive, Battery B, 998th CATB.

     d. I am not under orders for change of station or assignment.

/s/ Howard T. Jones
/t/ HOWARD T. JONES
1st Lt, CAC
0696564

201 Jones, Howard T. (O)   1st Ind   RRB/gon
Btry B, 998th CATB, Camp Hitchcock, Tex, Nov 11, 1941.
To: CO, 998th CATB, Camp Hitchcock, Tex.

    1. Approved.

    2. Authorized officer strength: four. Present on duty: four.

    3. There will be no other officer on leave from this battery during the period for which this leave is requested.

/s/ Robert R. Barlow
/t/ ROBERT R. BARLOW
Capt, CAC
Comdg

201 Jones, Howard T. (O)   2d Ind   AAP/lpo
Hq, 998th CATB, Camp Hitchcock, Tex, Nov 12, 1941.
To: Commanding General, 717th Coast Artillery Training Group, Camp Hitchcock, Tex.

    Approved.

    For the Commanding Officer:

/s/ Arnold A. Peters
/t/ ARNOLD A. PETERS
Capt, Inf
Adj

NOTE: If disapproved, this communication would be returned by indorsement showing disapproval by the Commanding General, 717th Coast Artillery Training Group, and would follow the same channels by which it reached that headquarters, each indorsement being in the form of a check indorsement, after the disapproving indorsement of the Headquarters 717th Coast Artillery Training Group.

If approved, the adjutant of the headquarters taking action would note in pencil below the last indorsement, in this case the 2d indorsement, the word: "Approved," followed by his initials. The communication would then go to the correspondence and orders section of the headquarters. There a special order would be issued granting the leave. The number of the order, and the paragraph number affecting Lieutenant Jones, would be informally noted in pencil on the communication immediately below the adjutant's initials. The communication then goes into the 201 file of Lieutenant Jones.

This is an approved solution, but not necessarily the *only* solution. Local commanders may require more or less information in requests for leave of absence, or may require a different form of request. The example given here conforms to the requirements of AR 340–15.

WAR DEPARTMENT

THE ADJUTANT GENERAL'S OFFICE

WASHINGTON

In reply
refer to:
  AG 201 Arnold, Wilbur E. (Enl)

May 15, 1942

SUBJECT: Identification of enlisted man
TO: Commanding General, 550th Infantry Division, Fort Washington, Maryland.

  1. Personal identification records on file in this office indicate that Salvatore Coco, 33043654, Company C, 999th

AG 201 Arnold, Wilbur E. (Enl)
May 15, 1942—continued.

Infantry, who was inducted August 17, 1941, at Fort George G. Meade, Maryland, is identical with Wilbur E. Arnold, 6946046, who enlisted December 10, 1938, at Fort Jackson, South Carolina, and deserted March 2, 1941, at Fort Bragg, North Carolina, while serving as a private, Headquarters and Military Police Company, 998th Infantry Division. Service record and allied papers are inclosed.

2. The correct Army serial number for Salvatore Coco is 6946046, and records on file in this office have been amended accordingly. Retained records should be amended accordingly but Army serial number 33043654 should not be held available for reassignment.

3. WD AGO Form 46 showing the return to military control of Wilbur E. Arnold, 6946046, Headquarters and Military Police Company, 998th Division, will be prepared in triplicate, the original pasted in the service record and the copies forwarded to this office.

4. This man will be dropped from all records showing him to have been inducted under the Selective Service and Training Act of 1940 (Par 35, AR 345–125, dated February 1, 1932). Action under the provisions of paragraph 21, AR 615–300, dated July 20, 1942, will be taken to dispose of the enlistment from which he is a deserter.

5. If photostatic copies of records are desired, request for them should be made by radio.

6. Report of action will be made by indorsement hereon.

By order of the Secretary of War:

/s/ John R. Smith
Adjutant General

6 Incls—

    Incl 1—Service Record
    Incl 2—Individual Clothing Record
    Incl 3—Report of Desertion
    Incl 4—Extract of Morning Report

AG 201 Arnold, Wilbur E. (Enl)
May 15, 1942—continued.

> Incl 5—List of clothing abandoned
> Incl 6—Report of probable cause of desertion
> > [*these incls assumed*]

201 Arnold, Wilbur E. (Enl)　　1st Ind　　　　BL/hhs
Hq, 550th Inf Div, Ft Washington, Md, May 18, 1942.
To: CO, 999th Inf, Ft Washington, Md.

> For immediate compliance and return to this head-
> quarters.

> > By command of Major General O'KEEFE:

> > > /s/ B. Lobovsky
> > > /t/ B. LOBOVSKY
> > > Capt, AGD
6 Incls—　　　　　　　　　　　Asst Adj Gen
> n/c

201 Arnold, Wilbur E. (Enl)　　2d Ind　　　　AWT/gk
Hq, 999th Inf, Ft Washington, Md, May 19, 1942.
To: Commanding General, 550th Inf Div, Ft Washington,
Md.

> 1. Complied with.
> 2. Charges will be preferred under the 58th Article
> of War.

> > For the Commanding Officer:

> > > /s/ A. W. Tolen
> > > /t/ A. W. TOLEN
> > > Capt, 99th Inf
1 Incl—　　　　　　　　　　　　Adj
> Withdrawn: 6 Incls—Incls 1 to 6
> Added: 1 Incl—
> > Incl 7—Report of Apprehension or Surrender of
> > > a Deserter (in trip)

AG 201 Arnold, Wilbur E. (Enl)
May 15, 1942—continued.

201 Arnold, Wilbur E. (Enl)　　　3d Ind　　BL/hhs
Hq, 550th Inf, Div, Ft Washington, Maryland, May 20, 1942.

To: The Adjutant General, Washington, DC.

/s/ B. L.
/t/ B. L.

1 Incl—
　　n/c

CAUTIONS IN MILITARY CORRESPONDENCE

23. **Cautions or "DO's": Always observe the following when writing Military Correspondence:**

1. Write only when necessary. Use personal conferences or the telephone for local matters.
2. Use good, clear, concise English.
3. Make sentences short and complete.
4. Arrange paragraphs in a natural and logical order.
5. Answer official communications within twenty-four hours.
6. Deal with only one subject in a letter.
7. Always be courteous.
8. Send letters on MESSAGEFORM BLANKS to obtain immediate action only when really necessary.
9. Follow precisely the prescribed form for military letters.
10. See that the sequence of arrangement of indorsements, inclosures, exhibits, and copies is correct.
11. Send letters to prominent civilians, such as congressmen and governors, only over the commanding general's or commanding officer's signature.
12. Be sure to send correspondence through proper channels.

24. Cautions or "DON'T's": Try to avoid the following common errors frequently found in Military Correspondence:

1. Don't write long involved letters or indorsements unless a long explanation is absolutely necessary.
2. Don't lose your temper.
3. Don't forget that as an adjutant you represent the commander.
4. Don't use stilted ("canned"), ponderous, and unusual words or phrases. (Ex.: "You are advised that . . .")
5. Don't punctuate the salutation of an official non-military letter with a comma (,) or a semi-colon (;). Both are incorrect. Use a colon (:). As: "My dear Senator Smith:"
6. Don't use the personal pronoun, *I,* except in an official letter concerning yourself, and in that case do not refer to yourself in the third person.
7. In letters to prominent civilians which you write for the commander's signature, do not use the personal pronoun, *I,* or the possessive pronoun, *my,* when you can avoid them.
8. Don't use the plural pronoun *we* in official communications. Use the expression, "the commanding officer" or "this headquarters."
9. Don't reveal the contents of official communications to anyone who is not entitled to receive them.
10. Don't under any circumstances use the expression, *in regards to.*
11. Don't "pass the buck." Take action whenever it is possible.

TELEGRAMS, RADIOGRAMS, AND CABLEGRAMS

25. Preparation

a. Prepare on Messageform Blanks. Type or print, double spacing, in all capitals.

b. Use telegraphic English, avoid unnecessary punctuation, use authorized abbreviations.

c. When using the negative, such as CAN NOT, after the word NOT write REPEAT NOT if the negative meaning is not suggested by the context.

d. Words to indicate numbers will be used in preference to figures and all punctuation or special marks must be spelled out in words. All sentences except the last will end with the punctuation mark STOP or PERIOD. The last sentence of a message will have the word END as the closing punctuation mark and that will be followed by the identifying symbol (see par g below).

e. When a reply is desired use these words in the text of the message: "REPLY REQUESTED."

f. Signature is always that of the Commander of the headquarters originating the message. The signature will consist of the Commander's last name only together with appropriate designation of the agency from which the message is being sent.

g. All War Department messages will include an identifying symbol of five letters written directly after the close of the text of the message. The first two letters of this symbol will be one of the following:

War Department General Staff.....WD
Army Ground Forces...............GN
Army Air Forces..................AF
Army Service Forces..............SP

The last three letters of the symbol will identify the subdivision of the sending agency within the particular agency.

h. Common practice requires the preparation of at least four copies of all messages: two for the Signal Office of the command, one for confirmation by mail, and one for headquarters files. *Par 57, AR 340–15,* as changed by C1.

SPECIMEN MESSAGES

26. **Model Telegrams (same form for Radio and Cable-grams):**

COMMANDING GENERAL   MARCH 17, 1942

TWENTY SECOND ARMY

SEC ONE WD CIR TWENTY EIGHT CS DOES
NOT REPEAT NOT RESCIND PAR SIX AR
SIX HUNDRED DASH FORTY TWO END
SPXPC

ULIO THE ADJUTANT GENERAL

COMMANDING GENERAL   JULY 23, 1942

TWENTY FIRST SERVICE COMMAND

EFFECTIVE DATE OF SEC ONE WD SIXTY
FOUR CS IS AMENDED BY SUBSTITUTING
EFFECTIVE DATE APRIL ONE NINETEEN
FORTY TWO PERIOD AMENDMENT IN
PROCESS OF BEING PUBLISHED END
SPPDD

ULIO THE ADJUTANT GENERAL

27. **The following is an example of a message as it might be written by letter and the same message condensed for transmission by radio.**

LETTER: Subject: Withdrawal movement.

To: Commanding Officer, 662d Cavalry
          Brigade, Camp Kelly, Missouri.

1. Preparation for the immediate withdrawal of 662d Cavalry Brigade will be made.
Further instructions will follow.

2. Your organization is authorized to draw additional supplies to bring it up to combat effectiveness in accordance with existing TBAs.

3. This headquarters will be notified by teletype if any further information is required.

By command of Major General SMITH:

JAMES T. JAMES,
Captain, AGD
Adjutant General

RADIOGRAM:

COMMANDING OFFICER JANUARY 7, 1943
SIX HUNDRED SIXTY SECOND
CAVALRY BRIGADE
BRIG WILL BE READIED FOR IMMEDIATE WITHDRAWAL STOP
FURTHER INSTRUCTIONS TO
FOLLOW STOP ADD SOK TO
BRING ORG TO COMBAT EFFECTIVENESS PER CUR TBA STOP
ADTELP IF FURTHER INFORMATION REQUIRED END GNABC
SMITH TWENTY SECOND
ARMY

NON-MILITARY CORRESPONDENCE

28. Definition

Non-military correspondence is official correspondence with offices or individuals not in or under the War Department or Navy Department. Non-military correspondence will be prepared in the general forms in use in proper civilian practice. *Par 55, AR 340-15.*

29. Preparation

a. Generally rules for the preparation of non-military correspondence are the same as for military correspondence except that the "Subject" and "To" lines are not used. In place of the "To" line use the three line address: name, street address, and city and state. This address will be typed beginning at the left margin in the third space below the date.

b. The body of the letter will be placed on the sheet so as to be centered from top to bottom. The salutation, which will be used, will appear in the second space above the first line of the first paragraph, typed beginning at the left margin, and the salutation will be followed by a colon (:).

c. Spacing within and between paragraphs will be the same as for military correspondence but main paragraphs will not be numbered ordinarily.

d. To continue on second and subsequent pages type the name of the addressee and the date of the letter beginning at the left margin.

e. A complimentary close will be used and should agree in degree of formality with the salutation.

f. The signature will be the same as in military correspondence but the command line will *not* be used.

g. Ordinarily only one carbon copy of non-military letters will be made, and that copy will be retained for file purposes. The exception to this rule is that all letters addressed to Senators, Congressmen, and Governors of States will be transmitted in duplicate. *Par 56, AR 340–15.*

SPECIMEN NON-MILITARY LETTERS

HEADQUARTERS   ALE/bf
200th ARMORED DIVISION

Fort Bixby, Arizona,
November 22, 1941.

Honorable William Linton Smith,
United States Senator,
New City, Arizona.

My dear Senator Smith:

I wish to take this opportunity to thank you for the courtesy of the informal visit which you made yesterday to this Division. Your many interesting questions showed that you are sincerely interested in the development of the Armored Force.

At this time the data on cost of construction of this post are very incomplete. As for the cost of operating and maintaining the vehicles of an armored division, this information will not be available until complete equipment has been received and in use for at least a month. I am writing today, however, to the Nth Armored division, and I shall send their operation and maintenance cost data to you within the next ten days.

Since you are so genuinely interested in the development of the Armored Force, and since this is the only armored division in the State of Arizona, the officers and men of this command would like to have you as a frequent visitor. On Saturday, December 6, at nine o'clock, the Division will have its first formal review. It would be a distinct privilege to hold this review in your honor.

Very truly yours,
/s/ A. L. Enhold
/t/ A. L. ENHOLD,
Major General, US Army,
Commanding.

[Note: Letters to members of Congress will be sent in duplicate]

Maran Village, N. H.,
May 20, 1942.

The General, Camp Madison,
New Jersey.

Dear General,

I am writing about my husband John, who is a soldier in your camp. His full name is John Baggott, and he is in the nine hundredth regiment. He was drafted into the army for one year and was married to me when he was home on furlough in July of last year. He was to be released from the army in January and had a job on a duck farm here. Now I am told that he cannot be released because there is a war on.

John can't send me any money because of his stomach. He can't eat the army food. So he has to eat in restaurants all the time, and uses up all his money.

You will have to let him out of the army so he can go to work on the duck farm so that he can support me and the baby as he should. I could feed him well and get his stomach trouble corrected. My folks won't give me food any more. They can't let me have any money, as they are on a farm and don't have more than enough to live on themselves.

You must let my John out of the army, as you said you were going to last July. You didn't do as you promised. He can work here and get our baby special medicines which the doctor says he should have. I can't buy them, because John can't send me money on account of his stomach.

Yours truly,

/s/ Mrs. John Baggott,

wife of Corporal John Baggott.

201—Baggott, John, 7483264 (Enl)   1st Ind   BC/blr
Hq, Camp Madison, NJ, May 22, 1942.

To: Co, 900th Inf, Camp Madison, NJ.

For investigation and direct reply, with report to this office.

By command of Brigadier General MARTIN:

/s/ Bernard Carter
/t/ BERNARD CARTER,
Maj, AGD,
Adj.

201—Baggott, John 7483264 (Enl)   2d Ind   HGW/ehs
Hq, 900th Inf, Camp Madison, NJ, May 24, 1942.

To: CO, Camp Madison, NJ.

1. First Indorsement complied with.

2. Copy of reply inclosed.

For the commanding officer:

/s/ Harold G. Walker
/t/ HAROLD G. WALKER
Capt, Inf
1 Incl—   Adj.

Note: A commanding officer, or adjutant in his official capacity, has frequent occasion to write to civilians. In this class of correspondence, an effort should be made always to be courteous and cooperative. The writer should remember at all times that civilians have little understanding of the inner workings of an army organization and may have an exaggerated idea of the hardships visited upon members of the armed forces. The writer should bear in mind that, to the civilian concerned, he is the voice of the Army. He should be always conscious of this responsibility.

Copy of letter to Mrs. John Baggott

HEADQUARTERS   HGW/ehs
900th Infantry

Camp Madison, N. J.,
May 24, 1942.

Mrs. John Baggott,
Maran Village, N. H.

My dear Mrs. Baggott:

Your letter to the Commanding General, Camp Madison, New Jersey, regarding your husband's discharge has been referred to me for reply.

Because the nation is at war and needs all its trained soldiers, discharges are now allowed only under most pressing circumstances.

I have talked with Corporal Baggott and he has seen the doctor here about his inability to eat the food provided. He now realizes that the food will not be injurious to his health. He has arranged to make an allotment to you from his pay of forty-five dollars a month. This will be sent to you directly each month by the finance officer.

I hope this will help to solve your problem. If I can be of

any further assistance in the future, do not hesitate to write me.

Yours most sincerely,

/s/ Harold G. Walker

/t/ HAROLD G. WALKER

Captain, Infantry

Adjutant

DEATHS OF MILITARY PERSONNEL

30. Deaths occurring within the continental United States

a. Telegram: The immediate commander will notify the nearest relative or other person designated to be notified in case of emergency. The telegram will include: the fact, date, place, and cause of death, and, when early shipment of the remains is practicable, will request the person notified to reply by telegraph (collect) whether it is desired to have the remains shipped home, and if such shipment is desired, to designate the destination and the name of the person to whom the remains are to be consigned. *Under no circumstances* will notification include a statement relative to line of duty status or misconduct. *Par 7, AR 600–550, Mar. 6, 1936,* as changed by C3.

b. Letter of condolence: The immediate commander will prepare such a letter addressed to the nearest relative or other person designated to be notified in case of emergency. The letter will include:

(1) Statement of date, place, and cause of death.

(2) If addressed to the widow or legal representative or other person designated in the 112th Article of War, will contain information relative to the following:

(*a*) Shipment of effects.

(*b*) The name, official designations, and post-office addresses of the officers and officials to whom application should be made for:

1 The effects.

    2 Settlement of accounts.

    3 Pensions.

    4 Gratuity pay (if applicable).

    5 Insurance (if applicable).

(3) Statement of sympathy, praise and offer of assistance.

(4) Statement relative to authorization of payment for burial expenses proper and for incidentals to interment (*Pars 3 and 4, AR 30–1830, Mar. 1, 1938, as changed by C1.*) *Pars 7 and 8, AR 600–550.*

c. Letter to undertaker: A statement relative to allowable expenses for burial as set forth in *Pars 3 and 4, AR 30–1830,* as changed by C1. This letter will be written only when applicable.

31. Deaths occurring outside the continental United States, including those occurring in Alaska

Execute W.D. A.G.O. Form No. 52 in duplicate and forward, together with necessary reports and records, to the commander of the overseas organization. *Par 5, AR 600–550,* as changed by C2.

SPECIMEN TELEGRAM AND LETTER OF CONDOLENCE

Memorandum request to post signal officer to transmit notification of death telegram.

HEADQUARTERS 1000th INFANTRY

Fort Dix, New Jersey,
April 30, 1942.

Memorandum to Post Signal Officer.

Request the following message be sent by commercial telegraph at Government rates—PRIORITY—:

MRS. JOHN DOE
114 COLLEGE AVENUE
PARIS ILLINOIS

I DEEPLY REGRET TO INFORM YOU OF THE
DEATH OF YOUR SON WILLIAM AS RESULT
OF LOBAR PNEUMONIA AT STATION HOS-
PITAL FORT DIX NEW JERSEY APRIL THIR-
TEENTH NINETEEN HUNDRED FORTY TWO
STOP KINDLY INFORM BY TELEGRAPH GOV-
ERNMENT RATE COLLECT WHETHER OR NOT
YOU WISH REMAINS SHIPPED HOME OR TO
WHAT DESTINATION AND TO WHOM SUCH
SHIPMENT SHOULD BE MADE STOP THE
GOVERNMENT WILL ALLOW FIFTY DOLLARS
TOWARD FUNERAL EXPENSES AFTER AR-
RIVAL OF REMAINS AT PLACE DESIGNATED
STOP THE OFFICERS AND MEN OF THIS
COMPANY JOIN ME IN EXPRESSING MOST
SINCERE SYMPATHY END

> MARTIN C WOODRING
> CAPT 1000th INFANTRY
> COMMANDING COMPANY K

OFFICIAL:
/s/ John A. Jones
JOHN A. JONES
2nd Lt, AGD
Asst Adj

COMPANY K, 1000th INFANTRY

Fort Dix, N. J.
April 30, 1942.

Mrs. John Doe,
144 College Avenue,
Paris, Illinois.

Dear Mrs. Doe:

Your son's death at 4 A.M. this morning came as a
great shock to me and to all of his comrades, for his con-

dition had shown a marked improvement. The end came suddenly and without suffering.

You have the deepest sympathy of the officers and men of this organization in your bereavement. William was held in high regard by all members of the command. He was a splendid soldier and an outstanding character. His loss will be deeply felt by his many friends. You may rest assured that everything possible was done for his recovery.

While it is realized that at this sad time you do not wish to be worried by business matters, you should be furnished certain information relative to personal effects, accounts, pensions, insurance, and gratuity pay. Upon your request Major John A. Hammond, Fort Dix, New Jersey, will ship William's personal effects to you. If you will write the General Accounting Office, Washington, D. C., all other accounts, including arrears of pay, will be settled. You may make application for pension and insurance to the director, Veterans Administration, Washington, D. C., if, after a reasonable period of time, you do not hear from the Veterans Administration. Six months gratuity pay will be paid by the Finance Officer, U. S. Army, Washington, D. C., without application by you.

May I express my own personal sympathy in your loss? Please feel free to call upon me for any additional information you may desire.

> Yours most sincerely,
> /s/ Martin C. Woodring
> /t/ MARTIN C. WOODRING,
>   Captain, 1000th Infantry,
>   Commanding.

ORDERS[2]

Section I

Part I

ORDERS, MEMORANDUMS, CIRCULARS, AND BULLETINS

Military orders are of several classes. There was a young second lieutenant who, in 1918, appeared before a promotion board. The president of the board, a gruff old colonel, asked the lieutenant to name the three great classes of military orders. The lieutenant gulped a couple of times and came up with this one:

"Orders, counter-orders, and disorders!"

The colonel looked at him pityingly, shook his head and murmured: "Out of the mouths of babes and sucklings . . ."

The lieutenant's reply stated a truth too frequently demonstrated: that carelessly and inexpertly drawn orders call for counter-orders—which inevitably produce disorder, confusion and uncertainty. A fundamental principle governing all military orders of whatever character is that all orders should be clear, concise, and subject *only* to that interpretation desired by the commander! They should also be definite, affirmative, positive. Avoid, as you would the plague, such expressions as "if practicable," and "as soon as practicable"; leave out the "ifs," the "ands" and the "buts." Avoid wherever possible such negative expressions as "will not"; rather express a prohibition in affirmative language, as "such and such is prohibited."

There is an interesting sentence in the Army Regulations

[2] Section I, Parts I and II, Part III (in part); Section V. From *Orders*, Instructional Pamphlet No. 1, The Adjutant General's School, Fort Washington, Maryland, Sixth Edition—Revised to March 26, 1943. Reprinted by permission.

of 1812: "It will be the duty of the Adjutant General to *form* all orders given by the Commanding General in a perspicuous manner . . ."

The routine orders of the War Department, of commanders of armies, corps, divisions, brigades, regiments, battalions and squadrons not organized into regiments, corps areas, departments, districts, harbor defense commands, posts, camps, and stations are designated "general orders," "general court-martial orders," "special court-martial orders," "special orders," "operations orders" (in the case of air corps stations and units), "bulletins," "circulars," and "memorandums" of the issuing commands, according to their character. These publications will be numbered consecutively in separate series for each calendar year.

Orders on routine matters issued by the commander of a battalion forming part of a regiment and serving with it, or of companies and detachments will be designated as "orders" without the term "general" or "special" and will be numbered in a single series for each calendar year.

Memorandums, circulars and bulletins may be issued by any headquarters which normally issues general or special orders. Memorandums usually contain matter directive, advisory, or informative in nature, and of temporary duration. They may also be used to convey directives and information received from higher headquarters. Memorandums may be issued in numbered series, or unnumbered memorandums may be issued to convey some directive of a temporary nature. For example, a division headquarters may issue a numbered memorandum to direct the submission of a periodic report, and to prescribe the method of preparation of the report. An unnumbered memorandum may be used to convey to those subordinate commanders concerned a specific directive of a transitory nature. Example: "Following the payment of troops of this command on June 30, scheduled drills will be suspended for the remainder of the day, and all men except necessary guard and fatigue details may be permitted to be absent from the post until reveille July 1."

A daily bulletin containing advisory or informative matter is normally issued by all administrative headquarters down to and including the regiment. This bulletin may contain a section devoted to official matter and a section containing useful and timely information, such as the program of post motion picture shows, announcement of athletic events, enlisted men's dances, and notices of articles lost and found on the reservation.

Military orders may be given orally or in writing in a variety of forms from the simple "Yes" or "No" of the commander, given in answer to a question, to the several types of written directives outlined above.

Go back for a moment to that 1812 regulation. It says that The Adjutant General will *form* all orders. That regulation, in principle, applies today. It is a somewhat trite saying, but true, that the adjutant is the mouthpiece of the commanding officer. He translates the commander's policies, decisions and plans into orders. He is the administrative executive. But he does more than write and publish orders; he follows through, and sees that the orders are executed.

The actual writing of an order is in itself an art to be acquired by careful attention to detail and an intimate knowledge of the policies and temperament of the commander. Recall, if you will, that phrase "orders must be clear, concise, subject only to that interpretation desired by the commander." Orders must mean exactly what they say, and nothing else. There must be no excuse for the recipient to ask himself: "Now, just what am I supposed to do? Does the commander want me to go here, or to go there, to do this, or to do that?"

How, then may this ideal of clarity be obtained?

Two processes are involved in the formulation of orders. First the mental process; and second, the mechanical. Obviously, to write a clear, understandable order, one must have a clear mental picture of what is desired. Remember Kipling's little verse:

> **"I keep six honest serving men**
> **(They taught me all I knew);**
> **Their names are What and Why and When**
> **And How and Where and Who . . ."**

Organize your mental processes. Decide *what* is to be done, *why* it is to be done, *when* it is to be done, *how* it is to be done, *where* it is to be done, and *who* is to do it. With those six things clearly in your mind you are ready to approach the mechanical process of writing an order.

Like most useful things, a completed order presents a harmonious whole, but upon closer examination you will find that it is divided into certain parts, which, when in logical sequence, make up the whole picture. There are four parts to a military order: the heading, the designation, the body, and the authentication. Taking them in that order, the heading is that part of the order which designates the headquarters from which the order originates, what office of that headquarters (optional), and where the headquarters is located. The date is also a part of the heading. For example:

HEADQUARTERS FIRST ARMY
Governors Island, N. Y.,
2 September, 1942.

Next comes the designation; like this:
SPECIAL ORDERS
NO. 210

Following is the body of the order. The body of the order may contain any number of paragraphs; or, if it is a general order, it may be divided into sections and the sections in turn may be broken into paragraphs. In a special order the paragraphs are numbered consecutively. In a general order which is divided into sections, the paragraphs are numbered consecutively within each section.

Each numbered paragraph of a special order often is

actually a complete order within itself. Each paragraph must contain the essential elements—the six honest serving men: the *what, why, when, how, where,* and *who.* Not always, nor even usually, in just that sequence. But all must be there. Each of these elements must be definitely stated or implied. There may be two or three *whats* or *whys* or *whens.* You may order someone to go *there* and return *here,* or to do this, and then do that. In any case, each of these six elements must be used or implied at least once in every order. Without them, the order will lack clarity and completeness.

The fourth component consists of three parts, but the three together constitute the authentication. First, there is the "order line," or "command line." That is, the line which reads "By order of Colonel BLANK:" or "By command of Major General DOE:" Why is one line "by order of" and the other "by command of"? Paragraph 13 *a,* AR 310–50, prescribes that all orders issued from a headquarters of which the commander is below the grade of brigadier general will be "by order of," and those issued from the headquarters of a general officer will be "by command of." The custom of the service is to write the name of the commander in capital letters, regardless of his grade. In a tactical unit commanded by a general officer which has a general staff group, the name, grade, arm or service, and title of the chief of staff will be typed below the command line. In the lower left corner of the page is written the word "Official," followed by a colon; and below that is typed the name, grade, arm or service, and title of the adjutant general, assistant adjutant general, or acting adjutant general of the command.

If the commander is below the grade of general officer, or if the command does not have a general staff group, orders are authenticated by the adjutant alone, his name appearing twice; once where, in a command having a general staff group, the name of the chief of staff would ordinarily appear, and once in the lower left corner. When the order is signed, the adjutant signs in the lower left corner.

The custom of placing the name of the executive officer in the authentication is followed in some commands, but this practice is forbidden in par 13 *b,* AR 310–50.

The authentication is not complete without the actual autographed signature of the adjutant general, the adjutant, or a duly appointed assistant, *or* the impression of the official seal of the headquarters issuing the orders. Where orders are mimeographed, the signature of the adjutant general, or the adjutant, may be written on the mimeograph stencil with a stylus, in which case those copies used for purposes of official record, or as supporting documents to a voucher for reimbursement of travel expenses, mileage, or any voucher involving the expenditure of public funds, should also bear the imprint of a rubber stamp facsimile of the official seal. Upon "extract copies" of orders, the actual impression of the seal itself should appear. This seal is usually a circular seal, bearing on the outer rim the words, "HEADQUARTERS —— INFANTRY DIVISION, U.S. ARMY" and in the center, the word: "OFFICIAL." It is made of metal, with raised letters on one face, and cutout letters on the reverse side, so that when the paper is placed between, and the two dies pressed together, the raised letters are impressed on the paper.

Orders are actually signed by the adjutant general or adjutant in the lower left corner, just under the word "Official," and just over his typed name. The chief of staff does not sign the orders. The commanding officer may dispense with the authentication of an order when in his judgment such dispensation will facilitate operations, and when there is no possibility of fraud.

As a matter of routine procedure, at least ten copies of every order of any kind should be kept in the files of the headquarters issuing the order. At least two copies of all orders should go to the personnel division, one to the enlisted section, one to the officers' section. In many headquarters, it is customary to indicate on the order itself, in the lower left corner, below the authentication, the distribution to be made. This may or may not be done. If this is not done, some responsible officer in the adjutant's or adjutant general's office should indicate by informal memorandum on the order itself the distribution desired.

When an order, memorandum, circular or bulletin is received from higher headquarters, and it is desired to distribute it to lower echelons but a sufficient number of copies of the original was not furnished, it may be reproduced, placing in the lower left corner a statement to the effect that it is reproduced; or the order may be incorporated in a memorandum or order originating in your own headquarters. A good form to use is the numbered memorandum, with the usual heading and designation, and an opening sentence something like this: "The following War Department General Orders No. ——, (date), are published for compliance by all concerned." Then repeat the War Department orders in their entirety, including heading and authentication. Then follows the usual authentication by your own headquarters.

While the regulations permit the authentication of orders by assistant adjutants general, and assistant adjutants, it is, nevertheless, a responsibility of the adjutant general or adjutant, and he should sign all orders, unless special circumstances make it impracticable to do so. At any rate, he should look them over before publication.

Have each order and each paragraph presented in draft form, so that necessary editing may be done before the order actually enters the reproducing process. Analyze the draft to be certain that each essential element is there, that the elements are arranged in proper sequence, that the order contains no ambiguity, that it can leave no doubt in the mind of the recipient as to what is desired. Remember this: grades of officers, Army nurses, warrant officers, and flight officers will be abbreviated with names and grades in capitals; grades, names, and Army serial numbers of enlisted men will be in italics when printed, but will not be underscored when reproduced by typewriter or mimeograph.

Any moderately intelligent clerk can learn the mechanics of fitting the various parts of an order together in proper sequence. The real job is in the body of the order—in fitting those six honest serving men together in logical and proper sequence so as to produce a clear, understandable directive. Proficiency, and even perfection, may come with practice; but no amount of practice will suffice without careful thought and constant study—study of Army Regulations, in order to make your orders consistent with those regulations, and study of orders received from other headquarters. Someone else may have found a phrase of an expression that is better than the one you commonly use. If you find such a phrase or expression, do not hesitate to adopt it, provided it conforms to Army Regulations. Try always for improvement, but keep in mind always simplicity and clarity of expression. In writing a military directive of any kind, never forget that it must conform to the principle of being subject only to that interpretation desired by the commander.

Copies of orders for The Adjutant General. The commands listed below will maintain files of numbered general orders, special orders, bulletins, circulars, memoranda, and training memoranda, with indexes thereto, issued from their headquarters:

Defense commands

Service commands and departments

Military District of Washington

Armies (in continental United States)

Corps (army, armored, amphibious) (in continental United States)

Tactical divisions (in continental United States)

Commands (antiaircraft, replacement and school, airborne, engineer amphibian, WAAC) (in continental United States)

Centers (tank destroyer, amphibious training, mountain training) (in continental United States)

Harbor defenses

Units of the Army Air Forces corresponding to the above.

At the completion of a series (which occurs normally at

the end of a calendar year), one copy of the series, securely bound, will be forwarded to The Adjutant General, attention Demobilized Records Branch, High Point, North Carolina, for permanent record. Commanders authorized to confer decorations and awards will furnish three copies of orders awarding such decorations to The Adjutant General, attention Decorations and Awards Branch, Washington, D. C. Commanders authorized to promote and demote officers will inform The Adjutant General, SPXPO, of such action by radio or other means.

In addition to the distribution of court-martial orders referred to in par 3 *d,* AR 310–50, all commanders having court-martial jurisdiction will forward without delay to The Adjutant General, attention Enlisted Branch, Washington, D. C., three copies of each general and special court-martial order issued at their headquarters for each person affected.

Part II

GENERAL ORDERS

General orders will usually include matter of importance which is directive in nature, general in application, and of *permanent* duration, not readily susceptible of immediate incorporation in established forms of regulations. General orders will contain the four parts common to all orders— heading, title, body, and authentication.

The body of a general order may be broken into sections, in which case the sections will be numbered consecutively from one, using Roman numerals, and the paragraphs under each section numbered consecutively from one, using Arabic numerals. Each section should be concerned with only one subject.

The following are a few of the most frequent purposes for which general orders are used:

1. To announce the activation of a unit, from a regiment up, including brigades, divisions, corps, armies, coastal and frontier commands, base commands, and so on.

2. To announce the closing of a headquarters and the opening of a new headquarters.

3. To announce the assumption of command by an officer.

4. To announce the death of the President of the United States, the Vice-President, a member of the cabinet, the Chief of Staff, or other military personnel in active service.

5. To announce the personal staff of a general officer (Aides de Camp).

6. To announce the naming of a military post, camp, or station.

7. To announce changes in the geographical divisions of command within the military establishment.

8. Within commands having a general staff group, to announce the appointment of the chief of staff, and assistant chiefs of staff G–1, G–2, G–3, and G–4.

9. To promulgate post or garrison regulations, or amendments to them.

There are also general court-martial orders used to promulgate the findings and sentences of general courts-martial. Such orders are issued only by officers having general court-martial jurisdiction, and who appointed the court whose action is being promulgated, and who reviewed the proceedings of such court.

General orders are usually authenticated in the same manner as are special orders. There is one exception: the assumption of command order is invariably signed by the officer who thereby assumes command. The name of the adjutant, the adjutant general, or chief of staff does not appear in assumption of command orders.

There is one important restriction on the use of orders, general and special, with which every adjutant must be familiar. It is contained in paragraph 20, AR 310–50, and reads: "Orders eulogizing the conduct of living officers will not be issued except in cases of gallantry in action or performance of especially hazardous service."

Use general orders sparingly. Think through each item to be covered, and construct each sentence carefully; be sure that you include every essential point; make each sentence and each directive positive and affirmative, rather than negative and prohibitive. Of course you will have to prohibit things, but in doing so try to make the sentence containing such prohibition an affirmative sentence.

Avoid reference to former orders and directives simply by identification symbols. That is, do not say: "Par 16 *b* (6) (c), Section I, General Orders No. 16, 1940, is rescinded and the following substituted therefor." Perhaps someone in the command hasn't read "Par 16 *b* (6) (c), Section I, General Orders No. 16, 1940." It is a pretty safe bet that even if everyone has read it, very few if any will be able to remember what that particular subparagraph contains. Even if most persons concerned have a complete file of 1940 General Orders, it will take some time to find the one referred to, to look up the particular paragraph referred to, and eventually decide just what you intend to rescind. You will earn kudos from everyone if you will put the matter simply, clearly. For example: "Paragraph 16 *b* (6) (c), Section I, General Orders No. 16, this headquarters, dated June 12, 1940, which reads: 'The garrison cap will be worn by officers and enlisted men when the service uniform, cotton, with blouse, is worn after retreat,' is rescinded, and the following is substituted therefor: 'The garrison cap will be worn with the service uniform, cotton. The service cap will be worn with the service uniform, wool, when the blouse is worn.'"

Avoid the use of stilted or pompous language or phraseology, such as: "The Commanding General directs . . ." or "The Commanding General notes with pride . . ." or "The Commanding General views with grave concern . . ." If the commanding general does not like something that everybody seems to be doing, and wants to stop it by a general order, get to the point; say "such and such is prohibited." The use of the phrase "The Commanding General directs" is redundant, since the order itself is a directive of the commanding general, as indicated by the authentication.

A general court-martial order has the same components as any other order, but its designation or title must be specific; that is: "General Court-Martial Orders," followed by the number. Bear in mind that general court-martial orders are numbered in a separate series for each calendar year. The body of the order differs from the usual body of a general or special order in that the paragraphs are *not numbered*. There is one exception (see Par 3(c) AR 310–50, dated August 8, 1942). When it is expeditious to announce the result of two or more trials of the same person at the same time, the related cases may be made the subject of separate, numbered paragraphs of the same order. Before writing a general or a special court-martial order, consult the model form shown in Appendix 11 of the Manual for Courts-Martial, 1928.

Part III

SPECIAL ORDERS

As an adjutant, or assistant adjutant of any command, you will find that of all classes of orders with which you will be concerned, the largest volume by far will be special orders.

Special orders are issued by all commands from a regiment on up to the War Department. Below the regiment, the battalion, except when operating as a separate unit, issues only "Orders" without the designation "General" or "Special." Likewise, companies and detachments issue only orders.

Special orders have to do with personnel—individuals and groups of individuals constituting any part of a command. Considering the definition given for general orders, it may be said that special orders are *directive* in nature, individual (or personal) in application, and of either temporary or permanent nature.

Appointment, assignment, promotion, transfer, relief, discharge, retirement of officers and enlisted men, warrant officers, and members of the Army Nurse Corps are accomplished by special orders. Officers and enlisted men are placed on detached service and special duty by special orders; courts-martial and boards of all kinds are appointed by special orders; staff officers are detailed by special orders, except that in a tactical command general staff officers are assigned by general orders. In fact, almost everything which effects a change in status or duty of an officer or enlisted man—except the appointment or reduction of privates first class, which is done by company orders—is done by special orders.

Special orders must contain the four components which are common to all orders. They are: the heading, the designation, the body, and the authentication. The heading, the designation, and the authentication will normally be the same as given for general orders.

Consider first the heading. That is always the headquarters from which the order issues. The location of the headquarters, with the date centered under it, is placed at the right of the page. The date is a part of the heading. Next comes the designation "Special Orders No.———." Special orders are numbered in series for each calendar year, beginning with the number one for the first day in the year on which an order is issued, and giving the next succeeding number to each succeeding day on which an order is issued. This does not mean that a number is assigned to every day in the year. For example, January 5, 1941 was on Sunday. If special orders No. 4 were issued on Saturday, and no order was issued on Sunday, the number for Monday the sixth would be No. 5. Only one "special orders" will be issued on any one day.

Pass now to the authentication, and then come back to the body. The authentication must contain the name of the commander who issued the order. If it is a colonel, a lieutenant colonel, or a major commanding the regiment, the "by line" would be "By order of Colonel BLANK," (Or By order of Lieutenant Colonel or Major BLANK) with the name of the officer written in capital letters—just the last name. Do not use such phrases as "By order of the regimental commander," or the "post commander," or "by command of the division commander." If the commander is a general officer, the "By line" is "By command of Major General ROE," with the general's name in capital letters—only the last name.

Consider now the body of the order. It is that one of the four components which tells What is to be done, Who is to do it, When, Where, How, and Why. Remember Kipling's Six Honest Serving Men:

> "I keep six honest serving men
>   (They taught me all I knew);
> Their names are *What* and *Why* and *When*
>   And *How* and *Where* and *Who* . . ."

All those six essential elements must be expressed or implied in the body of a special order. Under peace-time practice, orders were often heavy with qualifying phrases and with clauses which left no possibility for misunderstanding. Now, however, under the pressure of actual war and the urgent necessity for "streamlining" every administrative procedure, a shorter form has been adopted, using abbreviations and symbols in the place of stock phrases and words. While the shorter form of orders is to be used wherever possible, the fundamental principles which govern all military directives must not be violated. That principle, as already stated, is: all orders must be clear, concise, and subject only to that interpretation desired by the commander.

The new form for special orders is prescribed in AR 310–50, dated August 8, 1942.

It provides for a system of block paragraphing to obviate the use of identical opening phrases in orders affecting more than one person.

The new system does not change the other three component parts of a special order, except that the authorized abbreviations in the heading and authentication may be used.

Every administrative officer should familiarize himself with AR 310–50 dated August 8, 1942.

Below, are given two specimen orders. The first is written in the long form; the second in the abbreviated form, under AR 310–50. In the long form, those words or phrases which constitute one of the six elements—the six honest serving men—are separated by a diagonal line (/) and above the phrase is written the element which that word or phrase represents. In the short form the same method is followed, with the element underscored where it is expressed, and inclosed in parentheses, without underscoring, where it is implied.

Example No. 1, Long Form:

HEADQUARTERS 65TH MOTORIZED DIVISION

Fort Jackson, S. C.
1 September 1942

SPECIAL ORDERS
      NO. 209

Why

1. In Compliance with letter, The Adjutant General's Office, dated May 21, 1942, Subject: Student Officers, Adjutant General's School, file AG 320.4 AG

Who

School, (O-MA-M) / Captain JAMES A. HARDY,

What

O345678 A.G.D., / will proceed from this station / to

Where   *When*

Fort Washington, Md., / to arrive thereat not earlier than

What (2d time)

June 5 and not later than June 7, 1942, / reporting upon arrival to the Commandant, Adjutant General's School, /

Why (2d time)

for temporary duty for a period of approximately eight (8) weeks, as student, Administrative Course, / and, unless sooner relieved, will upon completion of the course of

What (3d time)

study, return to his proper station. The travel directed is

How

necessary in the military service. / FD 34 P 434-02 A 0425-23.

By Command of Major General STOUT:
          /t/ THOMAS J. HILL,
                Colonel, General Staff Corps,
                            Chief of Staff.

OFFICIAL:
    /s/ Robert B. Kelly
    /t/ ROBERT B. KELLY,
        Lieutenant Colonel, Adjutant General's
        Department, Adjutant General.

Example No. 2, Short Form

HEADQUARTERS 65TH MOTORIZED DIVISION

SPECIAL ORDERS   Fort Jackson, S. C.,
   NO. 209   1 September, 1942.

Who

    1. CAPT JAMES A HARDY O345678
  What   *Where*   *When*   *Why*

AGD / WP/Ft Washington Md / to rpt 7 June / temp dy
                      When (2d time) *What*

stu AG Sch approx 8 weeks / upon completion / course
(2d time)   *What (2d time)*   *How*

(Administrative) / will return proper sta. TDN /FD 34
                    Why (2d time)

P 434-02 A 0425–23 / Auth: ltr AG 320.4 (O-MA-M)
21 May 1942.

        By Comd of Maj Gen STOUT:
              /t/ THOMAS J. HILL
                Col GSC
                CofS

Official

   /s/ Robert B Kelly
   /t/ ROBERT B KELLY
     Lt Col AGD
     Adj Gen

This order is reduced from 10 typewritten lines in the long form, to three lines in the short form, thus saving seven lines of type, the time of the writer and the time of the reader.

The date in this Special Order is written: day, month, year—to conform to style used in War Department Special Orders. Throughout this pamphlet, this style is used for special orders; but the conventional style (month, day, year) is used in General Orders, letter orders and correspondence. Neither style is prescribed by Army Regulations.

If several changes in assignments and duties are to be

directed in the same special order, the block system of paragraphing is used. The example below shows how the order given above would appear in a block paragraph: (The heading, designation and authentication are not given, since they would be the same as in Example No. 2)

1.   The following changes in assignments and duties are directed. WP and return to proper sta as directed. TDN. FD 34 P 434-02 A 0425-23.

Name	Nature of Change	Assgd or atchd to	Auth
CAPT JAMES A HARDY O345678AGD	DS approx 8 weeks	AG Sch Ft Washington Md; will return to proper sta upon completion course	Ltr AG 320.4 (O-MA-M) Aug 21, 1942

Any number of officers or enlisted men, or both, might be included under the same paragraph number of this special order. The allotment numbers shown cover travel on temporary duty. If any of the officers or men are being ordered to make a permanent change of station, the allotment numbers for that change would be included with those already listed. In the example above the nature of the change is given as "DS approx 8 weeks." DS means detached service, and is a commonly used abbreviation or symbol.

Whenever it is necessary to quote the authority under which an order is issued, it will normally appear as the last sentence of the body of the order, as illustrated in Example No. 2 above.

Present regulations require that orders issued in the field, which direct travel, must cite the authority under which the order is issued, unless such authority is expressly delegated to the commander issuing the order. This authority has been extended by the War Department to commanders of service commands, departments, armies, defense commands, and certain other agencies of the War Department. These commanders are further authorized to delegate this authority as they may deem necessary to appropriate commanders within their chain of command. The regulations also specifically require that when an order is issued in compliance with a directive of The Adjutant General, The Adjutant General's directive must be cited.

When the local commander has what might be termed "original jurisdiction" to direct a thing, he may issue an order directing that thing without citing authority. For example, the Army Regulations give a regimental commander authority to grant leave of absence for not more than one month to those officers under his command. It is therefore not necessary for him to cite any authority when he grants leave within the limits imposed on him by Army Regulations, unless higher authority, such as a division commander, has issued instructions curtailing the privilege of the regimental commander to grant leaves. The same rule applies to post and other commanders to whom Army Regulations grant blanket authority to direct certain things.

Some examples of the application of these rules are:

a. Order granting leave of absence:

(1) Old Form: "Under the provisions of AR 605–115 leave of absence for ten days effective on or about June 10, 1942, is granted to CAPT PAUL A BROWN Oooooo Inf."

(2) New Form: "Lv of absence is granted CAPT PAUL A BROWN Oooooo INF for 10 days eff about 10 June 1942."

b. Order appointing a Regimental Claims Officer:

(1) Old Form: "Under the provisions of paragraph 7c, AR 25–20, dated March 15, 1943, CAPT JOSEPH A BOURDOW, Ooooooo Inf is appointed Regimental Claims Officer. Officer is authorized to act as the board of one officer in any case within the provisions of Article of War 105." and so forth.

(2) New Form: "CAPT JOSEPH A BOURDOW Oooooo Inf is aptd Regimental Claims O and is

authorized to act as board of one O under AW 105. Auth:
par 7c, AR 25–20 dated 15 Mar 1943."

c. Order assigning newly arrived officer to unit:

(1) Old Form: "Captain PAUL A BROWN
Oooooo having reported for duty in compliance with paragraph 19, War Department Special Orders No. 147, dated
May 27, 1942, is hereby assigned to the 100th Infantry and
will report to the commanding officer thereof for duty."

(2) New Form: "CAPT PAUL A BROWN
Oooooo INF is asgd to 100th INF."

Examples of orders given show the allotment number
when the order directs travel. What are allotments, and
why are they used in travel orders? The War Department
has greatly simplified the system of allotment numbers.
Under the system of showing allotments adopted by Section II of WD Circular 206, (1942) War Department ap-
propriations for travel were designated as "Finance Service, Army, 1942 and 1943." The allotment symbols "FD
31, 32, 33, 34, and 35," were adopted as the basic symbols
for travel of the Army. Only one symbol is used to indicate purpose and object of expenditure under the several
allotment number symbols, and this one symbol is followed
by the appropriation number as established by the Treas-
ury.

Extracts and true copies. Most special orders issued by
an active headquarters contain a number of paragraphs,
each of special import to some individual or to several
groups of individuals. If the orders involve travel, the individual will need a number of copies. In most commands
an officer or enlisted man involved in travel orders is
furnished with extract copies of the particular paragraph
concerning himself. An extract copy is made by simply
writing the heading, the designation, followed by the word
"extract," written in capital letters, and then the paragraph which you desire to extract, preceded by its proper
number. Then, of course, comes the authentication. In most
headquarters it is customary to prepare extract copies of
every travel order and of every order appointing a board

of officers. In addition to the typed signature of the adjutant or adjutant general on the extract copies, the official seal is placed just over the place left for the adjutant's signature. Such extract copies, bearing the imprint of the official seal of the headquarters, are all that is needed for the individual to collect his mileage or other travel allowance.

In case an officer or enlisted man wishes to make extra copies of his orders, or extract copies, he may make them himself. In the absence of the official seal, he may "true copy" the orders or the extract, simply by writing the words: "Certified a True Copy," or "True Copy," and signing his name, grade and organization, if he is an officer; or in the case of an enlisted man, by getting any commissioned officer to certify that it is a true copy.

Confirmatory orders. Paragraph 3, AR 35-4890, reads: "When it is impracticable by reason of the exigencies of the service to issue orders in advance . . . , confirmatory orders may be issued. Where travel for the performance of a military duty is performed in compliance with oral orders . . . such orders . . . will be confirmed by means of proper confirmatory orders so that the officer who has been required to travel may receive the statutory mileage allowance provided therefor.

"Confirmatory orders, when authorized, must meet the statutory provisions required of all mileage orders." Those statutory requirements are that all orders shall state the necessity for such travel by the phrase "the travel directed is necessary in the military service" (which is abbreviated "TDN"), and that all orders involving mileage shall state the special duty involved. "Where confirming oral orders . . . issued in advance, confirmatory orders will so recite, showing the date of such oral or other orders and source thereof. If issued for the purpose of confirming travel performed under exigencies which prevented the issuance of advance travel orders, they must so state."

In order to put that regulation into effect, an introductory sentence something like the following should be added to the usual order form:

"Oral orders of the commanding general, issued on August 15, 1942 directing CAPT ROBERT A BRUCE Oooooo (Inf) A.D.C., to proceed from this station to Atlanta, Georgia, for temporary duty in connection with so and so, and upon completion of such duty, to return to his proper station, are hereby confirmed as having been necessary in the military service, the exigencies of the service having been such as to prevent the issuance of travel orders in advance. FD————————.

This type of confirmatory order does not readily lend itself to shortening by use of abbreviations to a great extent. Let us see, however, what can be done with this one:

"VOCG 15 Aug directing CAPT ROBERT A BRUCE Oooooo (Inf) ADC to proceed from this sta to Atlanta Ga for temp duty in connection with so and so, and upon completion of temp duty to return to his proper sta, are hereby confirmed as TDN, the exigencies of the serv having been such as to prevent the issuance of orders in advance."

Secret or confidential orders involving travel may be issued as letter orders or as paragraphs of special orders. When the latter method is used, the paragraph which deals with the secret or confidential matter will appear in the consolidation only by number followed by the word "secret" or "confidential." In either case the directive will be handled as are other secret or confidential documents in the manner prescribed in AR 380–5. When such orders are issued, extract copies will be issued at the same time, without secret or confidential markings, and will be furnished to the unit personnel section or other reporting source in order to afford the necessary information for preparation of reports of change. The extract will include, when applicable, the name of the traveler, station from which transferred, date and mode of travel, port of embarkation, and in the case of Reserve officers, the date on which active duty will terminate.

Special orders appointing Boards of Officers. Great care must be used to make certain that the order states clearly and unequivocally the subject to be investigated, and includes all necessary instructions upon which the board can base its actions.

Special orders appointing General or Special Courts Martial should be written with extreme care if abbreviations are to be used, for upon the validity of the order appointing a court may depend the validity of all the actions of the court. The same caution applies to the writing of General or Special Court Martial orders promulgating the sentence of a court. Bear in mind that a court is appointed in Special Orders, and that the findings and sentence of the court and the action of the reviewing authority, are promulgated by General Court Martial Orders, or Special Court Martial Orders.

General. While it is highly desirable to reduce to a minimum the number of words, sentences, and lines of written or typed matter which make up an order, the urge for brevity must not be allowed to overshadow the necessity for clarity. In using abbreviations, be sure that the abbreviations do not permit the order being interpreted two or three ways. If abbreviations cannot be used without laying the order open to two or more constructions, do not use the abbreviations.

Letter orders. Occasionally an order involving an individual is directed by letter rather than by special order. Such an order is called a letter order and follows the rules pertaining to military correspondence so far as form is concerned. It must be remembered that the six essential elements must be contained in the letter just as they would be in a special order. Letter orders are sometimes used to place an officer on leave, to appoint an investigating officer, to direct a secret mission, or to accomplish similar directives which can be effectively handled in this manner.

Section V

MISCELLANEOUS

CHANGE OF STATION OF UNIT

CONFIDENTIAL

HEADQUARTERS 198TH INFANTRY DIVISION

SPECIAL ORDERS   Fort D A Russell, Tex.,
NO. 57   15 March, 1943

—EXTRACT—

6. The 555th Engr Hv Pon Bn consisting of 18 O 3 WO and 507 EM is reld fr attachment to this comd and WP Ft Brown Tex by rail and motor movement as indicated below. Movement will be completed not later than 25 March 1943.

BY RAIL (PASSENGER)

LT COL ROBERT E MOORE 0456876 CE (Train Commander)

     10 Officers
     2 Warrant Officers
     350 Enlisted Men

BY RAIL (FREIGHT)

CAPT JAMES C BARNES 0468364 CE (Train Commander)

     12 Enlisted Men (Guard Detail)

BY GOVERNMENT MOTOR

MAJ FRANKLIN C BRICE 0754762 CE (Commanding)

     5 Officers
     1 Warrant Officer
     145 Enlisted Men

T/BA equipment will be taken. Hv and track laying motor equipment will be moved by rail. TC will furn necessary T. In accordance with AR 35–4520 FD will pay in advance the monetary alws in lieu of rat a/r $2.25 per day for twelve (12) men (guard detail) for two and two-thirds (2 2/3 days and for qrs a/r $1.50 per day for twelve men for one (1) day. $5.00 per diem in lieu of subs is authorized for CAPT JAMES C BARNES 0468364 CE.

CAPT JAMES C BARNES 0468364 CE is aptd cl "A" Agent Fin O for MAJ HAROLD R ROSEN Disbursing O Ft D A Russell Tex for the purpose of making pmt of monetary alws authorized for guard detail.

CAPT JOHN Q ADAMS 0674532 CE and CAPT CHARLES B RITTER 0986735 CE are aptd cl "B" Agent Fin O for MAJ HAROLD R ROSEN Disbursing O Ft D A Russell Tex for the purpose of making necessary pmts incident to this movement. Maximum amt to be entrusted to each O $2500.00.

TDN. FD 34 P 43402 A 0425–23. QM 110 P 01 03 07 08 A 0500–23. Auth : ltr AGF 370.5, 10 Mar 1943.
By comd Maj Gen STRAHON :
/t/ ROBERT O RUPP
Lt Col GSC
CofS

Official :
/s/ Allan F Dummer
/t/ ALLAN F DUMMER
Maj AGD
Adj Gen

CONFIDENTIAL

Note. *The paragraph appointing Captain Barnes as class "A" Agent Finance Officer may be omitted if the members of the guard appear personally at the Finance Office for payment.*

DAILY BULLETIN

HEADQUARTERS FORT WHEREVER

Wherever, Va.,
September 2, 1942.

DAILY BULLETIN
  NO. 205

OFFICIAL

1. DETAILS FOR TOMORROW:
     Field Officer of the Day: LT COL ROB-
     ERT A TRASK Oooooo Inf
     Officer of the Day: CAPT S A HAMER
     Oooooo Inf
     Officer of the Guard: 2D LT J E HENRY
     Oooooo Inf
     Staff Duty Officer: MAJ HENRY T JOR-
     DAN Oooooo SC

2. USE OF OFFICIAL TELEPHONES:
Official telephones will be used only in the transaction of
official business. Those making calls to numbers outside the
Post will give the operator the name of the person calling,
and will state that the call is official. Calls not designated as
official will not be completed. Personal calls will be made
from public telephones installed for that purpose. This restriction does not apply to telephones installed in officers'
quarters, officers' messes or clubs, nor to telephones installed in noncommissioned officers' clubs.

3. UNAUTHORIZED OPERATORS OF
GOVERNMENT MOTOR VEHICLES: Only enlisted
men holding Government Motor Vehicle Operator's Permits issued by the Motor Transport Officer, this station,
will be permitted to drive Government motor vehicles. Officers will operate Government motor vehicles only in case
of emergency. The Provost Marshal will cause Government motor vehicles driven by officers to be stopped, and
the officer's name, rank and organization reported to this
headquarters, together with the number of the vehicle be-

ing driven, the time, and destination as given by the officer.

4. EMERGENCY CALLS—STATION HOSPITAL: The telephone number of the Emergency Room, Station Hospital, is Post 56. Telephone operators, however, will connect with the Emergency Room upon being signalled: "Hospital, Emergency."

5. OFF LIMITS: The establishment known as "Bide-a-Wee," located on Stoneman's Road, five miles east of the town of Moron, is declared "Off Limits" for members of this command until further notice.

By order of Col LANG:

Official: /t/ JAMES B HARDIN
/s/ James B Hardin   Maj AGD
/t/ JAMES B HARDIN   Adj
    Maj AGD
    Adj

INFORMATION

1. Mr. J. W. Sampson, representing the Acme Military Stores, will display uniforms and equipment for officers in the Post Complement Officers' Club Sept 5 to Sept 8.

2. Tickets for the Radio Show to be given in the Main Recreation Hall (Avenue B and 2d Sts) at 2000 Sept 4 may be obtained at the adjutant's office. First come, first served. The program will be broadcast on a national hook-up.

3. Military personnel and their families are cordially invited to attend community singing to be held on the grounds of the court house in Freehold next Friday night, from 1800 to 2100.

4. FOUND: Pair of gray kid gloves, size 8, men's. Owner may have them by applying to the Provost Marshal's office.

MEMORANDUM

HEADQUARTERS 200th INFANTRY DIVISION

Fort Clane, N.J.
September 2, 1942.

MEMORANDUM
NO. 192

APPEARANCE OF MILITARY PERSONNEL

1.   Recent observations of military personnel of this command, both in the Post and on pass in nearby civilian communities reveal the following improper wearing of the articles of uniform, and improper mixtures of uniform clothing:

a.   Garrison caps are being worn turned around, on the extreme back of head, with peak at angles several degrees off center.

b.   Various unauthorized ornaments are being worn on garrison caps.

c.   Shirts are being worn with sleeves rolled up to elbows, and with collars open when worn with neck-tie. Shirt pockets are not buttoned in many cases.

d.   Woolen trousers are being worn with cotton shirts without the blouse.

e.   Civilian type oxfords with fancy scroll work on toes are being worn by enlisted men. Service shoes are not properly cleaned and shined.

2.   The appearance of a large percentage of enlisted men observed on a recent Saturday night in several nearby communities was such as to reflect discredit on the military service. Commanders of all echelons are reminded that a soldierly appearance, neatness, cleanliness and proper uniform are essential elements of discipline and morale.

3.   The proper appearance of enlisted men on all occasions is a direct responsibility of organization commanders. Proper steps will be taken by all concerned to correct the faults noted above, and any other faults which reflect on the discipline and morale of the command.

4. The Provost Marshal will cause all enlisted men whose appearance is below the required standard of neatness and cleanliness to be returned to their organizations under guard, and the names, serial numbers and grades of enlisted men so returned will be reported to this headquarters by the Provost Marshal.

By command of Maj Gen ROE:

/t/ JOHN A DOE
Col GSC
CofS

Official:
/s/ John A Kind
/t/ JOHN A KIND
Lt Col AGD
Adj Gen

BATTALION AND COMPANY ORDERS

HEADQUARTERS DETACHMENT 2d BATTALION
100th INFANTRY

ORDERS
NO. 10

Fort Dix, N.J.,
September 1, 1942.

The following apmts are announced effective this date:

TO BE PRIVATES, 1st CLASS:
Pvt Joseph A Perdue 22345678
Pvt John T Ullman 22345987

/s/ William T White
/t/ WILLIAM T WHITE,
1st Lt 100th Inf
Comdg

COMPANY G, 100th INFANTRY

ORDERS   Fort Dix, N. J.,
  NO. 10   September 1, 1942.

    The following apmts and reductions in this co are
announced, effective this date:

        TO BE PRIVATES, 1ST CLASS:
           Pvt John J Warner 6755423
           Pvt Albert K Leese 32144842
        TO BE PRIVATE:
           Pfc Carl T Wixon 30455921

               /s/ Frank T Held
               /t/ FRANK T HELD
                   Capt 100th Inf
                   Comdg

INDEX

P 253 of This America
P 33-42 — read in this book

g — — 21
pp 22 - 55 } grtext
pp 84 - 98 }

Punct.
    esp. dialogue
    C.F. ; Terminal Punct.
    Participles
    Note taking
    " Univ Days "
    American Blend of Humor"
Page 551 This America for Wal.

{